101 Fabulous Rotary-Cut Quilts

JUDY HOPKINS

&

NANCY J. MARTIN

& COMPANY

Bothell, Washington

Credits

President . . . . .Nancy J. Martin
CEO/Publisher . . . . Daniel J. Martin
Associate Publisher . . . . .Jane Hamada
Editorial Director . . . . Mary V. Green
Technical Editor . . . . Ursula Reikes
Design and
    Production Manager . . . . .Cheryl Stevenson
Text Designer . . . . Kay Green
Cover Designer . . . . .Trina Stahl
Copy Editor . . . . Liz McGehee
Illustrator . . . . .Laurel Strand
Photographer . . . . Brent Kane

101 Fabulous Rotary-Cut Quilts
© 1998 by Judy Hopkins and Nancy J. Martin

Martingale & Company
PO Box 118
Bothell, WA 98041-0118 USA

Printed in Hong Kong
03 02 01 00 99 98   6 5 4 3 2 1

Library of Congress Cataloging-in-Publication Data
Hopkins, Judy
    101 fabulous rotary-cut quilts / Judy Hopkins and
      Nancy J. Martin.
      p. cm.
    ISBN 1-56477-240-3
    1. Patchwork—Patterns. 2. Rotary cutting.
      3. Patchwork quilts.
  I. Martin, Nancy J. II. Title.
TT835.H557 1998
746.46'041—dc21   98-28906
                        CIP

MISSION STATEMENT

We are dedicated to providing quality products and service by working together to inspire creativity and to enrich the lives we touch.

Contents

Introduction

In 1978, I used a rotary cutter only to cut fabric for making garments. When I began to make quilts on a regular basis in 1981, I quickly sought out ways to cut with the rotary cutter rather than use the traditional template-and-scissors method. I soon realized that accurate rulers and measuring devices were needed for these new techniques. To meet this need, I developed the Bias Square® ruler and cutting technique for making accurate half-square triangle units. Now after millions of bias squares and hundreds of quilts, I still find this technique invaluable for speed and accuracy.

Judy found herself working mainly from a scrap bag, so long cutting rulers or techniques that called for squares or rectangles of fabric wouldn't work with her small, irregularly shaped scraps. To solve this problem, she developed the ScrapMaster, a cutting guide that makes it fast and easy to cut individual patchwork pieces without a template.

As two quilting professionals who need to produce a lot of teaching samples and quilts within a short amount of time, we dedicate ourselves to uncovering easy and accurate techniques. Now we've gathered into one volume a grand collection of 101 quilts made with these techniques. Traditional patterns are given new life with interesting color combinations, unusual sets, and exciting quilting designs or tacking techniques. These designs have appeared in Judy's and my earlier books *Rotary Riot* and *Rotary Roundup*, as well as Judy's *Down the Rotary Road*.

Alphabetically arranged, these 101 rotary-cut quilts will prove to be an invaluable resource for beginning quilters, as well as a great refresher for more experienced quilters.

We're pleased to have been part of this rotary revolution, which enabled quilters to forsake more tedious methods for faster and more accurate techniques. We hope you enjoy the results.

Nancy J. Martin

About the Authors

Judy Hopkins is a prolific quilmaker whose fondness for traditional design goes hand in hand with an unwavering commitment to fast, contemporary cutting and piecing techniques. Judy has been making quilts since 1980 and working full-time at the craft since 1985. Her work has appeared in numerous exhibits and publications. She writes a regular mystery pattern series for *Lady's Circle Patchwork Quilts* magazine.

Teaching and writing are by-products of Judy's intense involvement in the process of creating quilts. She is the author of *One-of-a-Kind Quilts* and its revision, *Design Your Own Quilts; Fit To Be Tied; Around the Block with Judy Hopkins;* and *Down the Rotary Road with Judy Hopkins.*

Judy lives in Anchorage, Alaska, with her husband, Bill, and their Labrador retriever. She has two grown daughters and three adorable and brilliant grandchildren who like to help her sew.

Nancy J. Martin, talented author, teacher, and quiltmaker, has written more than twenty-five books on quiltmaking. Nancy is an innovator in the quilting industry and introduced the Bias Square cutting ruler to quilters everywhere. Having taught for more than eighteen years and with numerous classic quilting titles to her credit, Nancy is the founder and president of Martingale & Company, the publisher of America's Best-Loved Quilt Books®. Nancy and her husband, Dan, enjoy living in the Pacific Northwest.

Materials and Supplies

Rotary Cutter and Mat

A large rotary cutter enables you to quickly cut strips and pieces without templates. A mat with a rough finish holds the fabric in place and protects both the blade and table on which you are cutting. An 18" x 24" mat allows you to cut long bias strips. A smaller mat is ideal when working with scraps.

Rulers and Cutting Guides

You need a ruler for measuring and to guide the rotary cutter. There are many appropriate rulers on the market. Look for rulers made of ⅛"-thick acrylic that include lengthwise and crosswise guidelines, as well as lines for marking 45° angles.

The Bias Square is the tool most critical to bias strip piecing. This acrylic cutting guide is available in three sizes, 4", 6", or 8" square, and is ruled with ⅛" markings. It features a diagonal line, which is placed on the bias seam, enabling you to cut accurately sewn half-square triangle units. The Bias Square is convenient to use when cutting small quilt pieces, such as squares, rectangles, and triangles. The larger 8" size is ideal for quick-cutting blocks that require large squares and triangles as well as making diagonal cuts for quarter-square triangles. A 20cm-square metric version is also available for those who prefer to work in this format.

The ScrapMaster cutting guide is a tool designed for cutting individual half-square triangles, in a variety of sizes, from scraps.

Sewing Machine

You need a straight-stitch machine in good working order. Make sure the tension is adjusted so that you are producing smooth, even seams. A seam that is puckered causes the fabric to curve and distorts the size of your piecing. Use a new needle in the machine; an old needle may snag the fabric. (Old needles usually make a popping sound as they enter the fabric.)

Needles

Use sewing-machine needles sized for cotton fabrics (size 70/10 or 80/12). You also need hand-sewing needles (Sharps) and hand-quilting needles (Betweens #8, #9, or #10).

Pins

A good supply of glass- or plastic-headed pins is necessary. Long pins are especially helpful when pinning thick layers together.

Iron and Ironing Board

Frequent and careful pressing are necessary to ensure a smooth, accurately stitched quilt top. Place your iron and ironing board, along with a plastic spray bottle of water, close to your sewing machine.

Fabric

FABRIC SELECTION

For best results, select lightweight, closely woven, 100%-cotton fabrics. Polyester content may make small patchwork pieces difficult to cut and sew accurately.

While 100% cotton is ideal, it is not always possible with quilts created from fabric collections of long standing. Some of Nancy's most interesting prints were purchased before she followed the 100% rule—they are polyester-cotton blends of uncertain content. The colors and prints are unobtainable today and often serve a unique design purpose in a quilt.

FABRIC LIBRARY

Many of the quilts in this book are multifabric quilts, commonly referred to as "scrap quilts." The success of a multifabric quilt, which relies on color groups rather than the use of a single print in a certain color, is dependent upon a well-stocked "fabric library" or scrap bag. Making multifabric quilts can change the way you shop for fabric.

We rarely purchase specific fabric for a specific quilt. When we buy new fabric, it is with the goal of enriching our fabric libraries. We buy three to four yards of any fabric that would make a good background fabric.

FAT QUARTERS

Many of the yardage amounts specify fat quarters. This is an 18" x 22" piece of fabric (rather than the standard quarter yard that is cut selvage to selvage and measures 9" x 44"). The fat quarter is a more convenient size to use, especially when cutting bias strips for bias squares. For added convenience, most quilt shops offer fat quarters already cut and bundled. Look for a basket or bin of fat quarters when buying fabrics.

If you are having trouble choosing a color scheme, you might want to select a bundle of fat quarters that has been color-coordinated. Often, you can use this group of fabrics as the basis for an effective color scheme, purchasing additional background fabric and more of any fabric that you wish to feature in your quilt.

Color Palette

Some quilt patterns in this book specify fabrics in particular colors; others simply call for a combination of light, medium, and dark fabrics. Your fabric and color choices will depend on what appeals to you or what is available in your scrap bag or fabric collection. If you are using scraps or fat quarters, you may want to use a number of different fabrics to represent a single color, such as an assortment of dark red prints. An alternative is to use two, three, or more different dark colors (like reds, blues, purples, browns, and greens) when cutting the pieces shown as "dark" in the quilt plan. Give extra zing to your selection by adding a small amount of an adjacent color on the color wheel. A few pieces of orange, for example, will spice up a collection of reds.

Visual Texture

Textural variety adds interest to repeat-fabric quilts, such as "Gentleman's Fancy" on page 105. Create more interesting quilts by combining plaids and stripes with a floral fabric, or by mixing large- or medium-scale multicolored prints with quieter tone-on-tone designs. Experiment to find combinations that appeal to you.

Two-Fabric Quilts

Several of the quilts in this book are two-fabric quilts, such as "Bear's Paw" on page 40 and "Shaded Pinwheel" on page 189. The most important element in selecting fabric for a two-fabric quilt is contrast—the fabric used for the design must contrast strongly with the fabric used for the background. For maximum contrast, use solids, rather than prints, for two-fabric quilts. But don't rule out prints—even busy, multicolored prints will work if matched with low-key prints that "read" as solids. You'll know you have sufficient contrast if you can clearly see the "line" where patches of the two fabrics are joined.

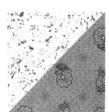

Sample Blocks

Once you have determined your color palette and pulled an assortment of fabric from your fabric library, it is time to test your color scheme by making sample blocks. Study the sample block illustration found with each quilt to cut the pieces needed for one sample block.

In a multifabric quilt, it is necessary to make several sample blocks to determine the effectiveness of the color palette. Overuse of a color, color integration, contrast, and unity are hard to determine from a single block.

Fabric Preparation

Wash all fabrics first to preshrink, test for colorfastness, and get rid of excess dye. Continue to wash fabric until the rinse water is completely clear. Add a square of white fabric to each washing of the fabric. When this white fabric remains its original color, the fabric is colorfast. A cupful of vinegar in the rinse water may also be used to help set difficult dyes.

Make it a habit to wash and prepare fabrics after they are purchased and before they are placed in the fabric library. Then, your fabric will be ready to sew when you are.

Rotary Cutting

GRAIN LINES

Yarns are woven together to form fabric, giving it the ability to stretch or remain stable, depending on the grain line you are using. Lengthwise grain runs parallel to the selvage and has very little stretch. Crosswise grain runs from selvage to selvage and has some give to it. All other grains are considered bias. True bias is a grain line that runs at a 45° angle to the lengthwise and crosswise grains.

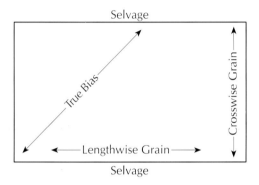

If fabric is badly off-grain, pull diagonally as shown to straighten. It is impossible to rotary cut fabrics exactly on the straight grain of fabric since many fabrics are printed off-grain. In rotary cutting, straight, even cuts are made as close to the grain as possible. A slight variation from the grain will not alter your project.

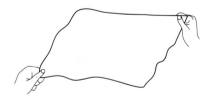

In most cases, the rotary-cutting directions follow these guidelines for grain-line placement:
- Strips are cut on the crosswise grain of fabric.
- Squares and rectangles are cut on the lengthwise and crosswise grain of fabric.

- Half-square triangles are cut with the short sides on the straight grain and the long side on the bias. Bias strip piecing produces sewn half-square triangles whose grain lines follow this guideline.
- Quarter-square triangles have the short sides on the bias and the long side on the straight grain. They are generally used along the outside edges of individual blocks or quilts where the long edge will not stretch.
- When you are working with striped fabric or directional prints, the direction of the stripe or print takes precedence over the direction of the grain. Handle these pieces carefully since they may not be cut on-grain and will therefore be less stable. If these pieces are to be used along the outside edges of the quilt, staystitch ⅛" from their raw edges to avoid stretching them.

STRAIGHT CUTS

Cutting dimensions given in the quilt plans include the ¼"-wide seam allowance. If accurate ¼" seams are sewn by machine, there is no need to mark stitching lines. To cut squares, rectangles, and triangles, you first need to cut straight strips of fabric.

1. Align the Bias Square with the fold of the fabric and place a ruler to the left. Place fabric to your right when making all cuts. (Reverse these techniques if you are left-handed.)

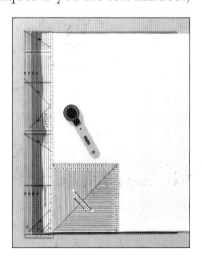

2. Remove the Bias Square and make a rotary cut along the right side of the ruler. Hold the ruler down with your left hand, placing the little finger off the edge of the ruler. This finger serves as an anchor and keeps the ruler from moving. Move your hand along the ruler as you make the cut, making sure the markings remain accurate. Use firm, even pressure as you rotary cut. Begin rolling the cutter before crossing the folded fabric edge and continue across the fabric. Always roll the cutter away from you; never pull the cutter toward you.

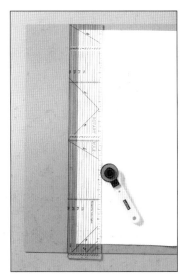

3. Fold fabric lengthwise again so that you will be cutting four layers at a time. (This means shorter cuts.) Open and check the fabric periodically to make sure you are making straight cuts. If fabric strips are not straight, use the Bias Square, ruler, and rotary cutter to straighten the edge again.

4. Place all fabric to the right and measure from the left straight edge. Rulers, or the Bias Square and rulers, can be combined to make wider cuts.

BIAS CUTS

To cut bias strips for binding:

1. Align the 45° marking on the ruler along the selvage and make a bias cut.
2. Measure the width of the strip from the cut edge of the fabric. Cut along the edge of the ruler.

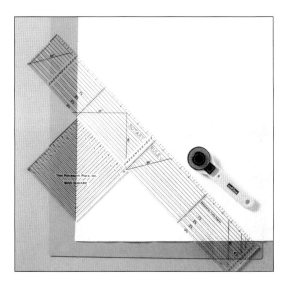

SQUARES AND RECTANGLES

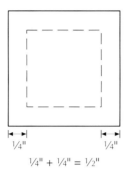

¼"   ¼"

¼" + ¼" = ½"

1. Cut fabric into strips the measurement of the square plus seam allowances. (Cutting dimensions in the quilt plans *include* seam allowances.)
2. Using the Bias Square, align the top and bottom edge of the strip and cut fabric into squares the width of the strip.

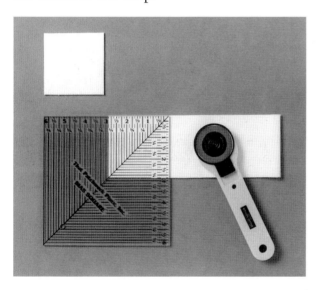

3. Rectangles are cut in the same manner, first cutting strips into the shortest measurement of the rectangle.

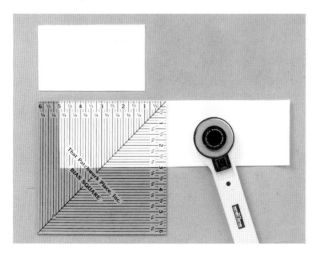

HALF-SQUARE TRIANGLES

Most of the triangles used in these quilts are half-square triangles. These triangles are half of a square, with the short sides on the straight grain of fabric and the long side on the bias. To cut these triangles, cut a square and then cut it in half diagonally. Cut the square ⅞" larger than the finished short side of the triangle to allow for seam allowances. (Cutting dimensions in the quilt plans *include* seam allowances.)

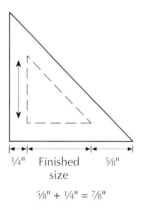

¼"   Finished   ⅝"
      size

⅝" + ¼" = ⅞"

1. Cut a strip the desired finished measurement plus ⅞".
2. Cut the strip into squares using the same measurement.
3. Cut a stack of squares diagonally, from corner to corner. Each square will yield two triangles with short sides on the straight grain.

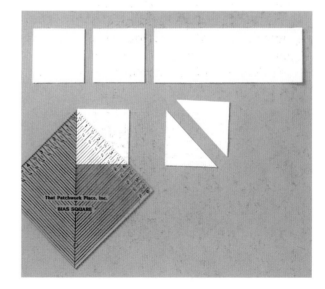

Trimming Points for Easy Matching

You can use the Bias Square to trim seam-allowance points on half-square triangles. The measurement to use is the finished short side of the triangle plus ½" (¼"-wide seam allowance on each side). The example shown here is a half-square triangle with a finished dimension of 4".

1. To quick-cut this triangle, cut a 4⅞" square of fabric and cut it in half once diagonally.
2. To trim the points for easy matching, set the Bias Square at the 4½" mark on the fabric triangle as shown. The points of the triangle will extend ⅜". Trim them off with the rotary cutter.

1. Cut a strip the desired finished measurement plus 1¼".
2. Cut the strip into squares using the same measurement.
3. Cut a stack of these squares (at least four) in half diagonally, lining up the ruler from corner to corner. Without moving these pieces, cut in the other direction to create the X cut. Each square will yield four triangles with the long side on the straight grain.

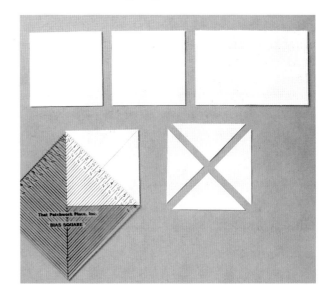

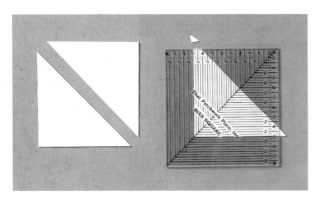

QUARTER-SQUARE TRIANGLES

Triangles that have their longest sides along the outside edges of blocks and quilts are usually quarter-square triangles. These triangles are cut from squares so their short sides are on the bias and the long side is on the straight of grain. This makes them easier to handle and keeps the outside edges of your quilt from stretching. Cut the square 1¼" larger than the finished long side of the triangle.

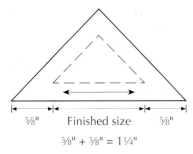

⅝"   Finished size   ⅝"

⅝" + ⅝" = 1¼"

TRIMMING TEMPLATES

Some quilt designs include squares or rectangles that have one or more corners trimmed at a 45° angle, allowing you to add a triangle from a different fabric. The traditional Snowball block is a typical example.

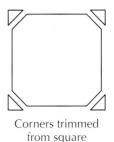 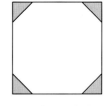

Corners trimmed
from square

Triangles added to
make Snowball block

In this book, a "trimming template" is provided with patterns that require these shapes. Carefully trace the template onto stiff, clear plastic and cut out the shape. The template is the correct size as given: *Never add seam allowances to a trimming template!*

Cut the needed squares or rectangles as described in the basic cutting instructions. Stack these in layers of four and place the trimming template in one corner, aligning the two short sides of the trimming template with the outside edges of the squares or rectangles. Hold the trimming template down firmly and push your Bias Square against the long edge of the template; the plastic will stop the ruler at the proper position. Move the trimming template out of the way and cut along the ruler to remove the corner. Repeat for other corners if instructed to do so.

Make trimming template from stiff plastic.

Stack squares or rectangles in four layers.

Align trimming template.

Push ruler against edge of trimming template.

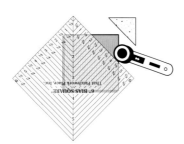
Remove trimming template and cut along ruler.

An alternate method is to lay your Bias Square upside down over the appropriate trimming-template outline, aligning the long side of the trimming template with the outside edge of the Bias Square. Then, outline the two short sides of the trimming template with masking tape on the underside of the Bias Square. You can also make a cutout from lightweight plastic or cardboard and tape it to the underside of the Bias Square. Align the edges of the masking tape or the cutout with the corner of your stack of squares or rectangles; remove the corner by cutting along the edge of the Bias Square.

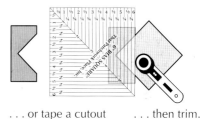

Outline the trimming template with masking tape . . .

. . . or tape a cutout to the underside of a ruler . . .

. . . then trim.

PAPER TEMPLATES

It is sometimes necessary to use a paper template while rotary cutting, especially if the template is a difficult shape or is cut in $1/16$" or $1/8$" increments. Using the templates found in this book, trace the desired shape, including seam allowances, onto paper. Cut the template from paper, and tape it to the underside of the rotary ruler, aligning the straight edge with the edge of the ruler. Use the paper template, rather than the ruler markings, to cut the desired shape.

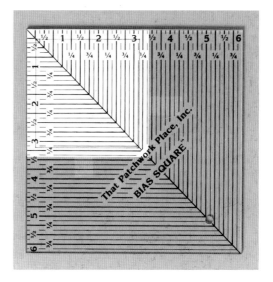

BIAS SQUARES

Many traditional quilt patterns contain squares made from two contrasting half-square triangles. The short sides of the triangles are on the straight grain of fabric while the long sides are on the bias. These are called bias-square units. Using a bias strip-piecing method, you can easily sew and cut large amounts of bias squares. This technique is especially useful for small bias squares, where pressing after stitching usually distorts the shape (and sometimes burns fingers).

NOTE: All directions in this book give the cut size for bias squares; the finished size after stitching will be ½" smaller.

Using Fat Quarters

You will need to cut a sizable amount of bias squares for most of the quilts in this book. Use the technique shown below to help conserve time and fabric. Cut strips from fat quarters (18" x 22") or fat eighths (9" x 22") of fabric. The directions specify the fabrics to use and the width of the strips to cut.

1. Layer two pieces of fabric, right sides facing up, and cut as shown. Starting at the *corner* of the fabric, make the first cut at a 45° angle.

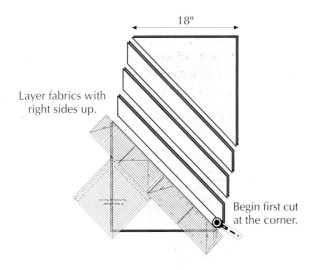

18"

Layer fabrics with right sides up.

Begin first cut at the corner.

2. Arrange the strips in the order you will sew them. Beginning with the triangular piece in either corner, select a strip from the top layer; then select the strip next to it from the bottom layer. Continue to select strips in this manner, alternating from the top and bottom layers as

you move toward the opposite corner of the strips. This will give you two sets of strips to sew together.

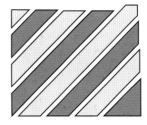 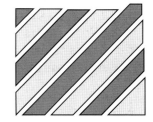

3. Sew the strips together along the long bias edge, right sides facing, with ¼"-wide seams. Offset the edges ¼" as shown.

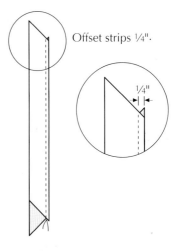

Offset strips ¼".

¼"

FAT QUARTERS CUTTING CHART FOR BIAS SQUARES
Based on 1 light and 1 dark fat quarter (18" x 22")

Strip Width	Cut Size of Bias Square	Yield	Finished Size of Bias Square
1¾"*	1½"	160	1"
2"*	1¾"	120	1¼"
2"	2"	100	1½"
2¼"	2¼"	80	1¾"
2½"	2½"	60	2
2¾"	3"	50	2½"
3"	3½"	38	3"
3¾"	4½"	24	4"

Press seams open rather than toward dark fabric.

The lower edge of the pieced rectangle and the adjacent side edge must form a straight line after sewing. The other two edges will be irregular. It is important to sew in this configuration if strip-pieced fabric is to yield the number of bias squares indicated in the chart. Press seams toward the darker fabric. (If cutting bias squares 1¾" or smaller, try pressing the seams open to evenly distribute fabric bulk.)

The illustrations below show the strip-pieced fabric shapes that result when strips are stitched for the most common sizes.

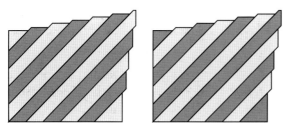

Strip-pieced fabric for 2½" cut (2" finished) bias squares

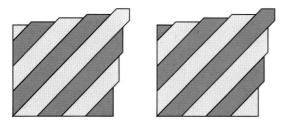

Strip-pieced fabric for 3½" cut (3" finished) bias squares

4. Begin cutting at the left side on the lower edge of each unit. Align the 45° mark of the Bias Square ruler on the seam line. Each bias square will require two cuts. The first cut is along the side and top edge. It removes the bias square from the rest of the fabric and is made slightly larger than the correct size, as shown in the series of illustrations below.

5. The second cut is made along the remaining two sides. It aligns the diagonal and trims the bias square to the correct size. To make the cut, turn the segment and place the Bias Square on the opposite two sides, aligning the required measurements on both sides of the cutting guide and the 45° mark on the seam. Cut the remaining two sides of the bias squares.

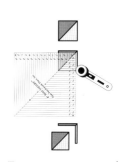

Turn cut segments and cut opposite two sides.

6. Continue cutting bias squares from each unit in this manner, working from left to right and from bottom to top, row by row, until you have cut bias squares from all usable fabric. The chart on page 14 specifies how many bias squares you can expect to cut from two fat quarters (18" x 22") of fabric.

TIP

Remember, when cutting bias squares, if you don't have enough fabric to cut a 2½" bias square, cut a smaller size, such as 2¼" or 2", for use in another project.

If you cut extra, smaller sizes of bias squares to finish off your bias-square strips, they will accumulate in no time, ready to make into a scrappy quilt.

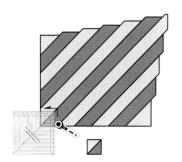

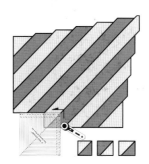

Align 45° mark on seam line and cut first two sides.

Scrappy Bias Squares

For bias squares with a scrappy look, use a variety of fabrics when you make them. Layer four fat quarters of fabric in two pairs and cut into bias strips. Consult the cutting specifications for the quilt you are making to determine the strip width.

Mix and match the cut bias strips from the four fabrics to form four strip-pieced fabric shapes. Arrange and sew strips by size, placing the left and lower edges as straight as possible. The remaining edges will be uneven.

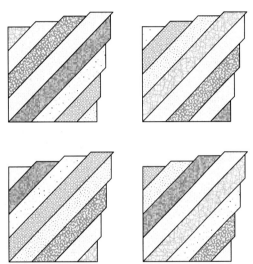

Using Squares of Fabric

You can also make bias squares starting with small squares of fabric. Refer to the chart at right for common sizes and yields.

1. Start with two small squares of fabric. Layer with right sides facing up and cut in half diagonally.

2. Cut the squares into strips, measuring from the previous cut.

3. Stitch the strips together using ¼"-wide seam allowances. Be sure to align the strips so the lower edge and one adjacent edge form straight lines.

4. Starting at the lower left corner and following the directions on page 15, cut bias squares.

Use the chart below to determine strip width and resulting yield.

Finished Size	Cut Size	Fabric Size	Strip Width	Yield
2"	2½" x 2½"	8" x 8"*	2½"	8
2"	2½" x 2½"	9" x 9"	2½"	14
2½"	3" x 3"	8" x 8"	2¾"	8
3"	3½" x 3½"	9" x 9"	3"	8

A pair of 7" x 7" squares will yield the same number of bias squares.

Square Two and Other Related Units

Marsha McCloskey and Nancy J. Martin discovered that they could construct other units by cutting the bias squares in half. Marsha introduced these units in her book *On to Square Two*. All of the units begin with the basic bias square, cut the size specified in the directions.

Square Two

1. Stack two bias squares right sides together, with opposing color placement and seam allowances.

2. Draw a diagonal line from corner to corner. Stitch ¼" from the drawn line on both sides.

Stitching lines

3. Cut diagonally along the drawn line.

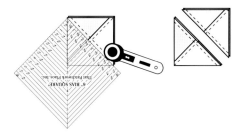

4. Press the seam to one side and trim the ends. You will have two Square Two units.

Unit 1.5

1. Cut a bias square in half diagonally.

2. Join each unit to a triangle of the same size. You will have a Unit 1.5 and a reverse Unit 1.5.

Unit .5

1. Cut a bias square in half diagonally.

2. You will have a Unit .5 and a reverse Unit .5.

HALF-SQUARE TRIANGLE UNITS FROM LAYERED STRIPS

Some of the patterns in this book call for half- and quarter-square triangle units made from layered strips. This is Judy's preferred quick-triangle technique. Yardage and yield calculations are simple and straightforward, and there is very little waste. You can make units in many different fabric combinations by using short strip pieces.

To make half-square triangle units:

When multiple half-square triangle units are needed for a block or quilt, the pattern instructions will tell you to "Make △" from precut strips or strip segments.

1. Make strip pairs by layering contrasting strips or strip segments right sides together. When you are working with several fabrics in each color or value group, use as many different fabric combinations as possible, unless otherwise instructed. If you press the strip pairs after you align the fabrics, they will stick together, reducing the possibility of slippage during the cutting process and making it unnecessary to pin when you sew.

2. Cut squares from each layered pair of strips, using the measurements given in the pattern instructions.

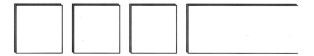

3. Cut the layered squares once diagonally from corner to corner.

4. Pick up and chain-piece the resulting triangle pairs along the long edges to make half-square triangle units; the pairs are matched and ready to sew. (See page 21 for a general description of chain piecing.) Cut the units apart and trim the corners before pressing.

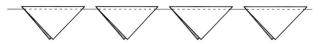

QUARTER-SQUARE TRIANGLE UNITS FROM LAYERED STRIPS

1. Start by making half-square triangle units as described previously, using the measurements given in the pattern instructions.
2. Cut the finished half-square triangle units once diagonally, perpendicular to the seam, and join the resulting pieces to make quarter-square triangle units.

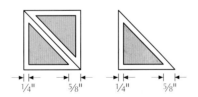

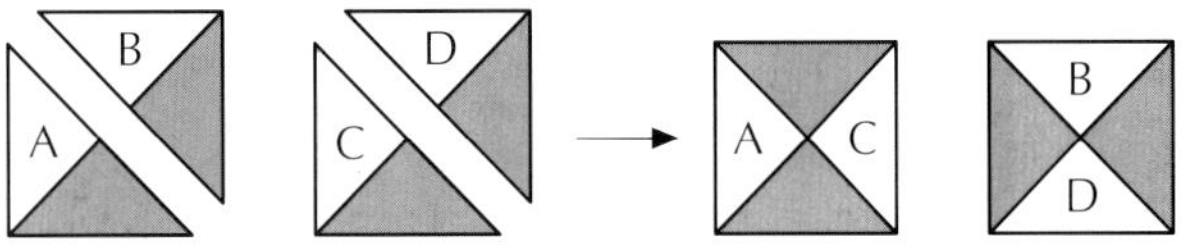

Note that two divided half-square triangle units will make two quarter-square triangle units, but you must mix and match the pieces cut from the half-square triangle units to make proper quarter-square triangle units.

MULTIFABRIC QUILTS FROM SCRAPS

Using the ScrapMaster cutting guide, you can quickly cut half-square triangles in an assortment of useful sizes from your odd-shaped scraps.

To quick-cut half-square triangles, we typically add ⅞" to the desired finished size of a short side of the triangle, cut a square to that measurement, and divide the square on the diagonal. This technique allows for ¼"-wide seam allowances and yields two half-square triangles, with the short sides on the straight grain of the fabric and the long side on the bias.

Finished size of short side
of triangle plus ⅞" = cut size

With the ScrapMaster, you can quick-cut individual half-square triangles without first cutting a square. The tool is marked for cutting 1⅞", 2⅜", 2⅞", 3⅜", and 3⅞" half-square triangles; with ¼"-wide seams, the short sides will finish to 1", 1½", 2", 2½", and 3".

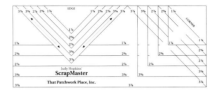

To use the ScrapMaster, you will need a rotary cutter and a cutting mat. A small cutting mat is ideal because you can rotate the mat to get the proper cutting angle without disturbing the fabric. Press your scraps before you begin, then cut as described in the following paragraphs. You can stack several scraps for cutting. Place the largest piece on the bottom and the smallest piece on top, aligning any square corners or true bias edges.

Remember the following guidelines:
For 1" (finished) triangles, use the 1⅞" lines.
For 1½ (finished) triangles, use the 2⅜" lines.
For 2" (finished) triangles, use the 2⅞" lines.
For 2½" (finished) triangles, use the 3⅜" lines.
For 3" (finished) triangles, use the 3⅞" lines.

For scraps with square corners (common with bias-square edge triangles):

Align the corner of the scrap with the proper edge-triangle lines of the ScrapMaster and cut along the straight edge to remove excess fabric.

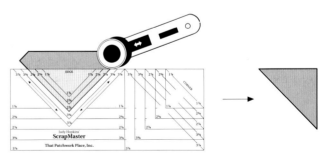

For scraps with true bias edges:

Align the bias edge of the scrap with the proper corner-triangle line of the ScrapMaster and cut along two straight edges to remove excess fabric.

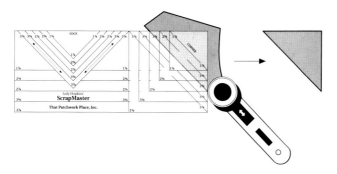

For scraps with no square corners or true bias edges:

Lay the corner triangle of the ScrapMaster over the scrap, aligning the ruler with the grain of the fabric and making sure that the corner-triangle line for the size you wish to cut does not extend beyond the fabric. Cut along the two straight edges, making a square corner.

NOTE: It may be easier to find the grain by looking at the wrong side of the fabric.

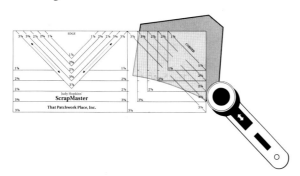

Align the square corner with the proper edge-triangle lines and cut along the straight edge to remove the excess fabric.

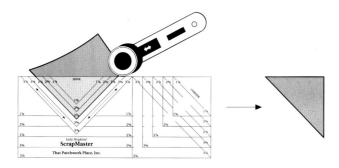

For larger scraps:

Lay the corner square of the ScrapMaster over the scrap, aligning the ruler with the grain of the fabric and making sure that the corner-square lines for the size you wish to cut do not extend beyond the fabric. Cut along the two straight edges, making a square corner.

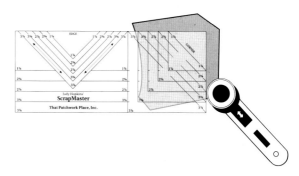

Rotate the cutting mat or turn the cut piece of fabric, align the corner you just cut with the proper corner-square lines, and cut along the two straight edges again to make a square.

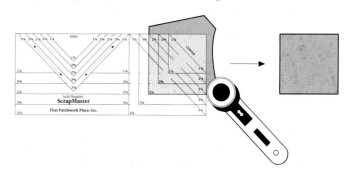

Align a corner of the square with the proper edge-triangle lines and cut along the straight edge to divide the square into two triangles.

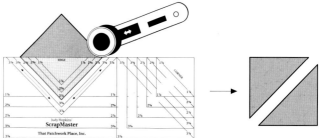

For large rectangular scraps:

Align a long edge of the ScrapMaster with the grain of the fabric and cut along the ruler to remove the uneven edge of the scrap.

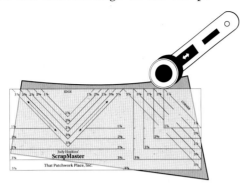

Rotate the cutting mat or turn the cut piece of fabric and align the proper long line with the straight cut you just made, letting the scrap extend just beyond the top of the ruler; cut along the two straight edges to make a square corner.

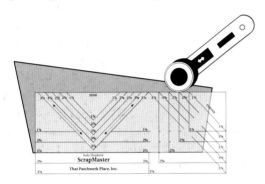

Align a square corner with the proper corner-square lines and cut along the straight edge to complete the square.

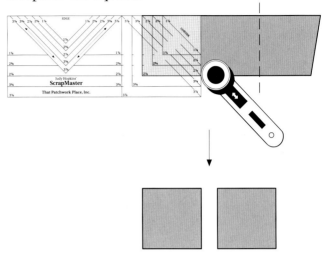

Repeat until you have cut as many squares as possible from the strip. Divide the squares, using the proper edge-triangle lines as shown above.

Machine Piecing

A well-maintained, straight-stitch sewing machine is adequate for most quiltmaking operations. If you are using a zigzag sewing machine, replace the zigzag throat plate with a plate that has a small, round hole for the needle to pass through, specially designed for straight stitching. If an even-feed ("walking") foot is available for your machine, it is worth buying one. You will find it invaluable for sewing on bindings and for straight-line machine quilting.

Use sewing-machine needles properly sized for cotton fabrics and change them frequently; dull or bent needles can snag and distort your fabric and cause your machine to skip stitches. Set the stitch length at 10 to 12 stitches per inch. Make sure the tension is adjusted properly so you are producing smooth, even seams. We recommend using 100% cotton thread; Judy uses a medium greenish-gray thread (the color you get when you mix all the Easter egg dyes together) for piecing all but the lightest and darkest fabrics.

Accurate cutting and piecing are critical elements of quiltmaking. Learn to machine stitch a straight, precise ¼"-wide seam. Find the ¼"-wide seam allowance on your machine by placing a Bias Square or a piece of accurate graph paper under the presser foot and lowering the needle onto the ¼" line. Place several layers of masking tape along the right-hand edge of the cutting square or graph paper to guide your fabric, making sure the tape does not interfere with the feed dog.

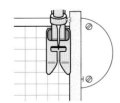

Put masking tape along edge
of graph paper to guide fabric.

Test your seam guide by cutting three short strips of fabric, each exactly 2" wide. Join the pieces into a strip unit, press the seams, and measure the finished width of the center strip. If you are sewing an accurate ¼"-wide seam, the center strip will measure exactly 1½".

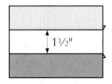

Seam 2" strips and measure the center.

You can save time and thread by chain piecing. Place the pieces that are to be joined right sides together with raw edges even; pin as necessary. Stitch the seam, guiding the pieces along the edge of your masking-tape guide, but do not lift the presser foot or cut the threads; just feed in the next set of pieces as close as possible to the last set. Sew as many seams as you can at one time; backstitching is not necessary. Clip the threads between the pieces either before or after pressing.

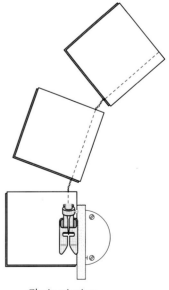

Chain piecing

Appliqué

The appliquéd circles on "State Fair" (page 220) were made with the freezer-paper method described below. Freezer paper has a plastic coating on one side; you can fold seam allowances over the freezer-paper edges and iron them to the plastic-coated side to make perfectly shaped appliqués with smooth edges.

Make a template from stiff plastic or cardboard. Do not add seam allowances to the template. Trace around the template on the plain side of a piece of freezer paper.

Cut out the freezer-paper shape on the pencil line. Do not add seam allowances. Pin the freezer-paper shape, plastic-coated side up, to the wrong side of the fabric. Cut the appliqué shape from the fabric, adding ¼"-wide seam allowances around the outside edges of the freezer paper.

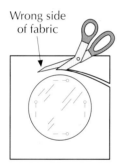

Add ¼" seam allowance all around.

Using a hot, dry iron, carefully turn and press the seam allowance over the freezer-paper edges, easing in any excess fabric. Clip inside points and fold outside points.

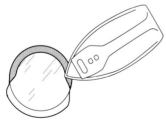

Press seam allowance over
freezer-paper edges.

Iron the design in place onto the background fabric and appliqué the shape to the background, using thread that matches the appliqué piece. Catch just a few threads at the edge of the appliqué piece. Only a tiny stitch should show on the front of the quilt; the "traveling" is done on the back.

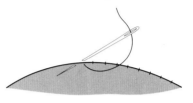

Appliqué stitch

After you have appliquéd the design, cut a small slit in the background fabric behind the appliqué. Cut away the background fabric, leaving a ¼"-wide seam allowance all around, and carefully remove the freezer paper.

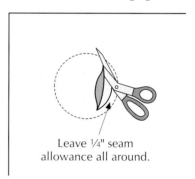

Leave ¼" seam
allowance all around.

Quilt Patterns

This section contains complete instructions for 101 rotary-cut quilts. All the patterns are written for rotary cutting; a few quilts require trimming, appliqué, or placement templates. Read the complete cutting and piecing directions for the quilt you are going to make before you begin. You may want to make a sample block to test the pattern and your fabric choices. The patterns are graded with symbols as to difficulty, so match the pattern to your skill level.

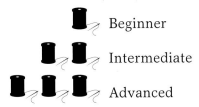

The "Materials" section of each pattern includes fabric and color suggestions. Fabric requirements are based on 44"-wide fabric that has 42 usable inches. If your fabric is not at least 42" wide after preshrinking, you may need to purchase more. The amounts given are adequate for the project; there will be little or no leftover fabric.

Cutting instructions are geared for rotary cutting. Quick-cutting and strip-piecing techniques sometimes yield more pieces than are actually needed to make a particular block or quilt; don't worry if you have a few more pieces than you need.

All measurements for block pieces include ¼"-wide seam allowances. Do not add seam allowances to the dimensions given in the cutting section. Instructions for cutting strips tell you to cut strips of a certain width and 42" long. Since 42" is the minimum length, it is fine if your strips are longer. Just cut selvage to selvage and proceed; do not trim the length to 42". Always cut the largest pieces from your fabric first, before cutting smaller pieces.

Some of the yardage specifications include a parenthetical note, for example, "1 strip, 6⅞" x 42", each of 12 different light-medium prints in assorted colors for blocks (Nearest cut is ¼ yd.)." The amount given in the parentheses is the nearest commercial cut. If you are using fabrics from your

collection, cut selvage-to-selvage strips the specified width. If you need to purchase fabric, buy the yardage specified and cut the needed strips; use the remaining fabric for another project.

Cutting specifications for triangles indicate the size of the square from which the triangles will be cut. Directions for half-square triangles instruct you to "cut once diagonally"; for quarter-square triangles, "cut twice diagonally." If you need a refresher, see the section that begins on page 11.

Use the photos and drawings that accompany the patterns as a reference while assembling your quilt. If you need help setting blocks on point, see the section that begins on page 240.

Borders with straight-cut corners rather than mitered corners are used, except where otherwise noted. Border strips are cut along the crosswise grain, except where otherwise noted, and seamed where extra length is needed; purchase additional fabric if you want to cut borders along the lengthwise grain. Border pieces are cut extra long, then trimmed to fit when the actual dimensions of the center section of the quilt are known. (See "Borders," beginning on page 242.)

Backings are pieced lengthwise or crosswise when seaming is necessary. (See "Backings" and "Batting" on page 244.)

Bindings are narrow, double-fold, and are made from straight-grain or bias strips. (See "Bindings," beginning on page 248, if you need basic information on applying bindings.)

In several of the patterns, the instructions result in a quilt that differs slightly from the quilt in the photograph; watch for the special notations that describe these differences. Though all the patterns have been written for strip piecing or bias squares, some of the photographed quilts have been made with individually cut pieces. The fabric requirements given should accommodate either method, but you will have to alter the cutting instructions if you prefer a more traditional approach.

General instructions for finishing your quilt begin on page 238. Specific quilting suggestions for the quilts in this book begin on page 252.

Amish Nine Patch Scrap

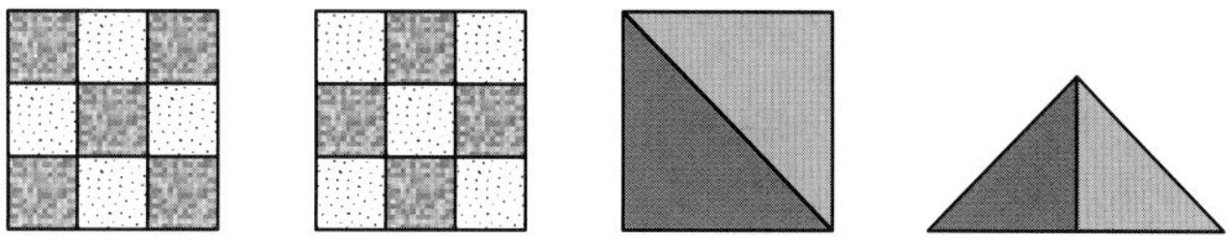

Block A
4½" block

Block B
4½" block

Block C
4½" block

Half Block D

Dimensions: 57" x 89"

126 blocks (33 Block A, 33 Block B, 50 Block C, and 10 Half Block D), 4½", set on point; 1½"-wide inner border with corner squares, 8"-wide outer border with corner squares.

NOTE: The pictured quilt has pieced corner squares in the inner border; the pattern calls for plain corner squares.

Materials: 44"-wide fabric

⅛ yd. *each* of 11 different light prints for Blocks A and B
⅛ yd. *each* of 11 different medium and/or dark prints for Blocks A and B
¼ yd. *each* of 10 different medium and/or dark solids for Block C, Half Block D, and side setting triangles
4½" x 9" medium or dark solid for corner setting triangles (Nearest cut is ⅛ yd.)
⅜ yd. bright pink solid for inner border
2" x 8" red solid for inner border corners (Nearest cut is ⅛ yd.)
2⅛ yds. blue-green solid for outer border
¼ yd. purple solid for outer border corners
5½ yds. fabric for backing (lengthwise seam)
⅝ yd. fabric for binding
Batting and thread to finish

Cutting: All measurements include ¼" seams.

From each of the 11 light and 11 medium and/or dark prints:

Cut 3 strips, 2" x 20", for a total of 33 light and 33 medium and/or dark strips for Blocks A and B.

From each of the 10 medium and/or dark solids:

Cut 1 square, 7⅝" x 7⅝", for a total of 10 squares. Cut twice diagonally into 40 quarter-square triangles for side setting triangles. You will have 20 triangles left over; save them for another project.

Cut 5 squares, 5⅜" x 5⅜", for a total of 50 squares. Cut once diagonally into 100 half-square triangles for Block C.

Cut 1 square, 4⅛" x 4⅛", for a total of 10 squares. Cut once diagonally into 20 half-square triangles for Half Block D.

From the 4½" x 9" solid:

Cut 2 squares, 4⅛" x 4⅛". Cut once diagonally into 4 half-square triangles for corner setting triangles.

From the bright pink solid:

Cut 6 strips, 2" x 42", for inner border.

From the 2" x 8" red solid:

Cut 4 squares, 2" x 2", for inner border corners.

From the blue-green solid:

Cut 4 strips, 8½" wide by the length of the fabric (2⅛ yds.) for outer border.

From the purple solid:

Cut 4 squares, 8½" x 8½", for outer border corners.

DIRECTIONS

1. Select 3 of the light print strips (all the same fabric) and 3 of the medium and/or dark print strips (all the same fabric) and join to make 2 strip units as shown. The units should measure 5" wide when sewn. Cut each unit into 9 segments, each 2" wide.

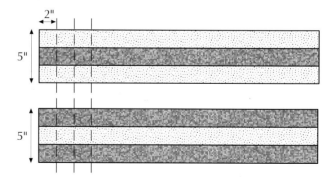

2. Join the segments to make 3 Block A and 3 Block B.
3. Repeat steps 1 and 2 with the remainder of the light print strips and the medium and/or dark print strips, for a total of 33 Block A and 33 Block B.

4. Join the 5⅜" assorted solid half-square tri-angles to make 50 Block C. Combine the fabrics at random.

5. Join the 4⅛" assorted solid half-square tri-angles to make 10 Half Block D. Combine the fabrics at random.

6. Set the blocks together in diagonal rows with the side and corner triangles as shown in the quilt photo. Join the rows. Trim and square up the outside edges after the rows are sewn if needed. See "Assembling On-Point Quilts" on page 240.

7. Add the pink inner border, seaming strips as necessary and adding red corner squares. See "Borders with Corner Squares" on page 243.

8. Add the blue-green outer border and purple corner squares as for inner border.

9. Layer with batting and backing; quilt or tie. See page 252 for a quilting suggestion.

10. Bind with straight-grain or bias strips of fabric.

Nine Patch Exchange *by George Taylor, 1993, Anchorage, Alaska, 57" x 89".*
George combined Nine Patch blocks acquired in a block swap with scraps of rich
Amish solids to make this lively quilt. Quilted by Peggy Hinchey in an original
wavy-line pattern that has become George's trademark.

Amsterdam Star

Amsterdam Star
16⅞" block

Dimensions: 77⅝" x 77⅝"

9 blocks, 16⅞", set 3 across and 3 down with 3¼"-wide sashing and sashing squares; 7"-wide border.

Materials: 44"-wide fabric

9 fat quarters of assorted beige prints for star backgrounds
10 fat quarters of assorted green prints for star "feathers" and sashing squares
5 fat quarters of assorted red prints for star tips
1½ yds. red print for sashing
2⅜ yds. striped fabric for border and star centers (must have at least 4 repeats across the width)
4⅞ yds. fabric for backing (lengthwise or crosswise seam)
⅝ yd. fabric for binding
Batting and thread to finish

Cutting: All measurements include ¼" seams.

From each fat quarter of beige print:
Cut 4 squares, 2½" x 2½", for Unit I.
Cut 4 squares, 2⅜" x 2⅜", for Unit II.
Cut 1 square, 6⅞" x 6⅞". Cut twice diagonally into 4 triangles (36 total) for Unit I.
Cut 4 squares, 4¼" x 4¼", for Unit II.

From each fat quarter of green print:
Cut 4 squares, 2⅞" x 2⅞". Cut once diagonally into 8 triangles (80 total) for Unit I.

Pair the remainder of the assorted fat quarters of green and beige prints:
Cut and piece 2½"-wide bias strips, following the directions for making bias squares on page 14. From this pieced fabric, cut 8 bias squares, 2½" x 2½", and 16 bias squares, 2⅜" x 2⅜". You will need a total of 72 bias squares, 2½", and 144 bias squares 2⅜".

NOTE: Be careful to keep these bias squares in two separate sets. The larger bias squares are used in Unit I, and the smaller bias squares are used in Unit II.

From the remaining fat quarters of green print:
Cut 16 squares, 3¾" x 3¾", for sashing squares.

From each fat quarter of red print:
Cut 8 squares, 3¾" x 3¾". Cut once diagonally into 16 triangles (80 total) for Unit I.

NOTE: You will need 8 matching triangles for each star. You will have 8 triangles left over.

From the red print for sashing:
Cut 24 pieces, 3¾" x 17⅜", for sashing strips.

From the striped fabric for border:
Cut 4 strips, 7¼" x 81", for striped border.
Cut 9 squares, 6⅛" x 6⅛", for star center.

DIRECTIONS

1. Piece 36 of Unit I, using the 2½" beige-and-green bias squares, 2½" beige squares, large beige and red triangles, and small green triangles.

NOTE: Use 8 matching red triangles, 16 matching bias squares, and 8 matching green triangles for each star.

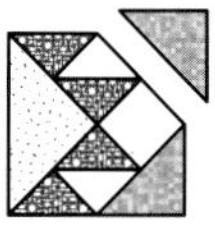

Unit I
Make 36.

2. Piece 36 of Unit II, using the 2⅜" beige-and-green bias squares, 2⅜" beige squares, and 4¼" beige squares.

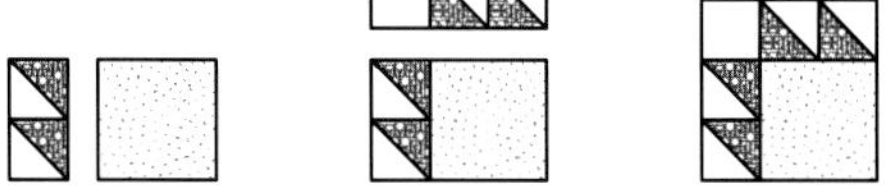

Unit II
Make 36.

3. Piece 9 Amsterdam Star blocks, using 1 center square of striped border fabric, 4 Unit I, and 4 Unit II squares for each block.

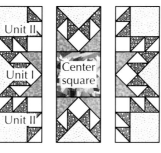

Make 9.

4. Join the blocks into rows, using 3 blocks and 4 sashing pieces.

5. Assemble 4 rows of sashing, using 3 sashing strips and 4 sashing squares.
6. Set the blocks into 3 rows of 3 with the sashing between them as shown in the quilt photo; join the rows. See "Straight Sets" on page 238.
7. Add the striped border, seaming strips as necessary. See "Borders with Mitered Corners" on page 243.
8. Layer with batting and backing; quilt or tie. See page 253 for a quilting suggestion.
9. Bind with straight-grain or bias strips of fabric.

Amsterdam Star *by Nancy J. Martin, 1992, Woodinville, Washington, 77½" x 77½". A wonderful reproduction striped chintz or "sitz" fabric purchased from* den haan *and* wagenmakers *in Amsterdam serves as the center of each Feathered Star and creates a graceful swirling border. Quilted by Alvina Nelson.*

Ann Orr's Rose Garden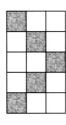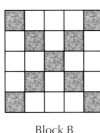

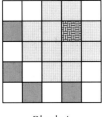

Block A
8¾" block

Block B
8¾" block

Block C
5¼" x 8¾"

Dimensions: 82¼" x 82¼"

65 blocks (25 Block A, 24 Block B, and 16 Block C), 8¾", set 7 across and 7 down with partial blocks at the outside edges; 1¾"-wide inner border, 3½"-wide outer border.

Materials: 44"-wide fabric

5¼ yds. muslin print for blocks and outer border
2 yds. pink solid for blocks and inner border
¼ yd. dark pink solid for blocks
⅝ yd. green print for blocks
1¼ yds. blue print for blocks
5⅛ yds. fabric for backing (lengthwise or crosswise seam)
⅝ yd. fabric for binding
Batting and thread to finish

Cutting: All measurements include ¼" seams.

From the muslin print:
Cut 54 strips, 2¼" x 42", for blocks.
Cut 10 strips, 4" x 42", for outer border.
Cut 4 strips, 5¾" x 42". Cut the strips into 12 rectangles, 5¾" x 9¼", for sides, and 4 squares, 5¾" x 5¾", for corners.

From the pink solid:
Cut 22 strips, 2¼" x 42", for blocks.
Cut 8 strips, 2¼" x 42", for inner border.

From the dark pink solid:
Cut 2 strips, 2¼" x 42", for blocks.

From the green print:
Cut 8 strips, 2¼" x 42", for blocks.

From the blue print:
Cut 19 strips, 2¼" x 42", for blocks.

DIRECTIONS

1. Join the 2¼" x 42" muslin, pink, dark pink, and green strips into strip units as shown. Make 2 each of Units A–E, for a total of 10 strip units. The units should measure 9¼" wide when sewn. Cut 25 segments, each 2¼" wide, from each of Units A–E; join the segments into 25 Block A.

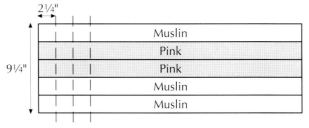

Unit A
Make 2.

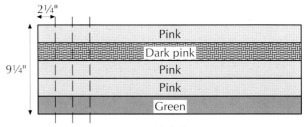

Unit B
Make 2.

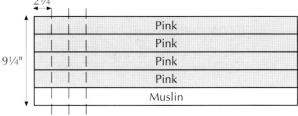

Unit C
Make 2.

Unit D
Make 2.

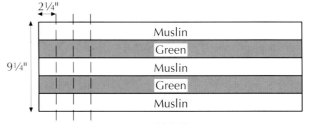

Unit E
Make 2.

2. Join the 2¼" x 42" muslin and blue strips into strip units as shown. Make 4 Unit F, 4 Unit G, and 3 Unit H. The units should measure 9¼" wide when sewn. Cut 64 segments, each 2¼" wide, from Unit F; 64 from Unit G; and 40 from Unit H. Join the segments into 24 Block B and 16 Block C.

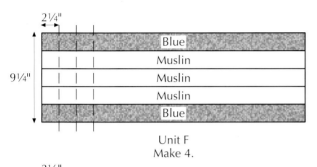

Unit F
Make 4.

Unit G
Make 4.

Unit H
Make 3.

3. Set the blocks and the muslin squares and rectangles together into 4 Row A, 3 Row B, and 2 Row C as shown.

4. Join the A and B rows, starting with Row A and alternating A and B. Add a Row C to the top and bottom of the quilt, completing the blue "chain" as shown in the photo on page 30.
5. Add the pink inner border, seaming the strips as necessary. See "Borders with Straight-Cut Corners" on page 243.
6. Add the muslin outer border as for the inner border.
7. Layer with batting and backing; quilt or tie. See page 253 for a quilting suggestion.
8. Bind with straight-grain or bias strips of fabric.

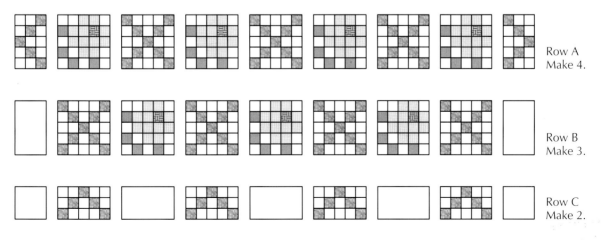

Row A
Make 4.

Row B
Make 3.

Row C
Make 2.

Anne Orr's Rose Garden *by Mimi Dietrich, 1989, Catonsville, Maryland, 82¼" x 82¼". Inspired by the design on an antique quilt, Mimi re-created this pleasing top, which combines Rose and Single Irish Chain blocks. It is reminiscent of the Anne Orr designs created during the 1930s.*

Anvil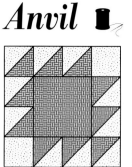

Anvil
8" block

Dimensions: 62" x 83"

35 blocks, 8", set 5 across and 7 down with 2½"-wide sashing; 6"-wide border.

Materials: 44"-wide fabric

1 fat quarter each of 12 assorted dark prints in navy, purple, burgundy, and black for blocks
1 fat quarter each of 12 assorted light prints for background
3½ yds. figured print for sashing and borders
5⅛ yds. fabric for backing (lengthwise seam)
⅝ yd. fabric for binding
Batting and thread to finish

NOTE: Directions are for cutting 12 groups of 3 identical blocks, which is the most economical way to purchase and use the fabric. If you have a large collection of scraps, don't hesitate to use them for a scrappier look as shown in the photo.

Cutting: All measurements include ¼" seams.

From each of the 12 dark prints:
Cut 4 squares, 8" x 8", for bias squares (48 total).
Cut 3 squares, 4½" x 4½", with 1 to match the dark print used in each Anvil block (36 total).

From each of the 12 light prints:
Cut 4 squares, 8" x 8", for bias squares (48 total). Pair each 8" light print with an 8" dark print, right sides up. Cut and piece 2½"-wide bias strips, following the directions for making bias squares on page 14. Cut 8 bias squares, 2½" x 2½", from each set of paired squares, for a total of 384 bias squares. You will use only 350, 10 matching bias squares for each block.
Cut 6 squares, 2½" x 2½", with 2 to match the light print in each Anvil block (72 total).

From the *length* of the figured print:
Cut 2 strips, 6½" x 71½", for side borders.
Cut 2 strips, 6½" x 62", for top and bottom borders.
Cut 28 rectangles, 3" x 8½", for vertical sashing strips.
Cut 6 strips, 3" x 50½", for horizontal sashing strips.

DIRECTIONS

1. Piece 35 Anvil blocks as shown.

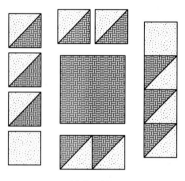

Make 35.

2. Set the blocks together in 7 rows of 5 with vertical sashing strips as shown in the quilt photo. Join the rows with a horizontal sashing strip between them.
3. Add the figured print border. See "Borders with Straight-Cut Corners" on page 243.
4. Layer with batting and backing; quilt or tie. See page 252 for a quilting suggestion.
5. Bind with straight-grain or bias strips of fabric.

Anvil *by Nancy J. Martin, 1991, Woodinville, Washington, 62" x 83". Inspired by a utility quilt made in Pennsylvania, Nancy used toile de Jouy fabric in the borders and sashing to frame contemporary fabrics that recall those printed in the late 1800s. Quilted by Freda Smith. (Collection of Martingale & Company).*

Anvil Star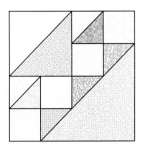

Anvil Star
8" block

Dimensions: 72" x 88"

48 blocks, 8", set 6 across and 8 down; 2"-wide inner border, 10"-wide outer border.

NOTE: Groups of 4 traditional Anvil blocks, set together in rotation, form the Anvil Star design.

Materials: 44"-wide fabric

¼ yd. *each* of 12 different light prints in assorted colors for blocks

1 strip, 6⅞" x 27", *each* of 12 different light-medium prints in assorted colors for blocks (Nearest cut is ¼ yd.)

1 strip, 2⅞" x 33", *each* of 12 different dark-medium prints in assorted colors for star points (Nearest cut is ⅛ yd.)

⅝ yd. light yellow print for inner border

2⅛ yds. multicolored print for outer border

5⅓ yds. fabric for backing (lengthwise seam)

¾ yd. fabric for binding

Batting and thread to finish

Cutting: All measurements include ¼" seams.

From each of the 12 light prints:

Cut 1 strip, 2½" x 42", for a total of 12 strips. Cut each strip into 16 squares, 2½" x 2½", for a total of 192 squares.

Cut 1 strip, 4⅞" x 11", for a total of 12 short strips.

Cut 1 strip, 2⅞" x 13", for a total of 12 short strips.

From each of the 12 light-medium strips:

Cut 2 squares, 6⅞" x 6⅞", for a total of 24 squares. Cut once diagonally into 48 half-square triangles.

From the remaining piece of each strip, cut 1 strip, 4⅞" x 11", for a total of 12 short strips.

From each of the 12 dark-medium strips:

Cut 6 squares, 2⅞" x 2⅞", for a total of 72 squares. Cut once diagonally into 144 half-square triangles.

From the remaining piece of each strip, cut 1 strip, 2⅞" x 13", for a total of 12 short strips.

From the light yellow print:

Cut 7 strips, 2½" x 42", for inner border.

From the *length* of the multicolored print:

Cut 4 strips, 10½" wide, for outer border.

DIRECTIONS

1. Make ◩: Layer the 2⅞" x 13" light and dark-medium strips, right sides together, to make 12 contrasting strip pairs. Cut 4 squares, 2⅞" x 2⅞", from each strip pair for a total of 48 layered squares. Cut the squares once diagonally and chain-piece the resulting triangle pairs to make 96 half-square triangle units.

2. Make ◩: Layer the 4⅞" x 11" light and light-medium strips, right sides together, to make 12 contrasting strip pairs. Cut 2 squares, 4⅞" x 4⅞", from each strip pair for a total of 24 layered squares. Cut the squares once diagonally and chain-piece the resulting triangle pairs to make 48 half-square triangle units.

3. Piece 48 Anvil blocks as shown. Combine the fabrics at random.

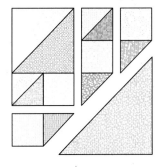

Make 48.

4. Set the blocks together in 8 rows of 6 as shown in the quilt photo, rotating every other block. Join the rows.

5. Add the light yellow inner border, seaming strips as necessary. See "Borders with Straight-Cut Corners" on page 243.

6. Add the multicolored print outer border as for the inner border.

7. Layer with batting and backing; quilt or tie. See page 252 for a quilting suggestion.

8. Bind with straight-grain or bias strips of fabric.

Anvil Star *by Ann Corkran, 1995, Anchorage, Alaska, 72" x 88". Clear pastels highlight this sentimental quilt. The anvil has a special meaning for Ann: her grandfather and great-grandfather were blacksmiths, and the one thing she has from their blacksmith shop is their anvil.*

Army Star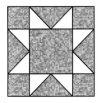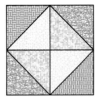

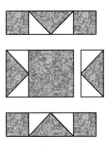

| Block A | Block B | Block C |
| 8" block | 8" block | 8" block |

Dimensions: 72" x 88"

63 blocks (12 Block A, 31 Block B, and 20 Block C), 8", set 7 across and 9 down; 2"-wide inner border, 6"-wide outer border.

Materials: 44"-wide fabric

⅜ yd. light yellow-green print for Block A

1⅞ yds. purple print for Blocks A and B

1¾ yds. yellow-green stripe for Block B and inner border

1 strip, 4⅞" x 27", *each* of 8 different medium yellow-green prints for Block C (Nearest cut is ¼ yd.)

1 strip, 4⅞" x 27", *each* of 8 different medium-to-dark purple prints for Block C (Nearest cut is ¼ yd.)

1⅝ yds. dark purple print for outer border

5⅓ yds. fabric for backing (lengthwise seam)

¾ yd. fabric for binding

Batting and thread to finish

Cutting: All measurements include ¼" seams.

From the light yellow-green print:

Cut 4 strips, 2⅞" x 42". Cut the strips into 48 squares, 2⅞" x 2⅞". Cut once diagonally into 96 half-square triangles.

From the purple print:

Cut 2 strips, 5¼" x 42". Cut the strips into a total of 12 squares, 5¼" x 5¼". Cut twice diagonally into 48 quarter-square triangles.

Cut 10 strips, 4½" x 42". Cut 2 of the strips into a total of 12 squares, 4½" x 4½". Leave the remaining 8 strips uncut.

Cut 3 strips, 2½" x 42". Cut the strips into a total of 48 squares, 2½" x 2½".

From the yellow-green stripe:

Cut 24 strips, 2½" x 42", for Block B and inner border.

From the dark purple print:

Cut 8 strips, 6½" x 42", for outer border.

DIRECTIONS

1. Join the light yellow-green and purple squares and triangles to make 12 Block A as shown.

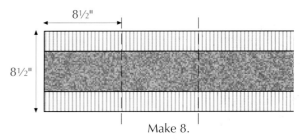

Make 12.

2. Join 16 of the 2½"-wide yellow-green striped strips and the 4½"-wide purple strips to make 8 strip units as shown. Cut the strip units into a total of 31 segments, each 8½" wide, for Block B.

Make 8.

3. Make ◺: Layer the 4⅞" x 27" medium yellow-green and medium-to-dark purple strips, right sides together, to make 8 contrasting strip pairs. Cut 5 squares, 4⅞" x 4⅞", from each strip pair for a total of 40 layered squares. Cut the squares once diagonally and chain-piece the resulting triangle pairs to make 80 half-square triangle units.

4. Piece 20 Block C as shown above.

5. Set the blocks together in 9 rows of 7 as shown in the quilt photo; join the rows.

6. Add the yellow-green striped inner border, seaming strips as necessary. See "Borders with Straight-Cut Corners" on page 243.

7. Add the dark purple outer border as for the inner border.

8. Layer with batting and backing; quilt or tie. See page 252 for a quilting suggestion.

9. Bind with straight-grain or bias strips of fabric.

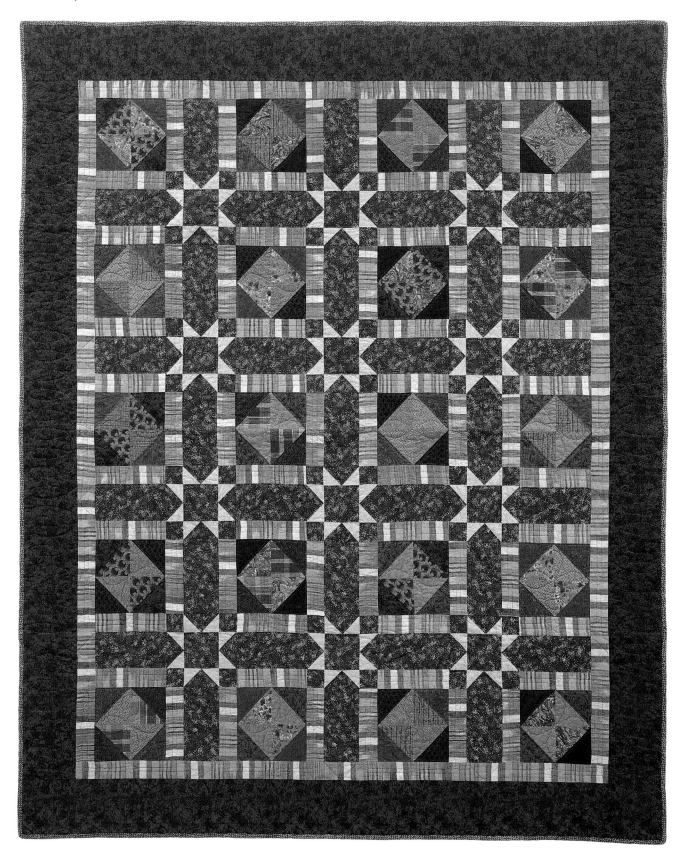

Top Brass *by Dee Morrow, 1995, Anchorage, Alaska, 71" x 85". Subtle stripes
and sparkling stars grace this elegant quilt. Dee has deftly showcased a fine
collection of green and plum prints.*

Attic Window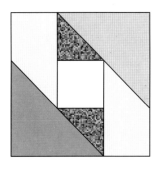

Attic Window
9" block

Dimensions: 58" x 76"

35 blocks, 9", set 5 across and 7 down; ½"-wide inner border, 6"-wide outer border.

Materials: 44"-wide fabric

1½ yds. light blue solid for blocks
⅞ yd. medium blue solid for blocks
¾ yd. dark blue solid for blocks and inner border
½ yd. peach solid for blocks
⅞ yd. lavender solid for blocks
1½ yds. mottled light blue fabric for outer border
3¾ yds. fabric for backing (crosswise seam)
⅝ yd. fabric for binding
Batting and thread to finish

Cutting: All measurements include ¼" seams.

From the light blue solid:

Cut 14 strips, 3½" x 42". Cut the strips into 70 rectangles, 3½" x 6⅞". Nip the lower right-hand corner of each rectangle at a 45° angle as shown.

From the medium blue solid:

Cut 4 strips, 6⅞" x 42". Cut the strips into 18 squares, 6⅞" x 6⅞". Cut once diagonally into 36 half-square triangles.

From the dark blue solid:

Cut 4 strips, 3⅞" x 42". Cut the strips into 35 squares, 3⅞" x 3⅞". Cut once diagonally into 70 half-square triangles.

Cut 8 strips, 1" x 42", for inner border.

From the peach solid:

Cut 4 strips, 3½" x 42". Cut the strips into 35 squares, 3½" x 3½".

From the lavender solid:

Cut 4 strips, 6⅞" x 42". Cut the strips into 18 squares, 6⅞" x 6⅞". Cut once diagonally into 36 half-square triangles.

From the mottled light blue fabric:

Cut 8 strips, 6½" x 42", for outer border.

DIRECTIONS

1. Piece 35 Attic Window blocks as shown.

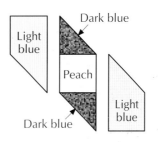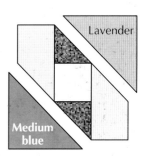

Make 35.

2. Set the blocks together in 7 rows of 5 as shown in the quilt photo; join the rows.
3. Add the dark blue inner border, seaming strips as necessary. See "Borders with Straight-Cut Corners" on page 243.
4. Add the mottled light blue outer border as for the inner border.
5. Layer with batting and backing; quilt or tie. See page 253 for a quilting suggestion.
6. Bind with straight-grain or bias strips of fabric.

Reflections *by Jacquelin Carley, 1991, Anchorage, Alaska, 58" x 76". This traditional Attic Window block may be unfamiliar to many quiltmakers; it's executed in soft lavenders, blues, and peaches and is finished with a multifabric binding.*

Bear's Paw

Bear's Paw
14" block

Dimensions: 72" x 92"

18 blocks (12 Bear's Paw blocks and 6 alternate blocks), 14", set on point; 2"-wide inner Sawtooth border, 4"-wide outer border.

Materials: 44"-wide fabric

5⅔ yds. ivory solid for blocks, alternate blocks, setting triangles, Sawtooth border, and outer border
1⅞ yds. red solid for blocks and Sawtooth border
5⅝ yds. fabric for backing (lengthwise seam)
¾ yd. fabric for binding
Batting and thread to finish

Cutting: All measurements include ¼" seams.

From the ivory solid:

Cut 12 strips, 2⅞" x 42".

Cut 4 strips, 2½" x 42". Cut the strips into a total of 52 squares, 2½" x 2½". You need 48 of these squares for the blocks; use the remaining 4 squares for the corners of the Sawtooth border.

Cut 4 strips, 6½" x 42". Cut 2 of the strips into a total of 24 segments, each 2½" wide, to make 2½" x 6½" rectangles. Leave the remaining 2 strips uncut.

Cut 3 strips, 14½" x 42". Cut the strips into a total of 6 squares, 14½" x 14½", for alternate blocks.

From the leftover pieces of the 14½"-wide strips, cut 2 squares, 11½" x 11½". Cut once diagonally into 4 half-square triangles for corner setting triangles.

From the length of the remaining piece of ivory solid, cut 4 strips, 4½" wide, for outer border.

From the remaining piece of ivory solid, cut 3 squares, 22½" x 22½". Cut twice diagonally into 12 quarter-square triangles for side setting triangles. You will have 2 triangles left over.

From the red solid:

Cut 12 strips, 2⅞" x 42".

Cut 6 strips, 4½" x 42". Cut the strips into a total of 48 squares, 4½" x 4½".

Cut 1 strip, 2½" x 42".

DIRECTIONS

1. Make 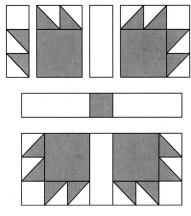: Layer the 2⅞"-wide ivory and red strips, right sides together, to make 12 contrasting strip pairs. Cut 14 squares, 2⅞" x 2⅞", from each strip pair for a total of 168 layered squares. Cut the squares once diagonally and chain-piece the resulting triangle pairs to make 336 half-square triangle units. You will use 192 units for the blocks and 140 units for the Sawtooth border, with 4 left over.

2. Join the 6½"-wide ivory strips and the 2½"-wide red strip to make 1 strip unit as shown. Cut the strip unit into 12 segments, each 2½" wide.

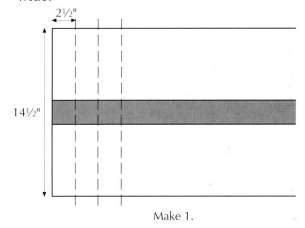

Make 1.

3. Piece 12 Bear's Paw blocks as shown.

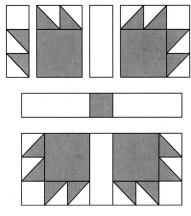

Make 12.

4. Set the blocks together in diagonal rows with the ivory alternate blocks and the side and corner triangles as shown in the quilt photo. Join the rows. Note that the setting triangles were cut large to allow some leeway in fitting the Sawtooth border to the quilt. See "Assembling On-Point Quilts" on page 240.

5. Piece the Sawtooth border, using 40 half-square triangle units for each of the 2 long edges and 30 half-square triangle units for each of the 2 short edges. Note that the Sawtooth units "turn" at the center of each pieced strip. Add a 2½" ivory square to each end of the 2 short pieces. Measure the pieced border strips and trim the patterned center section of the quilt as necessary to make the border fit properly. Join the Sawtooth border to the quilt.

6. Add the ivory outer border. See "Borders with Straight-Cut Corners" on page 243.

7. Layer with batting and backing; quilt or tie. See page 253 for a quilting suggestion.

8. Bind with straight-grain or bias strips of fabric.

Brian's Bear Paw *by Kathleen Herring, 1993, Anchorage, Alaska, 72" x 92". Flannel-backed for warmth, this classic red-and-white quilt is used daily by Kathleen's six-year-old son. The Sawtooth border adds a special touch. Quilted by Bobbi Moore.*

Birds in the Air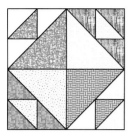

Birds in the Air
8" block

Dimensions: 45¼" x 56½"

31 blocks, 8", set on point with setting triangles and angled corners; finished without a border.

Materials: 44"-wide fabric

2 yds. assorted light prints for blocks
2 yds. assorted dark prints in blue and rust for blocks
⅜ yd. blue print or solid for setting triangles
3⅛ yds. fabric for backing (crosswise seam)
⅜ yd. fabric for binding
Batting and thread to finish

Cutting: All measurements include ¼" seams.

From the assorted light prints:

Cut 16 squares, 8" x 8", for bias squares.
Cut 31 squares, 4⅞" x 4⅞". Cut once diagonally into 62 half-square triangles.
Cut 62 squares, 2⅞" x 2⅞". Cut once diagonally into 124 half-square triangles. Cut 2 triangles to match each bias square.

From the assorted dark prints:

Cut 16 squares, 8" x 8", for bias squares. Pair each 8" dark print square with an 8" light print square, right sides up. Cut and piece 2½"-wide bias strips, following the directions for making bias squares on page 16. Cut 8 bias squares, 2½" x 2½", from each pair of squares for a total of 128 bias squares. You will have 4 bias squares left over.
Cut 31 squares, 4⅞" x 4⅞". Cut once diagonally into 62 half-square triangles.
Cut 62 squares, 2⅞" x 2⅞". Cut once diagonally into 124 half-square triangles. Cut 2 triangles to match each bias square.

From the blue fabric for setting triangles:

Cut 3 squares, 12⅝" x 12⅝". Cut twice diagonally into 12 quarter-square triangles for side setting triangles. You will have 2 triangles left over.

DIRECTIONS

1. Piece 31 Birds in the Air blocks as shown.

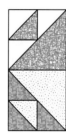 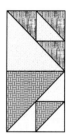

Make 4.

Make 31.

2. Set the blocks and side setting triangles into diagonal rows; join the rows. See "Assembling On-Point Quilts" on page 240.
3. Layer with batting and backing; quilt or tie. See page 253 for a quilting suggestion.
4. Bind with straight-grain or bias strips of fabric.

Hidden Stars *by Louise Bremner, 1989, Anchorage, Alaska, 45¼" x 56½".*
Classic Birds in the Air blocks, arranged on point, form hidden stars.

Blackford's Beauty

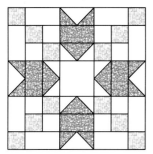

Blackford's Beauty
12" block

Dimensions: 73½" x 87½"

20 blocks, 12", set 4 across and 5 down with 2"-wide sashing; ¾"-wide inner border, 3"-wide middle border, 4"-wide outer border.

Materials: 44"-wide fabric

4⅛ yds. light print for background and middle border
1¼ yds. medium blue print for blocks, sashing squares, and inner border
2¼ yds. dark blue print for blocks and outer border
5½ yds. fabric for backing (lengthwise seam)
⅝ yd. fabric for binding
Batting and thread to finish

Cutting: All measurements include ¼" seams.

From the light print:

Cut 8 strips, 2" x 42", for blocks.

Cut 10 strips, 3½" x 42", for blocks. Cut 2 of the strips into 20 squares, 3½" x 3½". Cut 4 of the strips into 80 rectangles, 2" x 3½". Leave the remaining 4 strips uncut.

Cut 3 strips, 4¼" x 42". Cut the strips into 20 squares, 4¼" x 4¼". Cut twice diagonally into 80 quarter-square triangles for blocks.

Cut 5 strips, 2⅜" x 42". Cut the strips into 80 squares, 2⅜" x 2⅜". Cut once diagonally into 160 half-square triangles for blocks.

Cut 17 strips, 2½" x 42". Cut the strips into 49 rectangles, 2½" x 12½", for sashing.

Cut 8 strips, 3½" x 42", for middle border.

From the medium blue print:

Cut 12 strips, 2" x 42", for blocks.

Cut 2 strips, 2½" x 42". Cut the strips into 30 squares, 2½" x 2½", for sashing squares.

Cut 8 strips, 1¼" x 42", for inner border.

From the dark blue print:

Cut 3 strips, 4¼" x 42". Cut the strips into 20 squares, 4¼" x 4¼". Cut twice diagonally into 80 quarter-square triangles for blocks.

Cut 5 strips, 2⅜" x 42". Cut the strips into 80 squares, 2⅜" x 2⅜". Cut once diagonally into 160 half-square triangles for blocks.

Cut 4 strips, 3½" x 42". Cut the strips into 80 rectangles, 2" x 3½", for blocks.

Cut 8 strips, 4½" x 42", for outer border.

DIRECTIONS

1. Join the 2" x 42" light print strips and 8 of the 2" x 42" medium blue strips to make 8 strip units as shown. The units should measure 3½" wide when sewn. Cut the units into 160 segments, each 2" wide. Join the segments into 80 four-patch units.

Make 8.

2. Join the 2" x 3½" light print rectangles to the four-patch units. Make sure the medium blue corners of the four-patch units are oriented as shown.

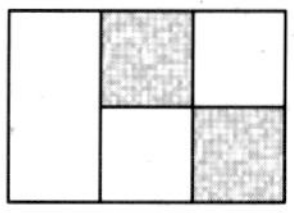

3. Join the uncut 3½" x 42" light print strips to the remaining 2" x 42" medium blue strips to make 4 strip units as shown. The units should measure 5" wide when sewn. Cut the units into 80 segments, each 2" wide.

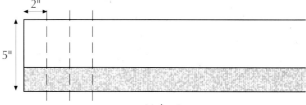

Make 4.

4. Join the segments to the four-patch units to make 80 Unit A as shown.

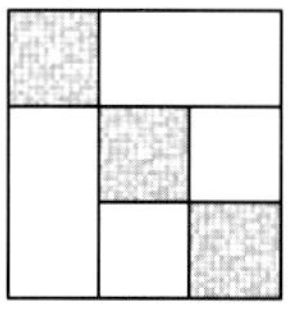

Unit A
Make 80.

5. Using the light print and dark blue half- and quarter-square triangles, piece 80 Unit B and 80 Unit C.

Unit B
Make 80.

Unit C
Make 80.

6. Join Units B and C with the dark blue rectangles to make 80 Unit D.

Unit D
Make 80.

7. Join Units A and D and light print squares to make 20 Blackford's Beauty blocks.

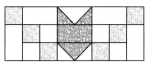

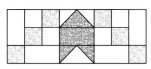

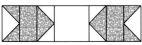

Make 20.

8. Set the blocks together in 5 rows of 4 with the light print sashing pieces and the medium blue sashing squares as shown in the quilt photo. The medium blue squares will form a "chain" across the surface of the quilt. Join the rows.

9. Add the inner border, seaming strips as necessary. See "Borders with Straight-Cut Corners" on page 243.

10. Add the middle border as for the inner border.

11. Add the outer border as for the previous borders.

12. Layer with batting and backing; quilt or tie. See page 254 for a quilting suggestion.

13. Bind with straight-grain or bias strips of fabric.

Blackford's Beauty
by Roxanne Carter, 1990, Edmonds, Washington, 73½" x 87½". The pastel color scheme is enhanced by the chain of blue squares across the quilt top.

Bridal Path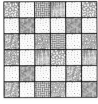

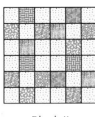

Block I
9" block

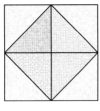

Block II
9" block

Block III
9" block

Dimensions: 51" x 63½"

32 blocks, (6 Block I, 6 Block II, and 20 Block III), 9", set on point with pieced side and corner setting triangles; finished without a border.

Materials: 44"-wide fabric

1½ yds. coral-print background fabric for nine-patch units and side and corner setting triangles

6 fat quarters of assorted teal prints for nine-patch units and side and corner setting triangles

5 fat quarters of assorted coral prints

1⅛ yds. light green fabric

3⅜ yds. coordinating fabric for backing (crosswise seam)

½ yd. fabric for binding

Batting and thread to finish

Cutting: All measurements include ¼" seams.

From the coral-print background fabric:

Cut 34 strips, 2" x 22", for nine-patch units.

Cut 1 strip, 2" x 42". Cut the strip into a total of 18 squares, 2" x 2", for pieced side and corner setting triangles.

Cut 1 strip, 3⅜" x 42". Cut the strip into 12 squares, 3⅜" x 3⅜". Cut 2 additional squares, 3⅜" x 3⅜", from a scrap, for a total of 14 squares. Cut twice diagonally into 56 quarter-square triangles. Use 54 for Corner Setting Triangle B and Side Setting Triangle B.

From the teal fat quarters:

Cut a total of 34 strips, 2" x 22", for nine-patch units.

Cut a total of 18 squares, 2" x 2", for pieced side and corner setting triangles.

Cut a total of 14 squares, 3⅜" x 3⅜". Cut twice diagonally into 56 quarter-square triangles. Use 54 for Corner Setting Triangle A and Side Setting Triangle A.

From each coral fat quarter:

Cut 8 squares, 5⅜" x 5⅜"(40 total). Cut once diagonally into 16 half-square triangles (80 total) for Block III.

From the light green fabric:

Cut 6 strips, 5⅜" x 42". Cut the strips into a total of 40 squares, 5⅜" x 5⅜". Cut once diagonally into 80 half-square triangles for Block III.

DIRECTIONS

1. Join 2 of the 2" x 22" teal strips and 1 of the 2" x 22" coral strips to make 10 strip units as shown. The units should measure 5" wide when sewn. Press seams toward the darker fabric. Cut the units into 93 segments, each 2" wide.

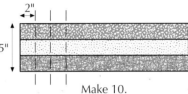

Make 10.

2. Join a 2" x 22" teal strip between 2 of the 2" x 22" coral strips to make 10 strip units as shown. The units should measure 5" wide when sewn. Cut the units into 93 segments, each 2" wide.

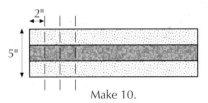

Make 10.

3. Stitch the units together to make 31 nine-patch units and 31 alternate nine-patch units. Press for opposing seams.

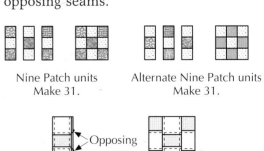

Nine Patch units
Make 31.

Alternate Nine Patch units
Make 31.

Opposing seams

Pressing

4. Join the nine-patch units and alternate nine-patch units into 6 of Block I and 6 of Block II. You will use the remaining segments in the pieced setting triangles.

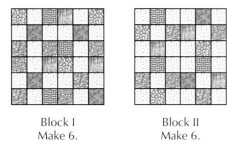

Block I
Make 6.

Block II
Make 6.

5. Join the coral and light green triangles to make 20 of Block III.

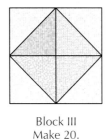

Block III
Make 20.

6. Join the remaining teal and coral strips to make 4 strip units as shown. The units should measure 3½" wide when sewn. Cut the units into 36 segments, each 2" wide.

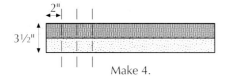

Make 4.

7. Join these segments with the remaining segments from step 4 and the teal and coral squares and triangles to make 7 Side Setting Triangle A and 7 Side Setting Triangle B.

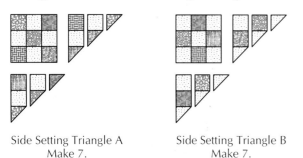

Side Setting Triangle A
Make 7.

Side Setting Triangle B
Make 7.

8. Join the remaining segments with the teal and coral squares and triangles to make 2 Corner Setting Triangle A (for lower corners) and 2 Corner Setting Triangle B (for upper corners).

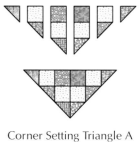

Corner Setting Triangle A
Make 2.

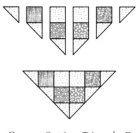

Corner Setting Triangle B
Make 2.

9. Set Blocks I, II, and III in diagonal rows with the side and corner setting triangles as shown; join the rows. See "Assembling On-Point Quilts" on page 240.

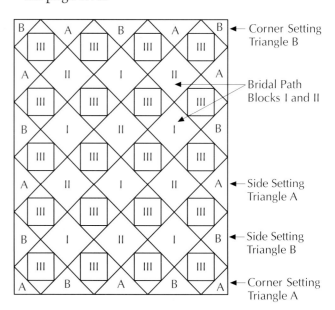

10. Layer with batting and backing; quilt or tie.
    See page 254 for a quilting suggestion.
11. Bind with straight-grain or bias strips of fabric.

Bridal Path *by Cleo Nollette, 1992, Seattle, Washington, 51" x 63½". Simple nine-patch units in two color families form chains across the quilt top. The delicate coral fabrics showcase an assortment of teal prints. Quilted by Roxanne Carter. (Collection of Martingale & Company.)*

A Brighter Day

This pattern was inspired by a Katherine Courtney quilt, original published in Old Fashioned Patchwork *magazine (Summer 1993, page 35); the design is used with Katherine's permission.*

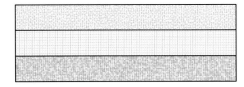

Nine Patch
3¾" block

Strip unit

Dimensions: 44¾" x 52¼"

28 Nine Patch blocks, 3¾", 17 strip units, 3¾" x 11¼", and 10 strip units, 3¾" x 7½", set together in 11 rows; 1¼"-wide inner border, ½"-wide middle border, 3¾"-wide outer border.

Materials: 44"-wide fabric

½ yd. light taupe print for blocks and inner border (Fabric 1)

⅓ yd. each of 2 more light taupe prints for blocks (Fabrics 2 and 3)

½ yd. medium taupe print for blocks (Fabric 4)

1⅛ yds. large-scale coral print for blocks and outer border (Fabric 5)

⅜ yd. each of 2 more medium coral prints for blocks (Fabrics 6 and 7)

¼ yd. purple print for middle border

3 yds. fabric for backing (crosswise seam)

½ yd. fabric for binding

Batting and thread to finish

NOTE: Paste a snip of each of Fabrics 1–7 to a card and number the snips. Use this for reference during the cutting and assembly process.

Cutting: All measurements include ¼" seams.

From Fabric 1:
    Cut 9 strips, 1¾" x 42", for blocks and inner border.

From *each* of Fabrics 2 and 3:
    Cut 5 strips, 1¾" x 42" (10 total).

From Fabric 4:
    Cut 7 strips, 1¾" x 42", for blocks.

From Fabric 5:
    Cut 6 strips, 4¼" x 42", for outer border.
    Cut 5 strips, 1¾" x 42", for blocks.

From *each* of Fabrics 6 and 7:
    Cut 6 strips, 1¾" x 42" (12 total).

From the purple print:
    Cut 5 strips, 1" x 42", for middle border.

DIRECTIONS

1. Join strips cut from Fabrics 7, 1, and 6 to make 4 strip units as shown. Cut the strip units into a total of 12 segments, each 11¾" wide.

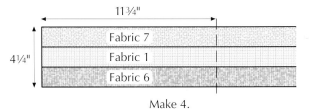

Make 4.

2. Join strips cut from Fabrics 2, 5, and 3 to make 4 strip units as shown. Cut 2 of the strip units into a total of 5 segments, each 11¾" wide. Cut the remaining 2 strip units into a total of 10 segments, each 8" wide.

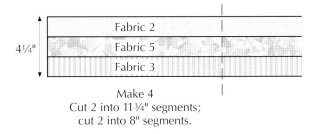

Make 4
Cut 2 into 11¾" segments;
cut 2 into 8" segments.

3. Join strips cut from Fabrics 7, 4, and 6 to make 2 strip units as shown. Cut the strip units into a total of 36 segments, each 1¾" wide.

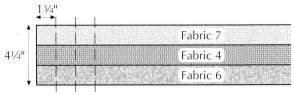

Make 2.

4. Join strips cut from Fabrics 4 and 5 to make 1 strip unit as shown. Cut the strip unit into 18 segments, each 1¾" wide.

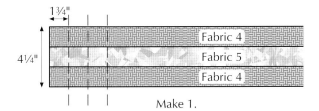

Make 1.

5. Join the segments you cut in steps 3 and 4 to make 18 Nine Patch blocks as shown.

7	4	6
4	5	4
6	4	7

Make 18

6. Join strips cut from Fabrics 2, 4, and 3 to make 1 strip unit as shown. Cut the strip unit into 20 segments, each 1¾" wide.

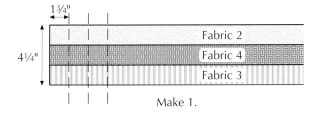

Make 1.

7. Join strips cut from Fabrics 4 and 1 to make 1 strip unit as shown. Cut the strip unit into 10 segments, each 1¾" wide.

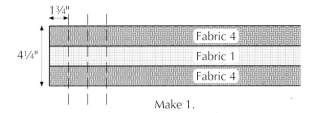

Make 1.

8. Join the segments you cut in steps 6 and 7 to make 10 Nine Patch blocks as shown.

2	4	3
4	1	4
3	4	2

Make 10.

9. Join the segments cut in steps 1 and 2 and the blocks assembled in steps 5 and 8 to make 11 rows as shown in the quilt photo. Be sure to orient the Nine Patch blocks and the strip-unit segments as shown. Join the rows.

10. Add the Fabric 1 inner border, seaming strips as necessary. See "Borders with Straight-Cut Corners" on page 243.

11. Add the purple print middle border as for the inner border.

12. Add the Fabric 5 outer border as for the previous borders.

13. Layer with batting and backing; quilt or tie. See page 252 for a quilting suggestion.

14. Bind with straight-grain or bias strips of fabric.

Fantasia *by Anne Richardson, 1994, Anchorage, Alaska, 42¾" x 50".
Sophisticated fabric and color choices make this simple quilt very special. The
narrow purple border is an important addition. Quilted by the Indiana Amish.*

Broken Dishes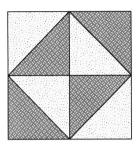

Broken Dishes
5" block

Dimensions: 75" x 86"

240 blocks (120 Broken Dishes blocks and 120 alternate blocks), 5", set 15 across and 16 down; 3"-wide top and bottom border.

NOTE: One of the Broken Dishes blocks in the antique quilt pictured is turned "wrong." Was it deliberate? You can either duplicate or correct this "error" when you set your blocks together.

Materials: 44"-wide fabric

⅛ yd. *each* of 7 different red prints for Broken Dishes blocks
⅛ yd. *each* of 7 different light and/or medium blue prints for Broken Dishes blocks
⅛ yd. *each* of 8 different dark blue prints for Broken Dishes blocks
½ yd. *each* of 5 different light prints for Broken Dishes blocks
2⅞ yds. light print A for alternate blocks
½ yd. light print B for top and bottom border
5⅜ yds. fabric for backing (lengthwise seam)
¾ yd. fabric for binding
Batting and thread to finish

Cutting: All measurements include ¼" seams.

From each red print:

Cut 1 strip, 3⅜" x 42" (7 total). Cut the strips into a total of 78 squares, 3⅜" x 3⅜". Cut once diagonally into 156 half-square triangles for Broken Dishes blocks.

From each light and/or medium blue print:

Cut 1 strip, 3⅜" x 42" (7 total). Cut the strips into a total of 74 squares, 3⅜" x 3⅜". Cut once diagonally into 148 half-square triangles for Broken Dishes blocks.

From each dark blue print:

Cut 1 strip, 3⅜" x 42" (8 total). Cut the strips into a total of 88 squares, 3⅜" x 3⅜". Cut once diagonally into 176 half-square triangles for Broken Dishes blocks.

From each of the 5 light prints:

Cut 4 strips, 3⅜" x 42" (20 total). Cut the strips into a total of 240 squares, 3⅜" x 3⅜". Cut once diagonally into 480 half-square triangles for Broken Dishes blocks.

From light print A:

Cut 18 strips, 5½" x 42". Cut the strips into 120 squares, 5½" x 5½", for alternate blocks.

From light print B:

Cut 4 strips, 3½" x 42", for top and bottom borders.

DIRECTIONS

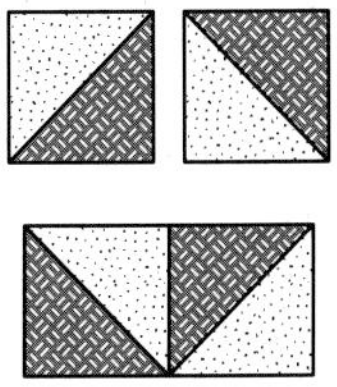

1. Join the red print half-square triangles and 156 of the light print half-square triangles to make 156 half-square triangle units. Join the half-square triangle units to make 39 Broken Dishes blocks as shown.

2. Join the light and/or medium blue print half-square triangles and 148 of the light print half-square triangles to make 148 half-square triangle units. Join the half-square triangle units to make 37 Broken Dishes blocks as shown above.

3. Join the dark blue print half-square triangles and the remaining light print half-square triangles to make 176 half-square triangle units. Join the half-square triangle units to make 44 Broken Dishes blocks as shown above.

4. Set the blocks together in 16 rows of 15 as shown in the quilt photo, alternating Broken Dishes blocks and 5½" light print A squares; join the rows.

5. Add the light print B top and bottom borders, seaming strips as necessary.

6. Layer with batting and backing; quilt or tie. See page 254 for a quilting suggestion.

7. Bind with straight-grain or bias strips of fabric.

Broken Dishes, *maker unknown, c. 1930, purchased in Nebraska, 68" x 78½".*
The maker arranged her colors in tidy diagonal rows but interrupted the flow by
turning one block the "wrong" way. NOTE: The pattern uses slightly larger blocks
and produces a 75" x 86" quilt. (Collection of Rosie Huntemann)

Broken Wheel

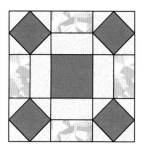

Broken Wheel
12¾" block

Dimensions: 69¼" x 86¼"

12 blocks, 12¾", set 3 across and 4 down with 4¼"-wide sashing and pieced sashing squares; 1"-wide inner border, 6"-wide outer border.

Materials: 44"-wide fabric

3 yds. light gold print for blocks and sashing
1⅛ yds. blue print for blocks and inner border
2¼ yds. red print for blocks and outer border
5¼ yds. fabric for backing (lengthwise seam)
¾ yd. fabric for binding
Batting and thread to finish

Cutting: All measurements include ¼" seams.

From the light gold print:
Cut 8 strips, 3" x 42". Cut the strips into a total of 108 squares, 3" x 3". Cut once diagonally into 216 half-square triangles.
Cut 7 strips, 2⅝" x 42".
Cut 13 strips, 4¾" x 42". Cut 6 of the strips into a total of 17 rectangles, 4¾" x 13¼"*, for sashing pieces. Leave the remaining 7 strips uncut.
*Your blocks may not measure exactly 13¼" square when sewn. Cut these rectangles a little longer and trim the sashing pieces to size after you piece the blocks if you wish.

From the blue print:
Cut 4 strips, 3½" x 42". Cut the strips into a total of 48 squares, 3½" x 3½".
Cut 2 strips, 4¾" x 42".
Cut 7 strips, 1½" x 42", for inner border.

From the red print:
Cut 1 strip, 3½" x 42". Cut the strip into 6 squares, 3½" x 3½".
Cut 7 strips, 2⅝" x 42".
Cut 8 strips, 6½" x 42", for outer border.

DIRECTIONS

1. Join the light gold triangles and the blue and red squares to make 48 gold and blue units (for blocks) and 6 gold and red units (for pieced sashing squares) as shown.

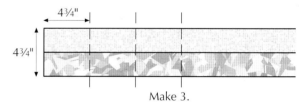

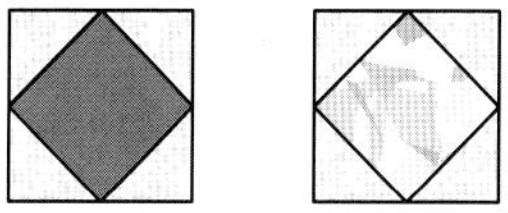

Make 48.   Make 6.

2. Join 3 each of the 2⅝"-wide light gold and red strips to make 3 strip units as shown. Cut the strip units into a total of 24 segments, each 4¾" wide.

4¾"

4¾"

Make 3.

3. Join the remaining 2⅝"-wide light gold and red strips and the 4¾"-wide blue strips to make 2 strip units as shown. Cut the strip units into a total of 12 segments, each 4¾" wide.

4¾"

13¼"

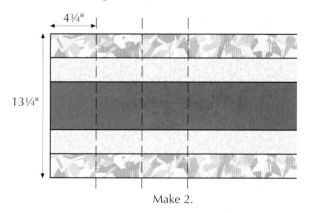

Make 2.

4. Piece 12 Broken Wheel blocks as shown.

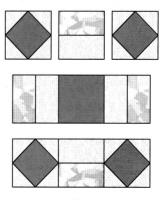

Make 12.

5. Set the blocks together in 4 rows of 3 with the light gold sashing pieces and the pieced sashing squares as shown in the quilt photo; join the rows. See "Straight Sets" on page 238. Seam the remaining 4¾"-wide light gold strips as necessary and add to the outside edges of the quilt.

6. Add the blue print inner border, seaming strips as necessary. See "Borders with Straight-Cut Corners" on page 243.

7. Add the red print outer border as for the inner border.

8. Layer with batting and backing; quilt or tie. See page 254 for a quilting suggestion.

9. Bind with straight-grain or bias strips of fabric.

Broken Wheel *by Trish DeLong, 1995, Fairbanks, Alaska, 64½" x 85". This design is also known as Rolling Stone and Wedding Ring. The dramatic Oriental print and the interesting background fabric combine to make a truly elegant quilt. Quilted by Janet Myers.*

Buckeye Beauty

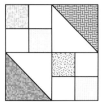 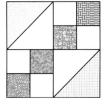

Block A
6" block

Block B
6" block

Dimensions: 66" x 84"

130 blocks (65 Block A and 65 Block B), 6", set 10 across and 13 down; 3"-wide border.

Materials: 44"-wide fabric

2 yds. assorted medium gray and tan prints for blocks
2 yds. assorted dark red and black prints for blocks
3¾ yds. assorted light prints for blocks
1 yd. black print for border
5⅛ yds. fabric for backing (lengthwise seam)
⅝ yd. fabric for binding
Batting and thread to finish

Cutting: All measurements include ¼" seams.

From the assorted medium gray and tan prints:
Cut 4 fat quarters, 18" x 22", for bias squares.
Cut 13 strips, 2" x 42", for blocks.

From the assorted dark red and black prints:
Cut 4 fat quarters, 18" x 22", for bias squares.
Cut 13 strips, 2" x 42", for blocks.

From the assorted light prints:
Cut 8 fat quarters, 18" x 22", for bias squares. Pair each light fat quarter with a medium or dark print fat quarter, right sides up. Cut and piece 3"-wide bias strips, following the directions for making bias squares on page 14. Cut a total of 130 light/medium bias squares, 3½" x 3½", and a total of 130 light/dark bias squares, 3½" x 3½:
Cut 26 strips, 2" x 42", for blocks.

From the black print:
Cut 8 strips, 3½" x 42", for border.

DIRECTIONS

1. Join the 2"-wide medium gray and tan strips to 13 of the 2"-wide light strips to make 13 strip units as shown. The strip units should measure 3½" wide when sewn. Cut a total of 260 segments, each 2" wide, from the strip units.

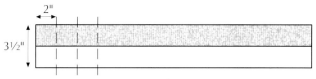

Make 13.

2. Join the segments into 130 light/medium four-patch units as shown.

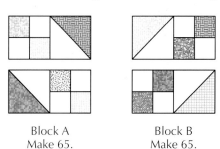

Make 130.

3. Join the 2"-wide red and black strips to the remaining 2"-wide light strips to make 13 strip units. The units should measure 3½" wide when sewn. Cut a total of 260 segments, each 2" wide, from the strip units. Join the segments into 130 light/dark four-patch units.

4. Piece 65 Block A, using the light/medium four-patch units and the light/dark bias squares. Piece 65 Block B, using the light/dark four-patch units and the light/medium bias squares.

Block A
Make 65.

Block B
Make 65.

5. Set the blocks together in 13 rows of 10 as shown in the quilt photo, alternating Block A and Block B. Start even-numbered rows with Block A and odd-numbered rows with Block B. Join the rows.
6. Add the black print border, seaming strips as necessary. See "Borders with Straight-Cut Corners" on page 243.
7. Layer with batting and backing; quilt or tie. See page 254 for a quilting suggestion.
8. Bind with straight-grain or bias strips of fabric.

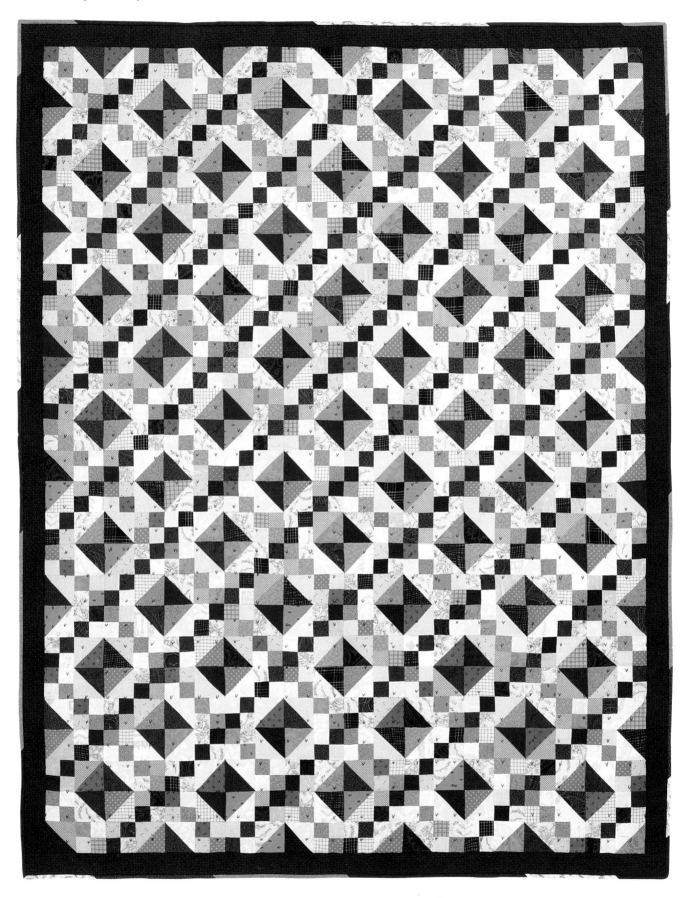

Mysterious Buckeye Beauty *by Carol Rhoades, 1991, Anchorage, Alaska, 66" x 84". This scrappy classic is made from an assortment of red, gray, black, and tan fabrics and is finished with crow footing and a multifabric binding.*

Charm Quilt

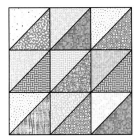

Charm Quilt
7½" block

Dimensions: 60" x 81¼"*

59 blocks, 7½", set on point with large setting triangles; finished without a border.

*Finished size will vary with size of setting triangles and trimming.

NOTE: In a charm quilt, no two fabrics are repeated. This quilt contains 1062 different triangles, which are rotary cut from scraps, using the ScrapMaster tool.

Materials: 44"-wide fabric

Scraps large enough to cut 177 light, 354 medium, and 531 dark 3⅜" ScrapMaster triangles for blocks
2⅛ yds. dark brown print for setting triangles
3⅞ yds. fabric for backing (crosswise seam)
⅝ yd. fabric for binding
Batting and thread to finish

Cutting: All measurements include ¼" seams.

From the scraps:

Cut 177 light, 354 medium, and 531 dark 3⅜" ScrapMaster triangles for blocks.

From the dark brown print:

Cut 5 squares, 19" x 19". Cut twice diagonally into 20 quarter-square triangles for side setting triangles.

Cut 2 squares, 13¼" x 13¼". Cut once diagonally into 4 half-square triangles for corner setting triangles.

DIRECTIONS

1. Piece 59 blocks. Each block contains 9 dark, 6 medium, and 3 light triangles as shown above right. In the pictured quilt, 16 of the blocks are primarily red, 16 are green, 14 are blue, 5 are purple, 4 are brown, and 4 are black. If you don't have enough scraps of a particular color to duplicate the pictured quilt exactly, use browns, purples, or rusts in place of reds, or substitute greens or blacks for blues. Or, ignore color completely and concentrate on achieving the desired value distribution in the individual blocks. Just do the best you can with what you have and enjoy the wonderful results!

Make 59.

2. Set the blocks together in diagonal rows with the dark brown side and corner setting triangles, arranging the colors as shown below. The setting triangles are cut large, to allow the blocks to "float." See "Assembling On-Point Quilts" on page 240.

B = blue
BL = black
BR = brown
G = green
P = purple
R = red

3. Join the rows. Trim and square up the outside edges after the rows are sewn if needed.
4. If desired, trim the corners of the quilt at a 45° angle as shown in the quilt photo.
5. Layer with batting and backing; quilt or tie. See page 255 for a quilting suggestion.
6. Bind with straight-grain or bias strips of fabric.

Charmed, I'm Sure *by Judy Hopkins, 1987, Anchorage, Alaska, 58" x 78½". Judy believes that the best way to become adept at combining printed fabrics is to make a charm quilt. This one includes 1061 different prints. Can you find the one fabric that appears twice? Hint: It's blue.*

Christmas Star

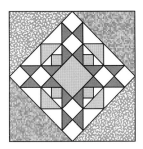

Christmas Star
12¾" block

Dimensions: 53¾" x 67½"

12 blocks, 12¾", set 3 across and 4 down; ¾"-wide inner border, ½"-wide middle border, 7"-wide outer border.

Materials: 44"-wide fabric

1 strip, 4½" x 13", *each* of 12 different red prints for blocks (Nearest cut is ⅛ yd.)
1 strip, 2⅜" x 21", *each* of 12 different green prints for blocks (Nearest cut is ⅛ yd.)
¼ yd. *each* of 6 different light gold prints for blocks
⅞ yd. dark green print for block corners and middle border
2 yds. red print for block corners and outer border
¼ yd. tan/red/green stripe for inner border
3½ yds. fabric for backing (crosswise seam)
1 yd. fabric for binding*
Batting and thread to finish

*To make the ¾"-wide finished double-fold binding shown in the quilt photo, cut 4¾"-wide strips.

Cutting: All measurements include ¼" seams.

From each of the 12 red strips:

Cut 1 square, 4¼" x 4¼" (12 total). Cut twice diagonally into 48 quarter-square triangles for blocks.

Cut 1 square, 3½" x 3½" (12 total).

Cut 4 squares, 1⁹⁄₁₆" x 1⁹⁄₁₆" (halfway between the 1½" and 1⅝" marks on your cutting square) (48 total).

From each of the 12 green strips:

Cut 8 squares, 2⅜" x 2⅜" (96 total). Cut once diagonally into 192 half-square triangles.

From each of the 6 light gold prints:

Cut 1 strip, 2" x 42" (6 total). Cut 16 squares, 2" x 2", from each strip for a total of 96 squares.

Cut 4 squares, 4¼" x 4¼" (24 total). Cut twice diagonally into 96 quarter-square triangles.

Cut 4 squares, 2¾" x 2¾" (24 total). Cut twice diagonally into 96 quarter-square triangles.

From the dark green print:

Cut 3 strips, 7¼" x 42". Cut the strips into a total of 12 squares, 7¼" x 7¼". Cut once diagonally into 24 half-square triangles.

Cut 5 strips, 1" x 42", for middle border.

From the red print:

Cut 1 strip, 7¼" x 42". Cut the strip into 5 squares, 7¼" x 7¼". Cut once diagonally into 10 half-square triangles.

From the length of the remaining piece of red print, cut 4 strips, 7½" wide, for outer border.

From the remaining piece of red print, cut 7 squares, 7¼" x 7¼". Cut once diagonally into 14 half-square triangles.

From the tan/red/green stripe:

Cut 5 strips, 1¼" x 42", for inner border.

DIRECTIONS

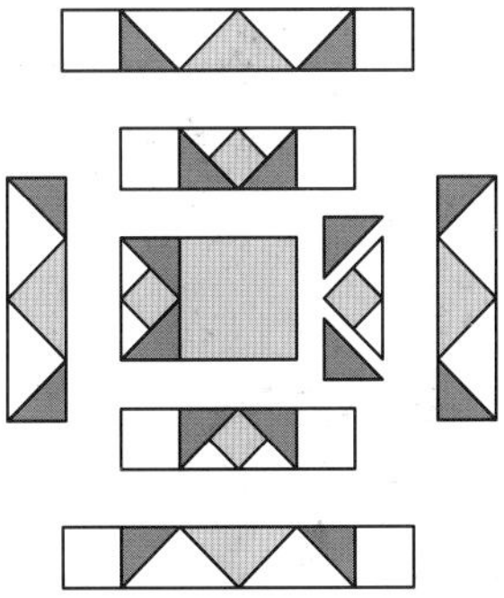

1. Piece 12 Christmas Stars as shown. Use just 1 red print, 1 green print, and 1 light gold print in each block.
2. Join the 7¼" red and green triangles to the stars as shown above.
3. Set the blocks together in 4 rows of 3 as shown in the quilt photo; join the rows.

Make 12.

4. Add the striped inner border, seaming strips as necessary. See "Borders with Straight-Cut Corners" on page 243.
5. Add the dark green middle border as for the inner border.
6. Add the red outer border as for the previous borders.
7. Layer with batting and backing; quilt or tie. See page 254 for a quilting suggestion.
8. Bind with straight-grain or bias strips of fabric.

Christmas Star *by Judy Dafoe Hopkins, 1995 Anchorage, Alaska, 53¾" x 67¼". This sparkling holiday quilt features a large assortment of red and green prints. The striped inner border is a surprising—but pleasing—addition. Quilted by Mrs. Emma Smucker.*

City Lights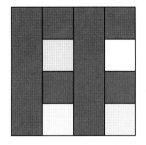

City Lights
8" block

Dimensions: 62" x 74"

20 blocks, 8", set 4 across and 5 down with 4"-wide sashing and pieced sashing squares; 1"-wide inner border, 4"-wide outer border.

Materials: 44"-wide fabric

2⅝ yds. black solid for blocks, pieced sashing squares, and outer border
1 strip, 2½" x 42", *each* of 8 different light solids (pinks, aquas, lavenders, light blues, light greens) for blocks and pieced sashing squares
1½ yds. medium blue print or solid for sashing
⅜ yd. purple solid for inner border
4 yds. fabric for backing (crosswise seam)
⅝ yd. fabric for binding
Batting and thread to finish

Cutting: All measurements include ¼" seams.

From the black solid:
Cut 10 strips, 4½" x 42". From 2 of the strips, cut a total of 30 segments, each 2½" wide, to make 2½" x 4½" rectangles for pieced sashing squares. Leave the remaining 8 strips uncut for outer border.
Cut 3 strips, 8½" x 42". Cut the strips into segments, each 2½" wide, to make 40 rectangles, each 2½" x 8½", for blocks.
Cut 8 strips, 2½" x 42", for blocks and pieced sashing squares.

From the medium blue print or solid:
Cut 6 strips, 8½" x 42". Cut the strips into segments, each 4½" wide, to make 49 rectangles, 4½" x 8½", for sashing.

From the purple solid:
Cut 8 strips, 1½" x 42", for inner border.

DIRECTIONS

1. Join any 6 of the 2½" x 42" light strips and 6 of the 2½" x 42" black strips to make 3 strip units as shown. The strip units should measure 8½" wide when sewn. Cut the units into a total of 40 segments, each 2½" wide.

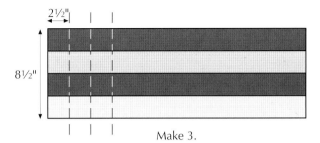

2½"

8½"

Make 3.

2. Join the segments with the 2½" x 8½" black rectangles to make 20 City Lights blocks as shown.

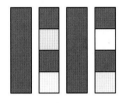

Make 20.

3. Join the remaining 2½" x 42" light and black strips to make 2 strip units as shown. The strip units should measure 4½" wide when sewn. Cut the units into a total of 30 segments, each 2½" wide.

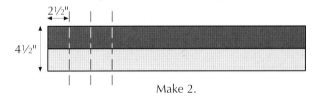

2½"

4½"

Make 2.

4. Join the segments with the 2½" x 4½" black rectangles to make 30 sashing squares as shown.

Make 30.

5. Set the blocks together in 5 rows of 4 with the 4½" x 8½" medium blue sashing pieces and the sashing squares as shown in the quilt photo; join the rows. See "Straight Sets" on page 238.

6. Add the purple inner border, seaming strips as necessary. See "Borders with Straight-Cut Corners" on page 243.

7. Add the black outer border as for inner border.

8. Layer with batting and backing; quilt or tie.

See page 255 for a quilting suggestion.

9. Bind with straight-grain or bias strips of fabric.

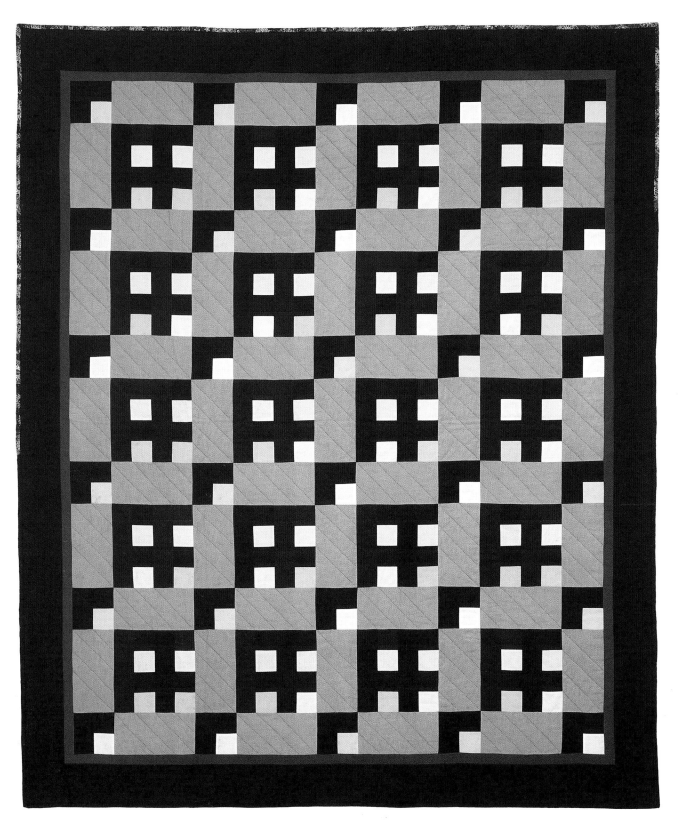

City Lights *by Jacquelin Carley, 1993, Anchorage, Alaska, 62" x 74". A Puss-in-the-Corner variation, Jackie's striking, cosmopolitan quilt is quick and easy to make and looks great in a variety of color combinations. Try it with fire-engine red sashing!*

Cleo's Castles in the Air

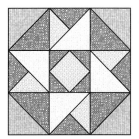

Cleo's Castles in the Air
9" block

Dimensions: 63" x 63"

16 blocks, 9", set 4 across and 4 down with 3"-wide sashing and sashing squares; 6"-wide border.

Materials: 44"-wide fabric

2 yds. blue-and-lavender print for block corners, sashing squares, and borders
1 yd. blue paisley fabric for star background
½ yd. periwinkle blue fabric for small star tip
1½ yds. light blue print for star tips and sashing
Scraps of blue fabrics for star centers
4 yds. fabric for backing (lengthwise or crosswise seam)
½ yd. fabric for binding
Batting and thread to finish

Cutting: All measurements include ¼" seams.

From the blue-and-lavender print:
Cut 2 strips, 3½" x 42". Cut the strips into 24 squares, 3½" x 3½". Cut 1 additional square from a scrap for a total of 25 sashing squares.
Cut 8 strips, 6¼" x 42", for borders.

From the blue paisley and the remaining blue-and-lavender print:
Cut 2 fat quarters (approximately 18" x 22") from each of the fabrics. Pair each blue paisley fat quarter with a lavender print fat quarter; you will have 2 pairs. Cut and piece 3"-wide bias strips, following the directions for bias squares on page 14. From this pieced fabric, cut 64 bias squares, 3½" x 3½".

From the blue paisley and periwinkle blue fabrics:
Cut a fat quarter (18" x 22") from each of the fabrics. Layer, cut, and piece 3½"-wide bias strips. From this pieced fabric, cut 32 bias squares, 3⅞" x 3⅞". Cut once diagonally into 64 of Unit .5, following the directions on page 17.

From the remaining blue paisley fabric:
Cut 32 squares, 2⅜" x 2⅜". Cut once diagonally into 64 triangles for star centers.

From the light blue print:
Cut 4 strips, 3⅞ x 42". Cut the strips into a total of 32 squares, 3⅞" x 3⅞". Cut once diagonally into 64 triangles for star tips.
Cut 10 strips, 3½" x 42". Cut the strips into a total of 40 pieces, 3½" x 9½", for sashing strips.

From the scraps of blue fabrics:
Cut 16 squares, 2⅝" x 2⅝", for star centers.

DIRECTIONS

1. Piece 16 star centers, using the 2⅝" blue squares and the blue paisley triangles.

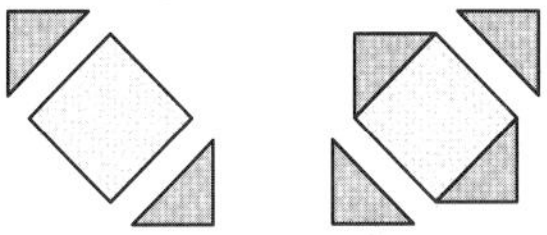

Make 16.

2. Join Unit .5 to light blue triangles to make Unit 1.5 as shown on page 17. You will have 32 of each configuration.

Unit 1.5
Make 32.

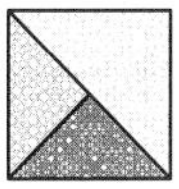

Alternate Unit 1.5
Make 32.

3. Piece 16 Cleo's Castles in the Air blocks, using the star centers, identical units of Unit 1.5, and bias squares. In 8 of the blocks, you will use one type of Unit 1.5, and in 8 you will use the alternate Unit 1.5.

   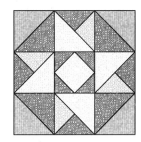

Make 8.   Make 8.

4. Set the blocks into rows, using 4 blocks (alternate configuration) and 5 sashing strips. See "Straight Sets" on page 238.

5. Assemble 5 rows of sashing, using 4 sashing strips and 5 sashing squares.

6. Join the rows of blocks with sashing between them as shown in the quilt photo.

7. Add the blue and lavender print border, seaming strips as necessary. See "Borders with Straight-Cut Corners" on page 243.

8. Layer with batting and backing; quilt or tie. See page 255 for a quilting suggestion.

9. Bind with straight-grain or bias strips of fabric.

Cleo's Castles in the Air *by Nancy J. Martin, 1992, Woodinville, Washington, 63" x 63". Delicate blue fabrics highlight the white center stars, which appear to spin in two directions. A Baptist Fan pattern was quilted in the border. Quilted by Marta Estes. (Collection of Martingale & Company)*

Comet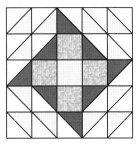

Comet
10" block

Dimensions: 55" x 70"

21 blocks, 10", set in 3 vertical strips with ½"-wide edge strips; four 5½"-wide bars.

Materials: 44"-wide fabric

1⅓ yds. ivory print for blocks
1 piece, 8" x 18", of bright gold solid for block centers (Nearest cut is ¼ yd.)
1 strip, 2⅞" x 42", *each* of 9 different yellow and gold solids for blocks (Nearest cut is ⅛ yd.)*
1 yd. dark blue print for blocks and seamed edge strips
2⅛ yds. multicolored print for blocks and bars
3½ yds. fabric for backing (crosswise seam)
⅝ yd. fabric for binding
Batting and thread to finish
*Use the same fabric more than once if you wish.

Cutting: All measurements include ¼" seams.

From the ivory print:
    Cut 15 strips, 2⅞" x 42".

From the bright gold solid:
    Cut 3 strips, 2½" x 18".

From the dark blue print:
    Cut 6 strips, 2⅞" x 42".
    Cut 12 strips, 1" x 42", for edge strips.

From the length of the multicolored print:
    Cut 4 strips, 6" wide, for bars.
    From the remaining piece of multicolored print, cut 12 strips, 2½" x 18". Cut 6 of the strips into a total of 42 squares, 2½" x 2½". Leave the remaining 6 strips uncut.

DIRECTIONS

1. Make 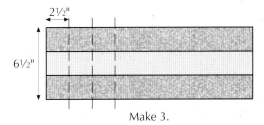: Layer the 2⅞"-wide yellow and gold strips and 9 of the ivory strips, right sides together, to make 9 contrasting strip pairs. Cut 14 squares, 2⅞" x 2⅞", from each strip pair for a total of 126 layered squares. Cut the squares once diagonally and chain-piece the resulting triangle pairs to make 252 half-square triangle units.

2. Make : Layer the 2⅞"-wide dark blue strips and the remaining ivory strips, right sides together, to make 6 contrasting strip pairs. Cut 14 squares, 2⅞" x 2⅞", from each strip pair for a total of 84 layered squares. Cut the squares once diagonally and chain-piece the resulting triangle pairs to make 168 half-square triangle units.

3. Join the 2½" x 18" gold and multicolored print strips to make 3 short strip units as shown. Cut the strip units into a total of 21 segments, each 2½" wide.

Make 3.

4. Piece 21 Comet blocks as shown.

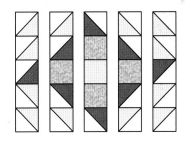

Make 21.

5. Set the blocks together in 3 vertical rows of 7 blocks each as shown in the quilt photo.
6. Join the 1"-wide dark blue strips to the long sides of each row of blocks, seaming the strips as necessary.
7. Measure one of the rows of blocks at the center and cut the 6"-wide multicolored print strips to that measurement. Join the bars and the block strips.
8. Layer with batting and backing; quilt or tie. See page 255 for a quilting suggestion.
9. Bind with straight-grain or bias strips of fabric.

Comet *by George Taylor, 1995, Anchorage, Alaska, 54¼" x 68½". The strippy set is a perfect foil for these delightful, whirling blocks. The triangle-studded background features many different yellow and gold solids. George quilted an original flame motif in the batik bars.*

Cracker Box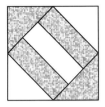

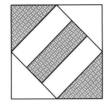

Block A
11¾" block

Block B
11¾" block

Dimensions: 60" x 94"

40 blocks (20 Block A and 20 Block B), 11¾", set 5 across and 8 down; finished without a border.

Materials: 44"-wide fabric

3 yds. muslin or light print fabric
½ yd. *each* of 5 different medium prints
⅓ yd. *each* of 5 different dark prints
5¾ yds. fabric for backing (lengthwise seam)
⅝ yd. fabric for binding
Batting and thread to finish

Cutting: All measurements include ¼" seams.

From the muslin or light print:
Cut 15 strips, 3¼" x 42".
Cut 8 strips, 6¾" x 42". Cut the strips into a total of 40 squares, 6¾" x 6¾". Cut once diagonally into 80 half-square triangles.

From each of the 5 medium prints:
Cut 2 strips, 3¼" x 42" (10 total).
Cut 1 strip, 6¾" x 42" (5 total). Cut the strip into 4 squares, 6¾" x 6¾" (20 total). Cut once diagonally into 8 half-square triangles (40 total).

From each of the 5 dark prints:
Cut 1 strip, 3¼" x 42" (5 total).
Cut 1 strip, 6¾" x 42" (5 total). Cut the strip into 4 squares, 6¾" x 6¾" (20 total). Cut once diagonally into 8 half-square triangles (40 total).

DIRECTIONS

1. Join 5 of the muslin strips with the 10 medium strips to make 5 strip units as shown. Use the same medium fabric for the 2 outer strips in each unit. The units should measure 8¾" wide

when sewn. Cut the units into 20 segments, each 8¾" wide.

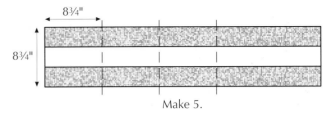

8¾"

8¾"

Make 5.

2. Add muslin and medium triangles to the segments to make 20 Block A, matching the medium triangles to the medium fabric in the strip segments.

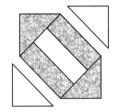

Block A
Make 20.

3. Join the remaining muslin strips with the 5 dark strips to make 5 strip units as shown. The units should measure 8¾" wide when sewn. Cut the units into 20 segments, each 8¾" wide.

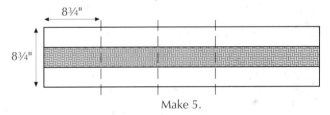

8¾"

8¾"

Make 5.

4. Add muslin and dark triangles to the segments to make 20 Block B as shown, matching dark triangles to dark fabric in the strip segments.

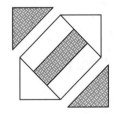

Block B
Make 20.

5. Set the blocks together in 8 rows of 5 as shown in the quilt photo, using only Block A in 4 of the rows and only Block B in the other 4 rows. Join the rows, alternating those that contain Block A with those that contain Block B.

6. Layer with batting and backing; quilt or tie. See page 256 for a quilting suggestion.

7. Bind with straight-grain or bias strips of fabric.

Cracker Box *by Della Currier Riley and Bernice Riley Smalley, 1952, Washington state, 60" x 94". Bernice Smalley finished the piecing and quilting begun by her mother, Della Currier Riley, after Della's death. The pattern is named for its shape, which resembles party crackers, the little packets filled with treats and tied together at each end.*

Crown of Thorns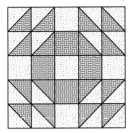

Crown of Thorns
10" block

Dimensions: 68" x 81½"

30 blocks, 10", set 5 across and 6 down with 3¼"-wide sashing; 3¼"-wide border.

Materials: 44"-wide fabric

½ yd. *each* of 8 assorted light-background prints for blocks
½ yd. *each* of 8 assorted dark prints in brown, navy, black, and purple for blocks
2½ yds. black print for sashing and border
5 yds. fabric for backing (lengthwise seam)
⅝ yd. fabric for binding
Batting and thread to finish

NOTE: Directions are for cutting 8 groups of 4 identical blocks (you will have 2 extra), which is the most economical way to purchase and use the fabric. If you have a large collection of scraps, don't hesitate to use them for a scrappier look as shown in the photo.

Cutting: All measurements include ¼" seams.

From each of the 8 light-background prints:

Cut 8 squares, 8" x 8", for bias squares (64 total).

Cut 20 squares, 2½" x 2½", matching 5 squares to the background fabric in each block (160 total). You will have 10 squares left over.

From each of the 8 dark prints:

Cut 8 squares, 8" x 8", for bias squares (64 total). Pair each 8" dark print square with an 8" light print square, right sides up. Cut and piece 2½"-wide strips, following the directions for making bias squares on page 16. Cut 8 bias squares, 2½" x 2½", from each pair of squares for a total of 512 bias squares. You will have 32 bias squares left over.

Cut 15 squares, 2½" x 2½", matching 4 squares to the dark print in each block (120 total).

From the *length* of the black print for sashing and border:

Cut 24 rectangles, 3½" x 10½", for vertical sashing strips.

Cut 7 strips, 3½" x 62½", for horizontal sashing strips.

Cut 2 strips, 3½" x 81½", for side borders.

DIRECTIONS

1. Piece 30 Crown of Thorns blocks.

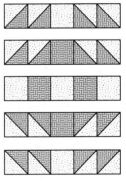

Make 30.

2. Set the blocks together in 6 rows of 5 with the vertical sashing strips as shown in the quilt photo. Join the rows with a horizontal sashing strip between them; add a sashing strip above and below the top and bottom rows.
3. Add the black print border to the sides of the quilt top.
4. Layer with batting and backing; quilt or tie. See page 256 for a quilting suggestion.
5. Bind with straight-grain or bias strips of fabric.

Crown of Thorns *by Ellen Vesper Gordon, c. 1900, South Dakota, 68" x 81". Leona Harleman taught the women of the Yakima Indian Mission to quilt, using this top pieced by her grandmother. A whisker cloth covers the top of the quilt to protect it from the abrasiveness of a man's beard. (Photo by Skip Howard)*

Delectable Mountains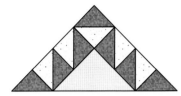

Delectable Mountains
8" x 8" x 11⅓"

Dimensions: 45¼" x 58¼"

20 pieced units, 8" x 8" x 11⅓", set strippy style with 4 units in each of 5 rows; 5"-wide strips between rows and at top and bottom edges.

Materials: 44"-wide fabric

5 fat quarters of assorted light prints in beige, tan, gray, and rust
5 fat quarters of assorted dark prints
⅞ yd. tan print for background
1½ yds. variegated striped fabric
3 yds. fabric for backing (crosswise seam)
½ yd. fabric for binding
Batting and thread to finish

NOTE: Directions are for cutting 5 groups of 4 identical blocks, which is the most economical way to purchase and use the fabric. If you have a large collection of scraps, don't hesitate to use them for a scrappier look as shown in the photo.

Cutting: All measurements include ¼" seams.

From each of the 5 light fat quarters:

Cut 3 squares, 8" x 8", for bias squares (15 total).

Cut 1 square, 7" x 7" (5 total). Cut twice diagonally into 20 half-square triangles.

From each of the 5 dark fat quarters:

Cut 3 squares, 8" x 8", for bias squares (15 total). Pair each 8" dark print square with an 8" light print square, right sides up. Cut and piece 2½"-wide strips, following the directions for making bias squares on page 16. Cut 8 bias squares, 2½" x 2½", from each pair of squares for a total of 120 bias squares. You will have 20 bias squares left over.

Cut 4 squares, 2⅞" x 2⅞" (20 total). Cut once diagonally into 40 half-square triangles.

From the tan print:

Cut 4 squares, 12⅝" x 12⅝". Cut twice diagonally into 16 quarter-square triangles for background. You will have 1 triangle left over.

Cut 5 squares, 6⅝" x 6⅝". Cut once diagonally into 10 half-square triangles for the ends of each row.

From the *length* of the variegated striped fabric:

Cut 6 strips, 5½" x 45½".

DIRECTIONS

1. Piece 20 Delectable Mountains units as shown.

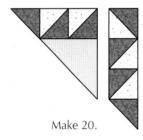

Make 20.

2. Set the Delectable Mountain units and background triangles in 5 rows as shown.

3. Join the rows, alternating pieced rows and strips of variegated striped fabric as shown in the quilt photo.
4. Layer with batting and backing; quilt or tie. See page 256 for a quilting suggestion.
5. Bind with straight-grain or bias strips of fabric.

Desert Storm *by Terri Shinn, 1991, Anchorage, Alaska, 45¼" x 58¼". Delectable Mountains blocks, arranged strippy style, give this quilt a Navajo-blanket look.*

Double Irish Chain

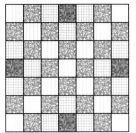 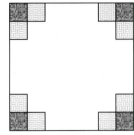

Double Irish Chain
10½" block

Alternate
10½" block

Dimensions: 75" x 75"

36 blocks (18 Chain blocks and 18 alternate blocks), 10½", set 6 across and 6 down; 6"-wide border.

Materials: 44"-wide fabric

2 yds. assorted black prints for alternate blocks

1½ yds. assorted indigo blue prints for Chain blocks

2 yds. light checked, striped, or print fabrics for Chain and alternate blocks

¾ yd. assorted black background fabrics for Chain blocks and corners of alternate blocks

1½ yds. black background fabric for border

4¾ yds. fabric for backing (lengthwise or crosswise seam)

⅝ yd. fabric for binding

Batting and thread to finish

Cutting: All measurements include ¼" seams.

NOTE: Corner squares of the alternate blocks were cut separately and appliquéd in place, so the checks and prints of the background squares were not interrupted by seams.

From the black prints for alternate blocks:
Cut 18 squares, 11" x 11".

From the indigo blue prints:
Cut 20 strips, 2" x 42", for Chain blocks.

From the light checked, striped, or print fabrics:
Cut 25 strips, 2" x 42", for Chain blocks.
Cut 144 squares, 2" x 2", for alternate blocks.

From the black background fabrics for Chain and alternate blocks:
Cut 4 strips, 2" x 42", for Chain blocks.
Cut 72 squares, 2" x 2", for corners of alternate blocks.

From the black background fabric for border:
Cut 8 strips, 6¼" x 42".

DIRECTIONS

1. Join the 2" x 42" strips into units as shown. Make 2 each of Units I, II, and III, and 1 of Unit IV. The units should measure 11" wide when sewn. Cut *each* strip unit into 18 segments, each 2" wide.

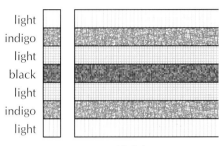

light
indigo
light
black
light
indigo
light

Unit I
Make 2.

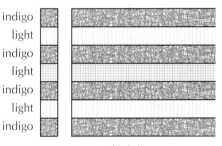

indigo
light
indigo
light
indigo
light
indigo

Unit II
Make 2.

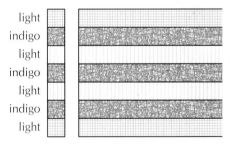

light
indigo
light
indigo
light
indigo
light

Unit III
Make 2.

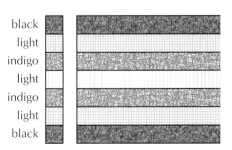

black
light
indigo
light
indigo
light
black

Unit IV
Make 1.

2. Appliqué the black background squares onto the corners of the alternate blocks. Appliqué 2 squares of light checked, striped, or print fabric to each corner.

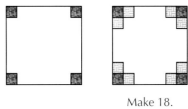

Make 18.

3. Set the blocks together in 6 rows of 6, alternating the blocks as shown in the quilt photo. Join the rows.

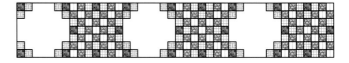

4. Add the black background border, seaming strips as necessary. See "Borders with Straight-Cut Corners" on page 243.
5. Layer with batting and backing; quilt or tie. See page 256 for a quilting suggestion.
6. Bind with straight-grain or bias strips of fabric.

Double Irish Chain, *maker unknown, c. 1900, Pennsylvania, 75" x 75". Dark indigo prints contrast with checks and stripes in this Irish Chain quilt. The dark checks and Shaker gray prints used in the alternate blocks give a masculine feel to this quilt. (Collection of Nancy J. Martin)*

Double Pinwheel

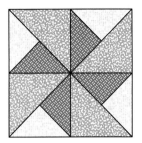

Double Pinwheel
8" block

Dimensions: 68" x 92"

70 blocks, 8", set 7 across and 10 down; 6"-wide border.

Materials: 44"-wide fabric

1½ yds. assorted light prints for background
⅓ yd. *each* of 10 different medium prints (rusts, browns, blues) for large pinwheels
¼ yd. *each* of 10 different dark prints (rusts, browns, blues) for small pinwheels
1½ yds. light print for border
5⅝ yds. fabric for backing (lengthwise seam)
⅝ yd. fabric for binding
Batting and thread to finish

Cutting: All measurements include ¼" seams.

From the light prints:
Cut 70 squares, 5¼" x 5¼". Cut twice diagonally into 280 quarter-square triangles for backgrounds.

From each of the medium prints:
Cut 2 strips, 4⅞" x 42" (20 total). Cut the strips into 14 squares, 4⅞" x 4⅞". When all 10 fabrics have been cut, you will have a total of 140 squares. Cut once diagonally into 280 half-square triangles for large pinwheels.

From each of the dark prints:
Cut 1 strip, 5¼" x 42" (10 total). Cut the strip into 7 squares, 5¼" x 5¼". When all 10 fabrics have been cut, you will have a total of 70 squares. Cut twice diagonally into 280 quarter-square triangles for small pinwheels.

From the light border print:
Cut 8 strips, 6½" x 42", for border.

DIRECTIONS

1. Piece 70 Double Pinwheel blocks as shown. Use a single fabric for the large pinwheel, a single fabric for the small pinwheel, and a single fabric for the background in each block.

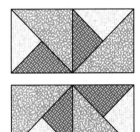

Piece 4
for each block.

Make 70.

2. Set the blocks together in 10 rows of 7 as shown in the quilt photo; join the rows.
3. Add the light print border, seaming strips as necessary. See "Borders with Straight-Cut Corners" on page 243.
4. Layer with batting and backing; quilt or tie. See page 256 for a quilting suggestion.
5. Bind with straight-grain or bias strips of fabric.

Scrappy Pinwheels *by Carol Rhoades, 1989, Anchorage, Alaska, 68" x 92". The scrappy Double Pinwheel blocks include several fabrics from the 1950s and '60s.*

Double Squares

Double Squares
9" block

Dimensions: 72" x 90"

80 blocks, 9", set 8 across and 10 down; finished without a border.

Materials: 44"-wide fabric

4½ yds. blue print for blocks
2⅛ yds. beige print for blocks
⅛ yd. *each* of 27 different red prints for blocks*
5½ yds. fabric for backing (lengthwise seam)
¾ yd. fabric for binding
Batting and thread to finish
*Note that the red prints in this quilt include clear reds, maroons, roses, corals, and red-violets in values ranging from medium to dark. Use the same fabric more than once if you wish.

Cutting: All measurements include ¼" seams.

From the blue print:
Cut 9 strips, 4⅜" x 42". Cut the strips into a total of 80 squares, 4⅜" x 4⅜". Cut twice diagonally into 320 quarter-square triangles.

Cut 38 strips, 3⅛" x 42". Cut 25 of the strips into a total of 320 squares, 3⅛" x 3⅛". Cut once diagonally into 640 half-square triangles. Leave the remaining 13 strips uncut.

From the beige print:
Cut 8 strips, 3⅝" x 42". Cut the strips into a total of 80 squares, 3⅝" x 3⅝".
Cut 13 strips, 3⅛" x 42".

From each of the 27 red prints:
Cut 2 strips, 1½" x 42" (54 total). From each strip, cut 3 rectangles, 1½" x 4⅞", and 3 rectangles, 1½" x 6⅞", for a total of 162 short rectangles and 162 long rectangles. You will have 2 short rectangles and 2 long rectangles left over.

DIRECTIONS

1. Make 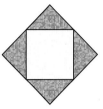: Layer the 3⅛"-wide blue and beige strips, right sides together, to make 13 contrasting strip pairs. Cut 13 squares, 3⅛" x 3⅛", from each strip pair for a total of 169 layered squares. Cut the squares once diagonally and chain-piece the resulting triangle pairs to make 338 half-square triangle units. You will have 18 triangles left over.

2. Join the 3⅝" beige squares and the 4⅜" blue quarter-square triangles to make 80 units as shown.

Make 80.

3. Join the blue/beige half-square triangle units and the 3⅛" blue triangles to make 320 units as shown.

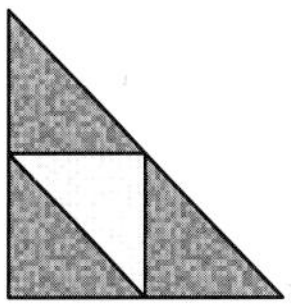

Make 320.

4. Piece 80 Double Square blocks as shown. Use rectangles cut from just 1 red print in each of the blocks.

Make 80.

5. Set the blocks together in 10 rows of 8 as shown in the quilt photo; join the rows.
6. Layer with batting and backing; quilt or tie. See page 257 for a quilting suggestion.
7. Bind with straight-grain or bias strips of fabric.

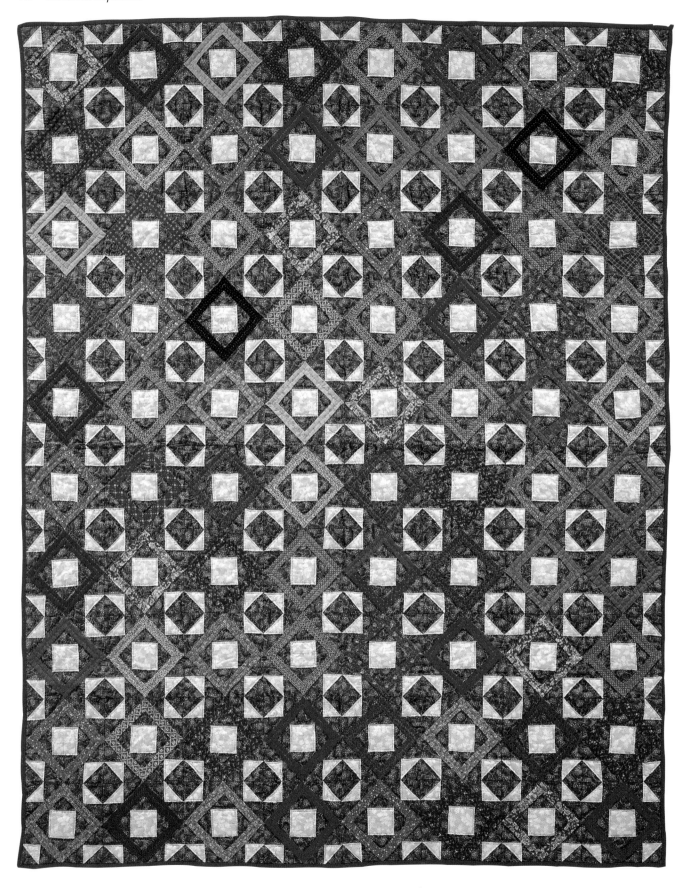

Jack in the Box *by Doris Rhodes, 1992, Anchorage, Alaska, 72" x 90". Doris adapted this pattern, also known as "Jack in the Pulpit," from a 100-year-old quilt in her collection. The eclectic array of red prints in many different values is balanced by the repetitive use of blue and beige background fabrics.*

Double T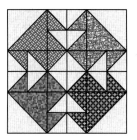

Double T
12" block

Dimensions: 77" x 84"

42 blocks, 12", set 6 across and 7 down; 2½"-wide side border strips.

Materials: 44"-wide fabric

½ yd. *each* of 14 assorted dark prints in brown, navy, red, purple, and black for blocks
5½ yds. pink print for background and side border strips
5⅛ yds. fabric for backing (lengthwise seam)
⅝ yd. fabric for binding
Batting and thread to finish

NOTE: The antique quilt in the photo was made using the template method and several striped fabrics. It is best to avoid striped fabrics for the bias squares, since careful cutting and matching of the stripes is required.

Cutting: All measurements include ¼" seams.

From each of the 14 dark prints:
Cut 1 fat quarter, 18" x 22", for bias squares (14 total).
Cut 6 squares, 4⅞" x 4⅞" (84 total). Cut once diagonally into 168 half-square triangles.

From the pink print:
Cut 14 fat quarters, 18" x 22", for bias squares. Pair each pink print fat quarter with a dark print fat quarter, right sides up. Cut and piece 2½"-wide bias strips, following the directions for making bias squares on page 14. Cut a total of 840 bias squares, 2½" x 2½".
Cut 11 strips, 4⅞" x 42". Cut the strips into a total of 84 squares, 4⅞" x 4⅞". Cut once diagonally into 168 half-square triangles.
Cut 4 strips, 3" x 42", for side borders.

DIRECTIONS

1. Piece 42 Double T blocks as shown. Use matching bias squares and 4⅞" triangles to form the shape of the letter "T." A background and 4 different fabrics are used in each block.

Make 4.

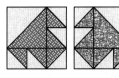
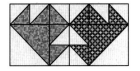
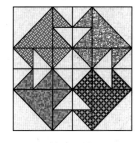

Make 42.

2. Set the blocks together in 7 rows of 6 as shown in the quilt photo; join the rows.
3. Add the pink print borders to each side.
4. Layer with batting and backing; quilt or tie. See page 257 for a quilting suggestion.
5. Bind with straight-grain or bias strips of fabric.

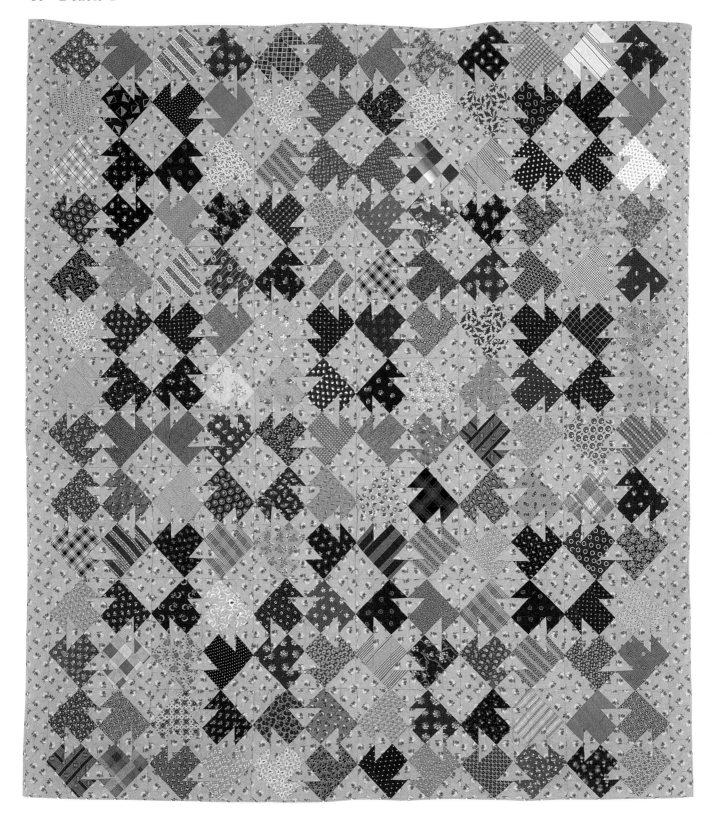

Double T, *maker unknown, c. 1900, Pennsylvania, 77" x 84". Scraps of brown, navy, red, and tan fabrics form the "T" units of each block. The double-pink print used in the background calms the myriad colors and prints. (Collection of Nancy J. Martin)*

Double Wrench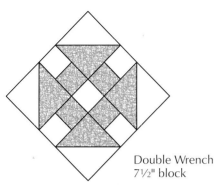

Double Wrench
7½" block

Dimensions: 64" x 85"

83 blocks, 7½", set on point; finished without a border.

Materials: 44"-wide fabric

4 yards muslin or light print for blocks and setting triangles

4¼" x 13" strip *each* of 83 different medium and/or dark fabrics for blocks (Nearest cut is ⅛ yd.)

5¼ yds. fabric for backing (lengthwise seam)

⅝ yd. fabric for binding

Batting and thread to finish

Cutting: All measurements include ¼" seams.

From the muslin or light print:

Cut 17 strips, 3⅞" x 42". Cut the strips into a total of 166 squares, 3⅞" x 3⅞". Cut once diagonally into 332 half-square triangles for blocks.

Cut 20 strips, 2" x 42". Cut the strips into a total of 415 squares, 2" x 2", for blocks.

Cut 6 squares, 11⅞" x 11⅞". Cut twice diagonally into 24 quarter-square triangles for side setting pieces.

Cut 2 squares, 6¼" x 6¼". Cut once diagonally into 4 half-square triangles for corner setting pieces.

From each of the 4¼" x 13" strips:

Cut 2 squares, 3⅞" x 3⅞". Cut once diagonally into 4 half-square triangles for blocks (332 total).

Cut 4 squares, 2" x 2", for blocks (332 total).

DIRECTIONS

1. Piece 83 Double Wrench blocks as shown. Each block is made by combining muslin or light print pieces with pieces cut from one of the 83 medium or dark scraps.

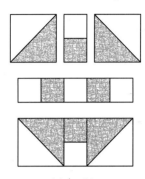

Make 83.

2. Set the blocks together in diagonal rows with the muslin or light print side and corner triangles as shown in the quilt photo; join the rows. Trim and square up the outside edges after the rows are sewn if needed. See "Assembling On-Point Quilts" on page 240.

3. Layer with batting and backing; quilt or tie. See page 257 for a quilting suggestion.

4. Bind with straight-grain or bias strips of fabric.

Fields of Calico *by Louise Pease, 1992, Anchorage, Alaska, 83" x 111". Double Wrench blocks set on point form an intriguing secondary dot-dash pattern. Each of the 83 blocks was made from a different fabric. NOTE: The pattern uses smaller blocks and produces a 64" x 85" quilt.*

Double X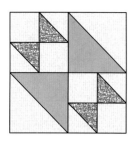

Double X
8" block

Dimensions: 40½" x 48"

24 blocks, 8", set 4 across and 6 down; 4"-wide side border strips from strip-pieced fabric.

Materials: 44"-wide fabric

1½ yds. tan print for blocks
⅞ yd. black print for blocks and border
¾ yd. red print for large triangles and border
1½ yds. fabric for backing
⅜ yd. fabric for binding
Batting and thread to finish

Cutting: All measurements include ¼" seams.

From the tan print:
    Cut 2 fat quarters, 18" x 22", for bias squares.
    Cut 96 squares, 2½" x 2½".
    Cut 24 squares, 4⅞" x 4⅞". Cut once diagonally into 48 half-square triangles.

From the black print:
    Cut 2 fat quarters, 18" x 22", for bias squares. Pair each black fat quarter with a tan fat quarter, right sides up. Cut and piece 2½"-wide bias strips, following the directions for making bias squares on page 14. Cut a total of 96 bias squares, 2½" x 2½".
    Cut 3 strips, 2½" x 42", for border.

From the red print:
    Cut 24 squares, 4½" x 4½". Cut once diagonally into 48 half-square triangles.
    Cut 3 strips, 2½" x 42", for border.

DIRECTIONS

1. Piece 24 Double X blocks as shown.

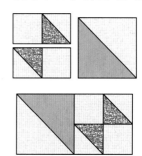

Make 24.

2. Set the blocks together in 6 rows of 4 as shown in the quilt photo; join the rows.
3. Stitch the 2½"-wide red and black strips together to make 3 strip units. Cut into a total of 24 segments, each 4½" wide.

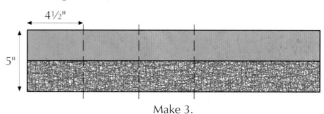

Make 3.

4. Join 12 red/black segments to make each of the side borders. Add to the sides of the quilt.
5. Layer with batting and backing; quilt or tie. See page 257 for a quilting suggestion.
6. Bind with straight-grain or bias strips of fabric.

Double X *by Judy Dafoe Hopkins, 1991, Anchorage, Alaska, 40½" x 48". Stripped side borders add spice to this simple quilt, which was utility quilted with red perle cotton.*

English Ivy

English Ivy
12" block

Dimensions: 84½" x 101"

32 blocks (20 English Ivy blocks and 12 alternate blocks), 12", set on point; 8"-wide border.

Materials: 44"-wide fabric

2⅜ yds. pink fabric for background
1¼ yds. burgundy solid for ivy tips and stems
⅞ yd. rose fabric for ivy
5⅛ yds. burgundy print for alternate blocks, set pieces, and border
7⅝ yds. fabric for backing (2 crosswise seams)
¾ yd. fabric for binding
Batting and thread to finish

Cutting: All measurements include ¼" seams.

From the pink fabric:
Cut 3 fat quarters, 18" x 22", for bias squares.
Cut 20 squares, 6⅞" x 6⅞". Cut once diagonally into 40 half-square triangles.
Cut 20 squares, 6½" x 6½".

From the burgundy solid:
Cut 3 fat quarters, 18" x 22". Pair each burgundy fat quarter with a pink fat quarter, right sides up. Cut and piece 2½"-wide strips, following the directions for making bias squares on page 14. Cut a total of 180 bias squares, 2½" x 2½".
Cut 20 bias strips, 1½" x 9", for stems.

From the rose fabric:
Cut 20 squares, 4⅞" x 4⅞". Cut once diagonally into 40 half-square triangles.
Cut 20 squares, 4½" x 4½".

From the burgundy print:
Cut 2 strips, 8½" x 85", on the lengthwise grain for side borders.
Cut 2 strips, 8½" x 84½", on the lengthwise grain for top and bottom borders.
Cut 12 squares, 12½" x 12½", for alternate blocks.
Cut 4 squares, 18¼" x 18¼". Cut twice diagonally into 16 quarter-square triangles for side setting triangles. You will have 2 triangles left over.
Cut 2 squares, 9⅜" x 9⅜". Cut once diagonally into 4 half-square triangles for corner setting triangles.

DIRECTIONS

1. Appliqué the ivy stems by stitching a burgundy bias strip to a pink background square.

Fold a 1½" x 9" strip of bias in thirds; baste. Appliqué diagonally from corner to corner.

2. Piece 20 English Ivy blocks as shown.

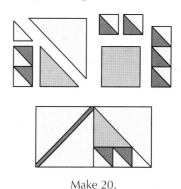

Make 20.

3. Set the English Ivy blocks into diagonal rows with the alternate blocks and the side and corner setting triangles as shown in the quilt photo; join the rows. See "Assembling On-Point Quilts" on page 240.
4. Add the burgundy print border. See "Borders with Straight-Cut Corners" on page 243.
5. Layer with batting and backing; quilt or tie. See page 257 for a quilting suggestion.
6. Bind with straight-grain or bias strips of fabric.

English Ivy *by Joyce Peaden, 1986, Prosser, Washington, 84" x 101". This traditional block is set in a dark-print background to mimic some of the quilts made in the late 1800s. Quilted by Buena Heights Quilters. (Photo by Skip Howard)*

Envelope

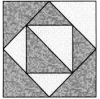 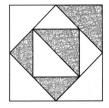

Block A
12" block

Block B
12" block

Dimensions: 72" x 72"

36 blocks (24 Block A and 12 Block B), 12", set 6 across and 6 down; finished without a border.

Materials: 44"-wide fabric

18 light and medium prints (tans, golds, rusts, lavenders, blues) for blocks: ¼ yd. *each* of 6 fabrics, and a "fat eighth" (9" x 22") *each* of 12 other fabrics

18 dark prints (browns, reds, purples, blues) for blocks: ¼ yd. *each* of 12 fabrics and a "fat eighth" (9" x 22") each of 6 other fabrics

4½ yds. fabric for backing (lengthwise or cross-wise seam)

⅝ yd. fabric for binding

Batting and thread to finish

Cutting: All measurements include ¼" seams.

From each of the ¼-yard pieces of fabric:

Cut 1 square, 7¼" x 7¼" (18 total). Cut twice diagonally into 4 quarter-square triangles (A) (72 total).

Cut 4 squares, 6⅞" x 6⅞" (72 total). Cut once diagonally into 8 half-square triangles (B) (144 total).

From each of the fat eighths of fabric:

Cut 1 square, 7¼" x 7¼" (18 total) . Cut twice diagonally into 4 quarter-square triangles (A) (72 total).

Cut 2 squares, 6⅞" x 6⅞" (36 total). Cut once diagonally into 4 half-square triangles (B) (72 total).

DIRECTIONS

1. Piece 24 Block A and 12 Block B as shown. Use a single fabric for all of the envelope pieces and a single fabric for all of the background pieces in each block.

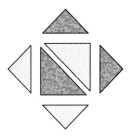 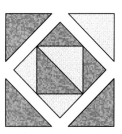

Block A
Make 24.

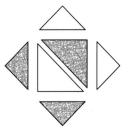 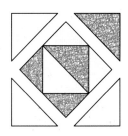

Block B
Make 12.

2. Set the blocks together in 6 rows of 6, rotating every other block as shown in the quilt photo. Join the rows.
3. Layer with batting and backing; quilt or tie. See page 258 for a quilting suggestion.
4. Bind with straight-grain or bias strips of fabric.

Mellow Motion *by Ramona Chinn, 1988, Anchorage, Alaska, 72" x 72".*
This traditional Envelope quilt features rich tans, browns, reds, and purples.

Flock of Geese

Flock of Geese
10" block

Dimensions: 58" x 78"

35 blocks, 10", set 5 across and 7 down; 4"-wide border.

Materials: 44"-wide fabric

½ yd. *each* of 6 different beige and tan prints
½ yd. *each* of 6 different blue and navy blue prints
1 yd. dark blue print for border
3¾ yds. fabric for backing (crosswise seam)
½ yd. fabric for binding
Batting and thread to finish

NOTE: Directions are for cutting 6 groups of 6 identical blocks (you will have 1 extra), which is the most economical way to purchase and use the fabric. If you have a large collection of scraps, don't hesitate to use them for a scrappier look as shown in the photo.

Cutting: All measurements include ¼" seams.

From each of the 6 beige and tan prints:

Cut 6 squares, 8" x 8", for bias squares (36 total).

Cut 6 squares, 5⅞" x 5⅞" (36 total). Cut once diagonally into 72 half-square triangles. You will have 2 triangles left over.

From each of the 6 blue and navy blue prints:

Cut 6 squares, 8" x 8", for bias squares (36 total). Pair each 8" blue or navy blue print square with an 8" beige or tan print square, right sides up. Cut and piece 2¾"-wide bias strips, following the directions for making bias squares on page 16. Cut 8 bias squares, 3" x 3", from each pair of squares for a total of 288 bias squares.

Cut 6 squares, 5⅞" x 5⅞" (36 total). Cut once diagonally into 72 half-square triangles. You will have 2 triangles left over.

From the dark blue print:

Cut 8 strips, 4" x 42", for border.

DIRECTIONS

1. Piece 35 Flock of Geese blocks as shown.

Make 35.

2. Set the blocks together in 7 rows of 5 as shown in the quilt photo; join the rows.
3. Add the dark blue border, seaming strips as necessary. See "Borders with Straight-Cut Corners" on page 243.
4. Layer with batting and backing; quilt or tie. See page 258 for a quilting suggestion.
5. Bind with straight-grain or bias strips of fabric.

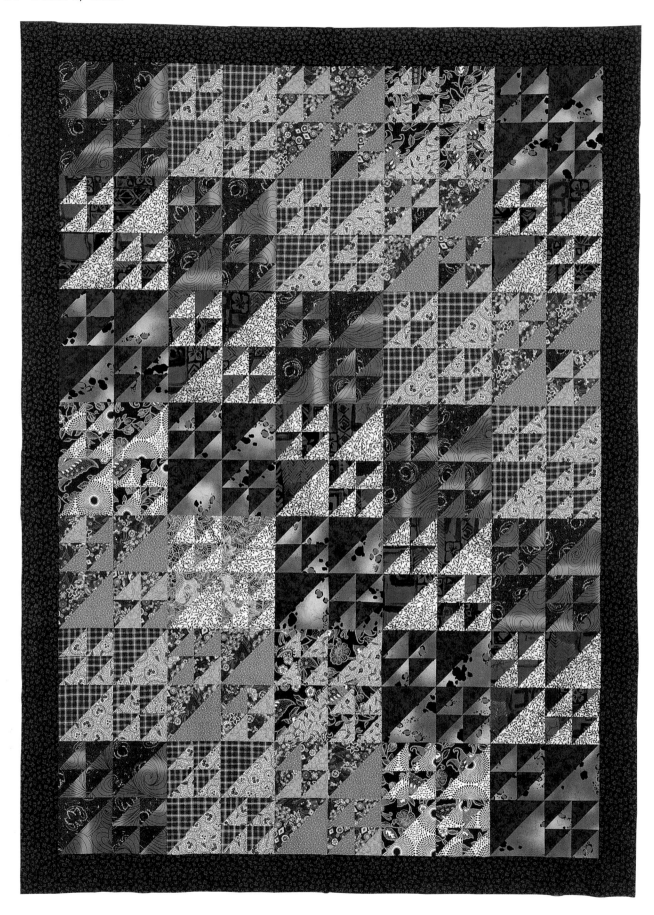

Flock of Geese *by Judy Hopkins, 1991, Anchorage, Alaska, 58" x 78".*
This brown-and-blue quilt was made from a collection of batik-like fabrics, plus a plaid.

Flying Birds

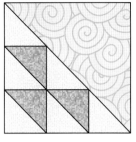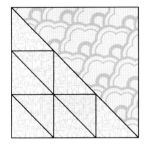

Block A
(red birds)
6" block

Block B
(blue birds)
6" block

Dimensions: 44¾" x 58¼"

48 blocks (36 Block A, "red birds," and 12 Block B, "blue birds"), 6", set 6 across and 8 down with ¾"-wide sashing; 2½"-wide border.

Materials: 44"-wide fabric

1 piece, 6⅞" x 15", *each* of 12 different large-scale red, gold, and blue-green prints for large triangles (Nearest cut is ¼ yd.)

1 strip, 2⅞" x 10", *each* of 18 different red prints or solids for Block A birds (Nearest cut is ⅛ yd.)*

1 strip, 2⅞" x 20", *each* of 18 different blue-green or gold prints for Block A backgrounds (Nearest cut is ⅛ yd.)*

1 strip, 2⅞" x 10", *each* of 6 more blue-green prints or solids for Block B birds (Nearest cut is ⅛ yd.)*

1 strip, 2⅞" x 20", *each* of 6 more red prints for Block B backgrounds (Nearest cut is ⅛ yd.)*

⅝ yd. medium blue print for sashing
⅝ yd. large-scale, multicolored print for border
3 yds. fabric for backing (crosswise seam)
½ yd. fabric for binding
Batting and thread to finish

*Use the same fabric more than once if you wish.

Cutting: All measurements include ¼" seams.

From each of the 12 large-scale prints:

Cut 2 squares, 6⅞" x 6⅞" (24 total). Cut once diagonally into 48 half-square triangles.

From the medium blue print:

Cut 14 strips, 1¼" x 42". Cut 7 of the strips into a total of 40 rectangles, 1¼" x 6½"**, for sashing pieces. Leave the remaining 7 strips uncut.

**Your blocks may not measure exactly 6½" square when sewn. Cut these rectangles a little longer than 6½" and trim the sashing pieces to size after you piece the blocks if you wish.

From the large-scale, multicolored print:

Cut 6 strips, 3" x 42", for border.

DIRECTIONS

1. Start by making 36 red bird blocks (Block A). Sort the 2⅞" x 10" red strips and the 2⅞" x 20" blue-green or gold strips into 18 pleasing sets, each containing 1 red and 1 blue-green or gold strip.

2. Work with 1 set at a time. From one end of the blue-green or gold strip, cut 3 squares, 2⅞" x 2⅞"; cut the squares once diagonally to make 6 loose half-square triangles. Now make ◿ by layering the red strip and the remaining piece of blue-green strip right sides together. From this strip pair, cut 3 squares, 2⅞" x 2⅞". Cut these layered squares once diagonally and chain-piece the resulting triangle pairs to make 6 half-square triangle units.

3. Join the loose half-square triangles and the half-square triangle units you made in step 2 with any 2 of the 6⅞" large-scale print triangles to make 2 Block A as shown. Repeat steps 2 and 3 with the remaining sets to make a total of 36 Block A.

Make 36.

4. Now make the blue bird blocks (Block B). Sort the 2⅞" x 10" blue-green strips and the 2⅞" x 20" red strips into 6 pleasing sets, each containing 1 red and 1 blue-green strip.

5. Work with 1 set a time. From one end of the red strip, cut 3 squares, 2⅞" x 2⅞"; cut the squares once diagonally to make 6 loose half-square triangles. Now make ◿ by layering the blue-green strip and the remaining piece of red strip, right sides together. From this strip pair, cut 3 squares, 2⅞" x 2⅞". Cut these layered squares once diagonally and chain-piece the resulting triangle pairs to make 6 half-square triangle units.

6. Join the loose half-square triangles and the half-square triangle units you made in step 5 with any 2 of the 6⅞" large-scale print triangles to make 2 Block B as shown on page 91. Repeat steps 5 and 6 with the remaining sets to make a total of 12 Block B.

7. Set the blocks together in 8 rows of 6 with the medium blue sashing pieces and strips as shown in the quilt photo, cutting the long sashing strips to size as needed. Join the rows. See "Straight Sets" on page 238.

8. Add the multicolored print border, seaming strips as necessary. See "Borders with Straight-Cut Corners" on page 243.

9. Layer with batting and backing; quilt or tie. See page 258 for a quilting suggestion.

10. Bind with straight-grain or bias strips of fabric.

Migration *by Emily R. McAlister, 1992, Anchorage, Alaska, 44¾" x 58¼". Exotic contemporary prints perk up this classic traditional design. The sashing fabric features tiny birds. Emily made this quilt—her fourth—as a way of shaking off "cabin fever," a common winter affliction in Alaska. (Collection of Wendy J. Talbott)*

Four Corners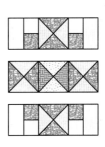

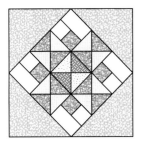

Four Corners
12¾" block

Dimensions: 52" x 52"

9 blocks, 12¾", set 3 across and 3 down; 4¾"-wide pieced inner border, 2"-wide outer border.

Materials: 44"-wide fabric

1½ yds. assorted light prints for stars and pieced inner border
1½ yds. assorted black prints for stars and pieced inner border
1½ yds. assorted tan and taupe fabrics for star corners and block corners
⅝ yd. medium fabric for outer border
3⅜ yds. fabric for backing (lengthwise or crosswise seam)
½ yd. fabric for binding
Batting and thread to finish

Cutting: All measurements include ¼" seams.

From the assorted light and black prints:

For the bias squares, cut 6 light and 6 dark pieces of fabric, each 10" x 10". Layer in pairs, right sides up. Cut and piece 3½"-wide bias strips, following the directions for making bias squares on page 16. Cut a total of 45 bias squares, 3⅞" x 3⅞".

Stack 2 bias squares, with seam allowances opposing, and cut once diagonally. Resew in pairs to make 45 Square Two units, following the directions on page 16.

From the remaining black prints:

Cut 36 squares, 2" x 2", for star corners.
Cut 17 squares, 6" x 6". Cut twice diagonally into 68 quarter-square triangles for pieced border.

From the remaining light prints:

Cut 15 squares, 6" x 6". Cut twice diagonally into 60 quarter-square triangles for the pieced border.

Cut 4 and 4r from Border Template 1, found on page 94, for pieced border corners.

From the assorted tan and taupe fabrics:

Cut 36 squares, 2" x 2", for star corners.
Cut 36 pieces, 2" x 3½", for star corners.
Cut 18 squares (2 matching for each block), 7½" x 7½". Cut once diagonally into 36 half-square triangles.

From the medium fabric:

Cut 8 strips, 2¼" x 42", for outer border.

DIRECTIONS

1. Piece 9 Four Corners blocks, using the Square Two units and corner pieces. Each "star" in the Four Corners blocks should have 4 matching Square Two units and an alternate coloration in the center. Trim blocks to 13¼".

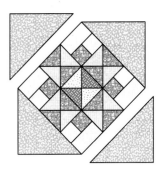

Make 9.

2. Set the blocks together in 3 rows of 3 as shown in the quilt photo; join the rows.
3. Join 9 dark triangles and 8 light triangles in a row for the inner section of the pieced border. Join 8 dark and 7 light triangles, adding light print border corners at each end of the strip for the outer section of the pieced border.

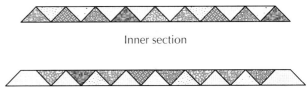

Inner section

Outer section

4. Join the 2 sections of the pieced inner border as shown. Then add the outer border to form a finished border strip for each side, top, and bottom.

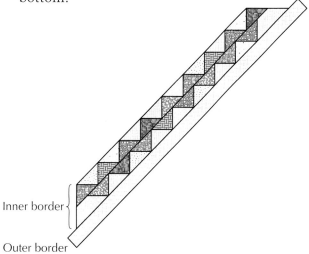

Inner border

Outer border

5. Add the finished borders to the quilt top, stopping ¼" from the outer edges. Miter the corners. See "Borders with Mitered Corners" on page 243.
6. Layer with batting and backing; quilt or tie. See page 258 for a quilting suggestion.
7. Bind with straight-grain or bias strips of fabric.

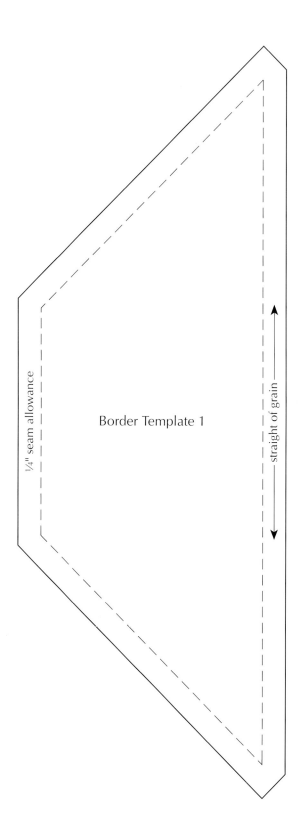

¼" seam allowance

Border Template 1

straight of grain

Four Corners *by Nancy J. Martin, 1992, Woodinville, Washington, 52" x 52". Black-and-white stars, set off by tan and taupe fabrics, emerge in the center of each Four Corners block. Black fabrics create an effective zigzag border surrounding the blocks. Quilted by Donna K. Gundlach. (Collection of Martingale & Company)*

Four-Four Time

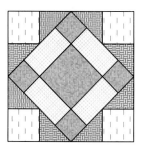

Four-Four Time
12" block

Dimensions: 54" x 68"

12 blocks, 12", set 3 across and 4 down with 2"-wide sashing and sashing squares; 5"-wide border with pieced corner squares.

Materials: 44"-wide fabric

⅞ yd. golf pictorial or other light print for blocks, sashing squares, and pieced border corners
⅔ yd. light plaid for blocks
1⅜ yds. butterscotch check for blocks and sashing
1¾ yds. dark green print for blocks and border
3½ yds. fabric for backing (crosswise seam)
⅝ yd. fabric for binding
Batting and thread to finish

Cutting: All measurements include ¼" seams.

From the golf print:

Cut 4 strips, 3½" x 42". Cut the strips into a total of 48 squares, 3½" x 3½".

Cut 2 strips, 2½" x 42". Cut the strips into a total of 20 squares, 2½" x 2½", for sashing squares.

Cut 2 squares, 5⅞" x 5⅞". Cut once diagonally into 4 half-square triangles for border corners.

From the light plaid:

Cut 2 strips, 4¾" x 42".
Cut 4 strips, 2⅝" x 42".

From the butterscotch check:

Cut 2 strips, 4¾" x 42".
Cut 4 strips, 2⅝" x 42".
Cut 2 strips, 12½"* x 42". Cut the strips into a total of 31 segments, each 2½" wide, to make 2½" x 12½" rectangles for sashing pieces.

*Your blocks may not measure exactly 12½" square when sewn. Cut this strip a little wider and trim the sashing piece to size after you piece the blocks if you wish.

From the *length* of the dark green print:

Cut 4 strips, 5½" wide, for border.

From the remaining piece of dark green print:

Cut 10 strips, 3⅞" x 20". Cut the strips into a total of 48 squares, 3⅞" x 3⅞". Cut once diagonally into 96 half-square triangles.

Cut 2 squares, 5⅞" x 5⅞". Cut once diagonally into 4 half-square triangles for border corners.

DIRECTIONS

1. Join the 2⅝"-wide butterscotch strips and the 4¾"-wide light plaid strips to make 2 strip units as shown. Cut the strip units into a total of 24 segments, each 2⅝" wide.

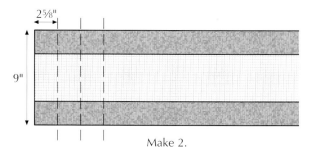

Make 2.

2. Join the 2⅝"-wide light plaid strips and the 4¾"-wide butterscotch strips to make 2 strip units as shown. Cut the strip units into a total of 12 segments, each 4¾" wide.

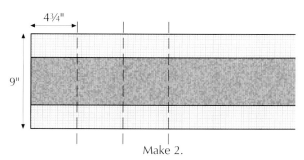

Make 2.

3. Join the segments you cut in steps 1 and 2 to make 12 units as shown.

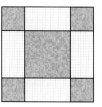

Make 12.

4. Join the units you made in step 3 with the 3½" golf print squares and the 3⅞" dark green triangles to make 12 Four-Four Time blocks as shown.

Make 12.

5. Join the 5⅞" golf print and dark green triangles to make 4 half-square triangle units for the pieced border corners as shown.

Make 4.

6. Set the blocks together in 4 rows of 3 with the butterscotch sashing pieces and golf print sashing squares as shown in the quilt photo. Join the rows. See "Straight Sets" on page 238.

7. Add the dark green border with half-square triangle corner squares. See "Borders with Corner Squares" on page 243.

8. Layer with batting and backing; quilt or tie. See page 258 for a quilting suggestion.

9. Bind with straight-grain or bias strips of fabric.

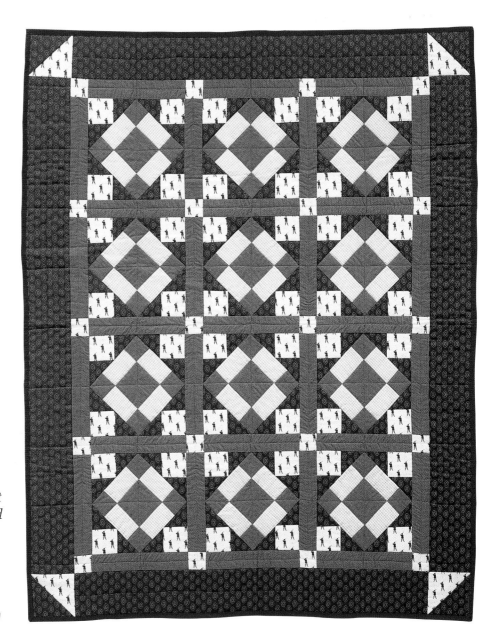

The Boss Can Golf
by Kay Dennis, 1994, Anchorage, Alaska, 54" x 67". The traditional Four-Four Time block might more appropriately be called "Fore-Fore Time" in this incarnation, which sports a charming golf pictorial print. Made in a Debbie Caffrey class. (Collection of Terry Cerney)

Friendship Star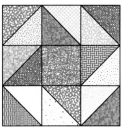

Friendship Star
6" block

Dimensions: 58" x 72"

99 blocks, 6", set 9 across and 11 down; 2"-wide pieced border.

Materials: 44"-wide fabric

1 fat quarter *each* of 8 assorted light prints for blocks
1 fat quarter *each* of 8 assorted medium prints for blocks
1 fat quarter *each* of 16 assorted dark prints for blocks
¾ yd. assorted dark prints for blocks
3¾ yds. fabric for backing (crosswise seam)
½ yd. fabric for binding
Batting and thread to finish

Cutting: All measurements include ¼" seams.

From the ¾ yd. of assorted dark prints:
    Cut 143 squares, 2½" x 2½", for blocks and pieced borders.

DIRECTIONS

1. Pair each light and medium print fat quarter with a dark print fat quarter, right sides up. Cut and piece 2½"-wide bias strips, following the directions for making bias squares on page 14. Cut a total of 872 bias squares, 2½" x 2½". Cut extra bias squares so you have some to play with when arranging the different values in your blocks.

2. Piece 99 Friendship Star blocks as shown.

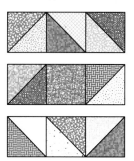

Make 99.

3. Set the blocks together in 11 rows of 9 as shown in the quilt photo. Orient the blocks so that the medium/dark bias squares are at the top of each block, and the light/dark bias squares are at the bottom. Join the rows.
4. Use the remaining bias squares and 2½" dark squares to make the pieced borders. Join 22 bias squares and 11 dark squares to make each of the side borders.

Side border
Make 2.

Join 18 bias squares and 11 dark squares to make each of the top and bottom borders.

Top and bottom borders
Make 2.

5. Add the side borders first, then the top and bottom borders.
6. Layer with batting and backing; quilt or tie. See page 258 for a quilting suggestion.
7. Bind with straight-grain or bias strips of fabric.

Harmony *by Paulette Peters, 1989, Elkhorn, Nebraska, 58" x 72". This Friendship Star variation made from gathered scraps symbolizes the interconnectedness of generations of women and the friendships that evolved through quilting. (Photo courtesy of Myron Miller, ©1990)*

Fruit Basket

Fruit Basket
10" block

Dimensions: 64½" x 64½"

13 blocks (9 Fruit Basket blocks and 4 alternate blocks), 10", set on point; 1"-wide inner border, 10"-wide outer border with corner squares.

Materials: 44"-wide fabric

1 fat quarter *each* of 9 bright-colored solids for baskets
2¼ yds. dark print for background, alternate blocks, and corner squares
¼ yd. bright-colored print for inner border
1½ yds. bright-colored print for outer border
4 yds. fabric for backing (lengthwise or crosswise seam)
½ yd. fabric for binding
Batting and thread to finish

Cutting: All measurements include ¼" seams.

From each of the 9 bright-colored fat quarters:

Cut 2 squares, 8" x 8", for bias squares (18 total). *Reserve an 8" square of each color.* Pair 2 bright-colored squares together, right sides up. Cut and piece 2½"-wide strips, following the directions for making bias squares on page 16. Cut 8 bias squares, 2½" x 2½", from each pair of squares for a total of 32 bias squares.

Cut 1 triangle for baskets, 6⅞" along the straight grain (9 total).

Cut 3 squares, 2⅞" x 2⅞" (27 total). Cut once diagonally into 54 half-square triangles. You will have 1 triangle of each color left over.

From the dark print:

Cut 9 squares, 8" x 8", for bias squares. Pair each dark print square with a bright-colored square, right sides up. Cut and piece 2½"-wide strips. Cut 8 bias squares, 2½" x 2½", from each pair of squares for a total of 72 bias squares.

Cut 5 squares, 4⅞" x 4⅞". Cut once diagonally into 10 half-square triangles. You will have 1 triangle left over.

Cut 18 rectangles, 2½" x 6½", for blocks.

Cut 8 squares, 10½" x 10½", for alternate blocks and corner squares.

Cut 2 squares, 15½" x 15½". Cut twice diagonally into 8 quarter-square triangles for side setting triangles.

Cut 2 squares, 8" x 8". Cut once diagonally into 4 half-square triangles for corner setting triangles.

From the bright-colored print for inner border:

Cut 5 strips, 1½" x 43".

From the bright-colored print for outer border:

Cut 4 strips, 10½" x 45", from the length of the fabric.

From any bright-colored fabric:

Cut 4 squares, 1½" x 1½", for small corner squares.

DIRECTIONS

1. Piece 9 Fruit Basket blocks as shown. Mix and match the bias squares inside the basket shape.

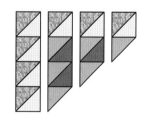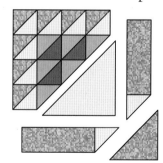

Make 9.

NOTE: Not all solid-colored fabrics in the handle match the basket.

2. Set the Fruit Basket blocks, alternate blocks, and side and corner setting triangles in diagonal rows; join the rows. See "Assembling On-Point Quilts" on page 240.

3. Attach the inner border, seaming strips as necessary and adding the small corner squares. See "Borders with Corner Squares" on page 243.

4. Attach the outer border, adding the large corner squares as for the inner border.
5. Layer with batting and backing; quilt or tie. See page 259 for a quilting suggestion.
6. Bind with straight-grain or bias strips of fabric.

Celebration *by Joyce Stewart, 1988, Rexberg, Idaho, 64½" x 64½". Brightly colored baskets are set against the wrong side of an electrifying dark print. The right side of this same print was used for the corner squares.*

Gaggle of Geese

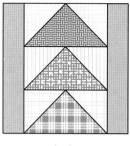

Block A
9" block

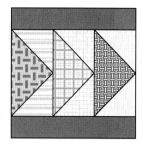

Block B
9" block

Dimensions: 73½" x 100½"

70 blocks (35 Block A and 35 Block B), 9", set 7 across and 10 down; 5¼"-wide border.

Materials: 44"-wide fabric

⅓ yd. *each* of 11 different light plaid flannels for block backgrounds*

1 piece, 7¼" x 16", *each* of 27 different dark plaid flannels (reds, blues, browns, golds, greens) for "geese" (Nearest cut is ¼" yd.)*

1⅛ yds. red flannel (a tiny check) for block edge strips

1⅛ yds. black flannel for block edge strips

1¾ yds. red-and-black checked flannel for border

6 yds. fabric for backing (lengthwise seam)

¾ yd. fabric for binding

Batting and thread to finish

*Use the same fabric more than once if you wish.

Cutting: All measurements include ¼" seams.

From each of the 11 light plaid flannels:

Cut 2 strips, 3⅞" x 42" (22 total). Cut the strips into a total of 210 squares, 3⅞" x 3⅞". Cut once diagonally into 420 half-square triangles.

From each of the 27 dark plaid flannels:

Cut 2 squares, 7¼" x 7¼" (54 total). Cut twice diagonally into 216 quarter-square triangles. You will have 6 triangles left over.

From the red flannel:

Cut 18 strips, 2" x 42". Cut the strips into a total of 70 rectangles, 2" x 9½"*.

From the black flannel:

Cut 18 Strips, 2" x 42". Cut the strips into a total of 70 rectangles, 2" x 9½"*.

*Your blocks may not measure exactly 9½" long when sewn. Cut these rectangles a little longer and trim to size after you piece the blocks if you wish.

From the red-and-black checked flannel:

Cut 10 strips, 5¾" x 42", for border.

DIRECTIONS

1. Join the light plaid half-square triangles and the dark plaid quarter-square triangles to make 210 flying-geese units as shown. Each unit uses 1 quarter-square triangle and 2 matching light plaid half-square triangles.

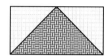

Make 210.

2. Join the flying-geese units into 70 groups of 3 as shown, combining the fabrics at random.

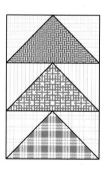

Make 70.

3. Join 2"-wide red rectangles to each side of 35 units to make 35 Block A as shown above.
4. Join 2"-wide black rectangles to each side of the remaining units to make 35 Block B.
5. Set the blocks together in 10 rows of 7 as shown in the quilt photo; join the rows.
6. Add the red-and-black checked border, seaming strips as necessary. See "Borders with Straight-Cut Corners" on page 243.
7. Layer with batting and backing; quilt or tie. See page 259 for a quilting suggestion.
8. Bind with straight-grain or bias strips of fabric.

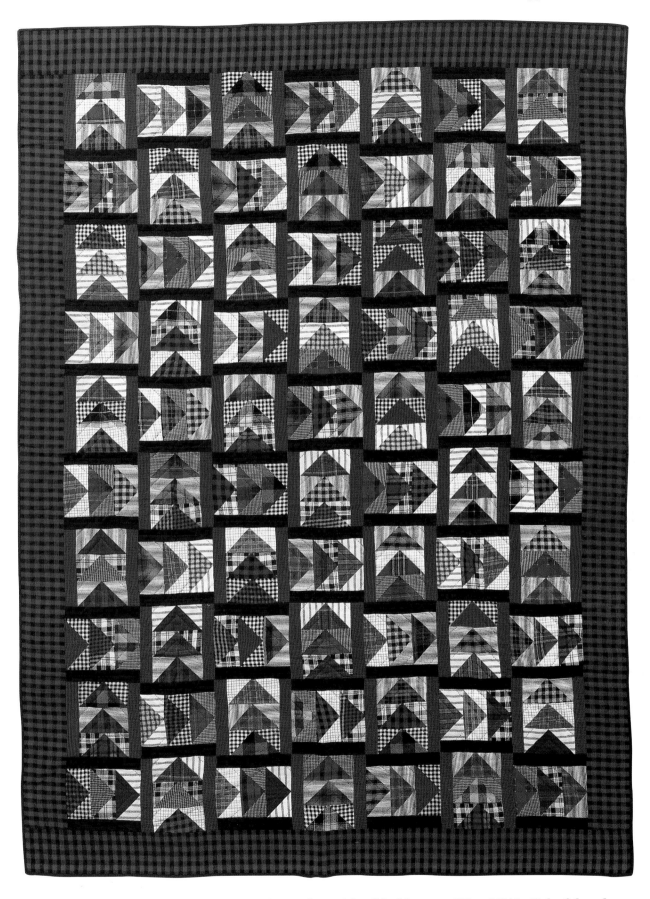

Northwood Gaggle *by Deb Coates, 1995, Brush Prairie, Washington, 72" x 98½". Colorful and cozy, this flannel quilt has that great "lodge" look we all admire. Deb had to scramble to find enough plaid flannels in the light value range. You may know the block as "Return of the Swallows."*

Gentleman's Fancy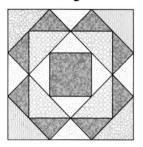

Gentleman's Fancy
12" block

Dimensions: 60" x 72"

20 blocks, 12", set 4 across and 5 down; 6"-wide border.

Materials: 44"-wide fabric

⅞ yd. beige print for block backgrounds
⅞ yd. multicolored floral print for blocks
½ yd. *each* of 2 different red-violet prints for block corners
2½ yds. dark green print for blocks and border
3¾ yds. fabric for backing (crosswise seam)
⅝ yd. fabric for binding
Batting and thread to finish

Cutting: All measurements include ¼" seams.

From the beige print:
Cut 5 strips, 5¼" x 42". Cut the strips into a total of 40 squares, 5¼" x 5¼". Cut twice diagonally into 160 quarter-square triangles.

From the multicolored floral print:
Cut 5 strips, 4⅞" x 42". Cut the strips into a total of 40 squares, 4⅞" x 4⅞". Cut once diagonally into 80 half-square triangles.

From each of the 2 red-violet prints:
Cut 3 strips, 4⅞" x 42" (6 total). Cut the strips into a total of 40 squares, 4⅞" x 4⅞" (20 from each fabric). Cut once diagonally into 80 half-square triangles.

From the dark green print:
Cut 3 strips, 4½" x 42". Cut the strips into a total of 20 squares, 4½" x 4½".

From the *length* of the remaining dark green print, cut 4 strips, 6½" wide, for border.

From the remaining piece of dark green print, cut 14 strips, 5¼" x 16". Cut the strips into a total of 40 squares, 5¼" x 5¼". Cut twice diagonally into 160 quarter-square triangles.

DIRECTIONS

1. Using 80 of the 5¼" beige quarter-square triangles and the 4½" dark green squares, make 20 units.

Make 20.

2. Using the 5¼" dark green quarter-square triangles and the 4⅞" floral half-square triangles, make 80 units.

Make 80.

3. Join 40 of the units made in step 2 to the units made in step 1 to make 20 units.

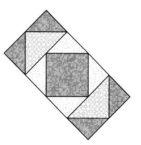

Make 20.

4. Join 80 beige quarter-square triangles to the remaining units you made in step 2 to make 40 units.

Make 40.

5. Piece 20 Gentleman's Fancy blocks as shown.

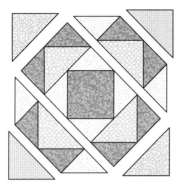

Make 20.

6. Set the blocks together in 5 rows of 4 as shown in the quilt photo; join the rows.
7. Add the dark green border. See "Borders with Straight-Cut Corners" on page 243.
8. Layer with batting and backing; quilt or tie. See page 259 for a quilting suggestion.
9. Bind with straight-grain or bias strips of fabric.

Gentleman's Fancy *by Mary Jo Wenrick, 1995, Girdwood, Alaska, 60" x 72½". This is one of the many traditional designs that form stars when the blocks are set together. Mary Jo's use of prints in a variety of visual textures is very effective. The quilt was crow-footed with perle cotton.*

Harmony Square

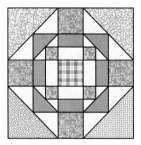

Harmony Square
12½" block

Dimensions: 67½" x 80"

20 blocks, 12½", set 4 across and 5 down; 2¼"-wide inner border, ¼"-wide second border, 1¼"-wide third border, 5"-wide outer border with corner squares.

Materials: 44"-wide fabric

1⅝ yds. yellow print for block backgrounds and second border
¼ yd. green plaid for block centers
1 strip, 5⅞" x 42", *each* of 6 different yellow-orange, gold, and green prints for block corners (Nearest cut is ¼ yd.)
1⅛ yds. rust print for blocks and third border
2¾ yds. multicolored print for blocks, inner and outer borders, and corner squares
4⅞ yds. fabric for backing (lengthwise seam)
⅝ yd. fabric for binding
Batting and thread to finish

Cutting: All measurements include ¼" seams.

From the yellow print:
Cut 7 strips, ¾" x 42", for second border.
Cut 7 strips, 1¾" x 42".
Cut 5 strips, 2⅛" x 42". Cut the strips into a total of 80 squares, 2⅛" x 2⅛". Cut once diagonally into 160 half-square triangles.
Cut 7 strips, 3⅜" x 42". Cut the strips into a total of 80 squares, 3⅜" x 3⅜". Cut once diagonally into 160 half-square triangles.

From the green plaid:
Cut 2 strips, 3" x 42".

From each of the 6 yellow-orange, gold, and green prints:
Cut 7 squares, 5⅞" x 5⅞" (42 total). Cut once diagonally into 84 half-square triangles. You will have 4 triangles left over.

From the rust print:
Cut 14 strips, 1¾" x 42", for blocks and third border.
Cut 4 strips, 3⅜" x 42". Cut the strips into a total of 40 squares, 3⅜" x 3⅜". Cut once diagonally into 80 half-square triangles.

From the multicolored print:
Cut 7 strips, 3" x 42".
Cut 4 strips, 1¾" x 42". Cut the strips into a total of 80 squares, 1¾" x 1¾".
Cut 7 strips, 2¾" x 42", for inner border.
Cut 7 strips, 5½" x 42", for outer border.
Cut 1 strip, 9¼" x 42". Cut the strip into 4 squares, 9¼" x 9¼", for border corners.

DIRECTIONS

1. Join 4 each of the 3"-wide multicolored print strips, the 1¾"-wide rust strips, and the 1¾"-wide yellow strips with the two 3"-wide green plaid strips to make 2 strip units as shown. Cut the strip units into a total of 20 segments, each 3" wide.

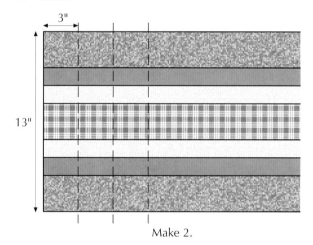

Make 2.

2. Join 3 of the 1¾"-wide rust strips and the remaining 3"-wide multicolored and 1¾"-wide yellow strips to make 3 strip units as shown. Cut the strip units into a total of 40 segments, each 3" wide.

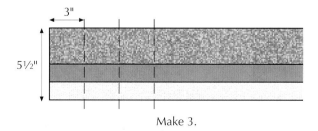

Make 3.

3. Join the yellow triangles, the rust triangles, the small multicolored squares, and the yellow-orange, gold, and green triangles to make 80 units as shown.

Make 80.

4. Piece 20 Harmony Square blocks as shown on page 106. Use 4 different prints for the outside corners of each block.
5. Set the blocks together in 5 rows of 4 as shown in the quilt photo; join the rows.
6. Piece the borders. Seam the yellow, rust, and multicolored border strips as needed to make 4 strips of each fabric, each about 65" long.

Join these long strips to make 4 stripped border pieces as shown.

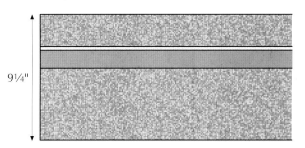

9¼"

Make 4.

7. Cut the border pieces to size and join to the quilt with the multicolored corner squares. See "Borders with Corner Squares" on page 243.
8. Layer with batting and backing; quilt or tie. See page 259 for a quilting suggestion.
9. Bind with straight-grain or bias strips of fabric.

Grandpa's Dream *by Janet Glen Wilson, 1995, Girdwood, Alaska, 68" x 78". Janet has a special facility with the warm side of the color wheel. Note the unusual strip-pieced borders with corner squares. Quilted by Janet Glen Wilson and Jonnie Lazarus.*

Hearts and Hourglass

Hourglass 4" block	Heart 4" block

Dimensions: 68" x 92"

391 blocks (288 Hourglass blocks and 103 appliqué Heart blocks), 4", set 17 across and 23 down; finished without a border.

Materials: 44"-wide fabric

1⅔ yds. muslin or light-background print for appliqué heart backgrounds

1¼ yds. or 103 squares, 4", assorted red, blue, and brown prints or solids for appliqué hearts

4¼ yds. or 36 squares, 12", assorted light and light-medium prints for bias squares

4¼ yds. or 36 squares, 12", assorted medium and dark prints (predominantly reds, blues, and browns) for bias squares

5⅝ yds. fabric for backing (lengthwise seam)

¾ yd. fabric for binding

Batting and thread to finish

Cutting: All measurements include ¼" seams.

From the muslin or light-background print:

Cut 12 strips, 4½" x 42". Cut the strips into a total of 103 squares, 4½" x 4½", for Heart backgrounds.

From the assorted light and light-medium prints:

Cut 36 squares, 12" x 12", for bias squares.

From the assorted medium and dark prints:

Cut 36 squares, 12" x 12", for bias squares. Pair each 12" medium or dark print square with a 12" light or light-medium print square, right sides up. Cut and piece 4¼"-wide bias strips, following the directions for making bias squares on page 16. Cut 8 bias squares, 4⅞" x 4⅞", from each pair of squares for a total of 288 bias squares.

DIRECTIONS

1. Use the template below to make 103 bond-paper or freezer-paper hearts as shown on page 22. Pin the paper patches to the wrong side of the 4" assorted red, blue, and brown squares; cut out the hearts, adding a ¼"-wide seam allowance. Turn the seam allowance over the edge of the paper patch and press or baste.

2. Appliqué a heart to each of the 4½" muslin or light background print squares. See "Appliqué" on page 22.

3. Match pairs of 4⅞" bias squares, right sides together, to make Square Two units, following the directions on page 16. When you have cut and stitched all the bias squares, you will have a total of 288 Hourglass blocks.

4. Set the Hourglass and appliqué Heart blocks together in 23 rows of 17 as shown in the quilt photo. Note that the center blocks are arranged to form a small star-and-heart medallion, with the hearts turned in various directions. Join the rows.

5. Layer with batting and backing; quilt or tie. See page 259 for a quilting suggestion.

6. Bind with straight-grain or bias strips of fabric.

Appliqué Template
Add seam allowance when cutting fabric.
(See "Appliqué," page 22.)

Hearts and Hourglass *by Sarah Kaufman, 1991, West Linn, Oregon, 72" x 96".*
This is an adaptation of an early-nineteenth-century quilt. The blocks are arranged
to form a small star-and-heart medallion in the center. Note: The pattern uses
slightly smaller blocks and produces a 68" x 92" quilt.

Holly's Houses

Little Quilts All Through the House by Alice Berg, Mary Ellen Von Holt, and Sylvia Johnson (That Patchwork Place, Inc.) features a 5" x 5" version of this House block, made entirely from strips, in a number of appealing projects.

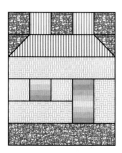

House
5" x 6" block

Dimensions: 30½" x 28"

12 blocks, 5" x 6", set 4 across and 3 down with ½"-wide sashing; 4"-wide border.

Materials: 44"-wide fabric

1 strip, 6" x 42", of black star print for sky (Nearest cut is ¼ yd.)
1 strip, 5½" x 42", of gray stripe for roofs and chimneys (Nearest cut is ¼ yd.)
¼ yd. gray-and-blue plaid for houses
⅓ yd. blue strip for doors, windows, and sashing
⅛ yd. dark gray print for grass or gravel
⅔ yd. black tree print for border (directional fabric)
1 yd. fabric for backing
⅜ yd. fabric for binding
Batting and thread to finish

Cutting: All measurements include ¼" seams.

From the black star print:

Cut 2 strips, 1½" x 42". Cut the strips into a total of 36 squares, 1½" x 1½".

Cut 1 strip, 1⅞" x 42". Cut the strip into 12 squares, 1⅞" x 1⅞". Cut once diagonally into 24 half-square triangles.

From the gray stripe:

Cut 3 strips, 1½" x 42". Cut 1 of the strips into 24 squares, 1½" x 1½".

Cut the remaining strips into a total of 12 segments, each 6¼" wide, to make 1½" x 6¼" rectangles. Trim the corners of the rectangles at a 45° angle as shown.

Trim the corners at a 45° angle.

From the gray-and-blue plaid:

Cut 5 strips, 1½" x 42". Cut 2 of the strips into a total of 12 segments, each 5½" wide, to make 1½" x 5½" rectangles. Cut 1 of the strips into 12 segments, each 3½" wide, to make 1½" x 3½" rectangles. Cut 1 of the strips into 24 squares, 1½" x 1½". Leave the remaining strip uncut.

From the blue stripe:

Cut 2 strips, 1½" x 42". Cut 1 of the strips into 12 squares, 1½" x 1½". Leave the remaining strip uncut.

Cut 7 strips, 1" x 42". Cut 2 of the strips into a total of 8 segments, each 5½" wide*, to make 1" x 5½" rectangles for sashing pieces. Leave the remaining 5 strips uncut.

*Your blocks may not measure exactly 5½" wide when sewn. Cut these rectangles a little longer and trim to size after you piece the blocks if you wish.

From the dark gray print:

Cut 2 strips, 1½" x 42". Cut the strips into a total of 12 segments, each 5½" wide, to make 1½" x 5½" rectangles.

From the *length* of the black tree print:

Cut 2 strips, 4½" wide, for side borders.

From the *width* of the remaining black tree print:

Cut 2 strips, 4½" x 33", for top and bottom borders.

DIRECTIONS

1. Join the 1½" black star and gray stripe squares to make 12 units as shown; keep the gray stripe running vertically in each unit.

Make 12.

2. Join the black star triangles to the trimmed gray stripe rectangles to make 12 units as shown.

Make 12.

3. Join the 1½" blue stripe and gray-and-blue plaid squares to make 12 units as shown. Keep the blue stripe running horizontally in each unit. Join a 1½" x 3½" gray-and-blue plaid rectangle to each of the units as shown.

 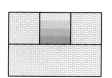

Make 12.

4. Join the 1½"-wide gray-and-blue plaid and blue stripe strips to make 1 strip unit as shown. Cut the strip unit into 12 segments, each 2½" wide.

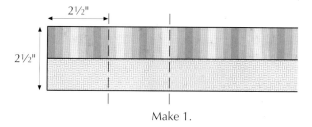

Make 1.

5. Piece 12 House blocks as shown.

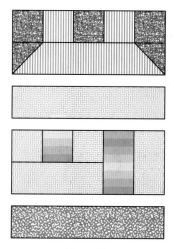

Make 12.

6. Set the blocks together in 3 rows of 4 with the blue stripe sashing pieces and sashing strips as shown in the quilt photo, cutting the long sashing strips to size as needed. Join the rows. See "Straight Sets" on page 238.
7. Add the black tree-print border. See "Borders with Straight-Cut Corners" on page 243.
8. Layer with batting and backing; quilt or tie. See page 259 for a quilting suggestion.
9. Bind with straight-grain or bias strips of fabric.

Holly's Houses *by Holly Rebekah Layton, 1994, Anchorage, Alaska, 29½" x 27½".*
Rows of inviting little houses, done up in plaids and stripes, nestle in a fairy-tale forest.
What a wonderful quilt for a child's room—or your own!

Homeward Bound to Union Square

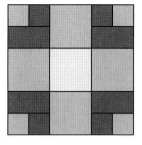 

Homeward Bound
9" block

Union Square
9" block

Dimensions: 46" x 64"

15 blocks (8 Homeward Bound blocks and 7 Union Square blocks), 9", set 3 across and 5 down; 1½"-wide inner border, 6"-wide middle border, 2"-wide outer border.

Materials: 44"-wide fabric

2 yds. black solid for block backgrounds and middle border
1⅜ yds. turquoise solid for blocks and inner and outer borders
¾ yd. blue solid for blocks
3 yds. fabric for backing (crosswise seam)
½ yd. fabric for binding
Batting and thread to finish

Cutting: All measurements include ¼" seams.

From the black solid:
Cut 6 strips, 6½" x 42", for middle border.
Cut 8 strips, 2" x 42". Cut 2 of the strips into a total of 28 squares, 2" x 2". Leave the remaining 6 strips uncut.
Cut 2 strips, 2⅜" x 42".
Cut 2 strips, 4¼" x 42". Cut the strips into a total of 14 squares, 4¼" x 4¼". Cut twice diagonally into 56 quarter-square triangles.

From the turquoise solid:
Cut 5 strips, 2" x 42", for inner border.
Cut 6 strips, 2½" x 42", for outer border.
Cut 1 strip, 3½" x 42".
Cut 2 strips, 3⅞" x 42". Cut the strips into a total of 14 squares, 3⅞" x 3⅞". Cut once diagonally into 28 half-square triangles.
Cut 4 strips, 2⅜" x 42". Cut 2 of the strips into a total of 28 squares, 2⅜" x 2⅜". Cut once diagonally into 56 half-square triangles. Leave the remaining 2 strips uncut.

From the blue solid:
Cut 2 strips, 2" x 42".
Cut 5 strips, 3½" x 42". Cut 1 of the strips into 7 squares, 3½" x 3½". Leave the remaining 4 strips uncut.

DIRECTIONS

1. Join 2 of the 2"-wide black strips and the 2"-wide blue strips to make 2 strip units as shown. Cut the strip units into a total of 32 segments, each 2" wide.

Make 2.

2. Join the remaining 2"-wide black strips and 2 of the 3½"-wide blue strips to make 2 strip units as shown. Cut the strip units into a total of 16 segments, each 3½" wide.

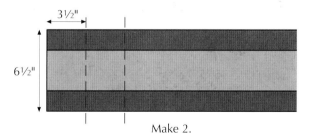

Make 2.

3. Join the remaining 3½"-wide blue strips and the 3½"-wide turquoise strip to make 1 strip unit as shown. Cut the strip unit into 8 segments, each 3½" wide.

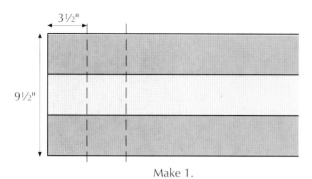

Make 1.

4. Piece 8 Homeward Bound blocks as shown on page 113.
5. Make ◿: Layer the 2⅜"-wide black and turquoise strips, right sides together, to make 2 contrasting strip pairs. Cut 14 squares, 2⅜" x 2⅜", from each strip pair for a total of 28 layered squares. Cut the squares once diagonally and chain-piece the resulting triangle pairs to make 56 half-square triangle units.
6. Join the 3½" blue squares, the 4¼" black quarter-square triangles, and the 3⅞" turquoise half-square triangles to make 7 units as shown.

Make 7.

7. Piece 7 Union Square blocks as shown.

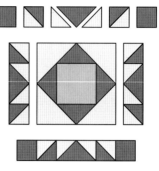

Make 7.

8. Set the blocks together in 5 rows of 3 as shown in the quilt photo, alternating Homeward Bound and Union Square blocks. Join the rows.
9. Add the turquoise inner border, seaming strips as necessary. See "Borders with Straight-Cut Corners" on page 243.
10. Add the black middle border as for the inner border.
11. Add the turquoise outer border as for the previous borders.
12. Layer with batting and backing; quilt or tie. See page 260 for a quilting suggestion.
13. Bind with straight-grain or bias strips of fabric.

Halfway There *by Judy Dafoe Hopkins, 1994, Anchorage, Alaska, 45½" x 64". Classic Amish colors illuminate this two-block quilt. It's big enough to nap under, but small enough for the wall. Quilted by Mrs. Ella Miller. (Collection of Andrew Seidlitz)*

Indian Trails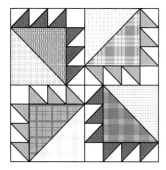

Indian Trails
16" block

Dimensions: 56" x 74"

12 blocks, 16", set 3 across and 4 down with 2"-wide sashing; 2"-wide border.

Materials: 44"-wide fabric

6 fat quarters of assorted black, brown, blue, and pink plaids for triangles

⅝ yd. *each* of 5 assorted light plaids or checks for background

1½ yds. black solid for bias squares and sashing

1¼ yds. blue solid for bias squares and border

3⅝ yds. fabric for backing (crosswise seam)

½ yd. fabric for binding

Batting and thread to finish

Cutting: All measurements include ¼" seams.

From the 6 fat quarters of assorted black, brown, blue, and pink plaids:

Cut a total of 24 squares, 6⅞" x 6⅞". Cut once diagonally into 48 half-square triangles.

From each of the 5 light plaids or checks:

Cut 1 fat quarter, 18" x 22", for bias squares (5 total).

Cut 5 squares, 6⅞" x 6⅞" (25 total). Cut once diagonally into 50 half-square triangles. You will have 2 triangles left over.

Cut 10 squares, 2½" x 2½" (50 total). You will have 2 squares left over.

From the black solid:

Cut 3 fat quarters, 18" x 22", for bias squares.

Cut 8 strips, 2½" x 16½", for vertical sashing.

Cut 4 strips, 2½" x 42", for horizontal sashing.

From the blue solid:

Cut 2 fat quarters, 18" x 22", for bias squares. Pair a blue or black solid fat quarter with a light plaid or check fat quarter, right sides up. Cut and piece 2½"-wide bias strips, following the directions for making bias squares on page 14. Cut a total of 288 bias squares, 2½" x 2½".

Cut 8 strips, 2½" x 42", for border.

DIRECTIONS

1. Piece 12 Indian Trails blocks as shown.

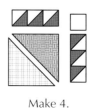

Make 4.

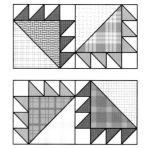

Make 12.

2. Set the blocks together in 4 rows of 3 with vertical sashing strips between the blocks as shown in the quilt photo; join the rows with horizontal sashing strips between them, seaming strips as necessary. See "Straight Sets" on page 238.

3. Add the blue border, seaming strips as necessary. See "Borders with Straight-Cut Corners" on page 243.

4. Layer with batting and backing; quilt or tie. See page 260 for a quilting suggestion.

5. Bind with straight-grain or bias strips of fabric.

Indian Trails *by Evelyn Bright, 1991, Bremerton, Washington, 56" x 74". A lively quilt, featuring plaids and stripes, is accented by a bold black in the bias squares and sashing. (Photo by Brian Kaplan)*

Jack-in-the-Box

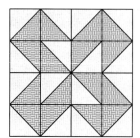

Jack-in-the-Box
10" block

Dimensions: 82" x 92"

56 blocks, 10", set 7 across and 8 down; 6"-wide border.

Materials: 44"-wide fabric

18 fat quarters of assorted light fabrics in white, pink, or checks
18 fat quarters of assorted dark fabrics in red, blue, or black
2 yds. black fabric for border
5⅝ yds. fabric for backing (lengthwise seam)
⅝ yd. fabric for binding
Batting and thread to finish

Cutting: All measurements include ¼" seams.

From the light and dark fat quarters:

Pair light and dark fat quarters, right sides up. Cut and piece 2¾"-wide bias strips, following the directions for making bias squares on page 14. Cut a total of 896 bias squares, 3" x 3".

From the black fabric for border:

Cut 10 strips, 6¼" x 42".

DIRECTIONS

1. Piece 56 Jack-in-the-Box blocks. Note in the quilt photo that not all the blocks have matching fabrics within the bias squares.

Make 4.   Make 4.

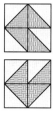 

Join.

Make 56.

2. Set the blocks together in 8 rows of 7 as shown in the quilt photo; join the rows.
3. Add the black border, seaming strips as necessary. See "Borders with Straight-Cut Corners" on page 243.
4. Layer with batting and backing; quilt or tie. See page 260 for a quilting suggestion.
5. Bind with straight-grain or bias strips of fabric.

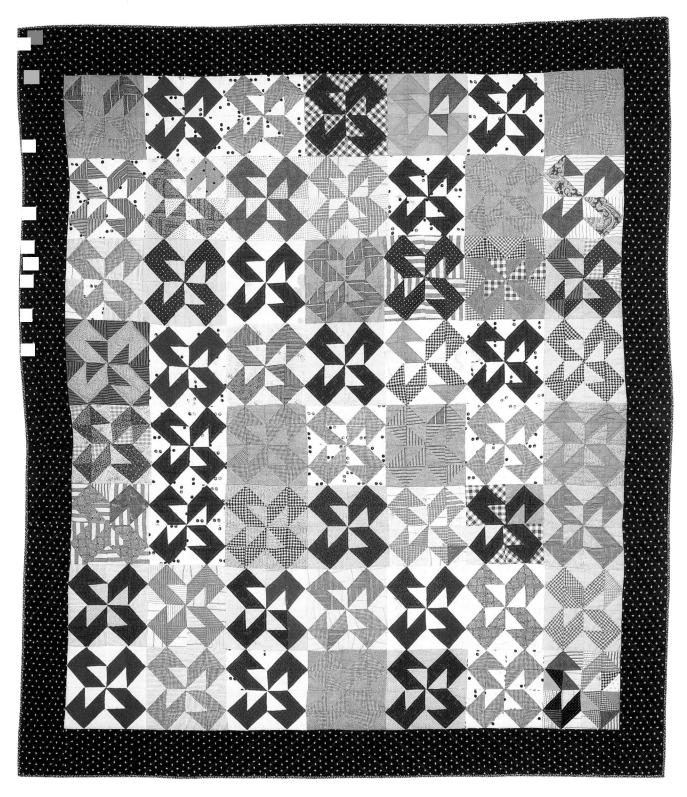

Jack-in-the-Box, *maker unknown, c. 1923, Colorado, 82" x 92". This lively scrap quilt is energized by the striped and checked fabrics that are randomly placed across the quilt top. Quilted by Beverly Payne. (Collection of Martingale & Company.)*

Jacob's Ladder

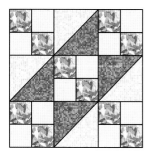

Jacob's Ladder
12" block

Dimensions: 60" x 84"

24 blocks, 12", set 4 across and 6 down; 2"-wide inner border, 1"-wide middle border, 3"-wide outer border.

Materials: 44"-wide fabric

1¼ yds. ivory print for blocks and middle border
1½ yds. dark gray print for blocks and inner border
1⅛ yds. light gold print for blocks
2 yds. multicolored print (gray, tan, maroon, gold, ivory) for blocks and outer border
5⅛ yds. fabric for backing (lengthwise seam)
⅝ yd. fabric for binding
Batting and thread to finish

Cutting: All measurements include ¼" seams.

From the ivory print:
Cut 6 strips, 4⅞" x 42". Cut the strips into 48 squares, 4⅞" x 4⅞". Cut once diagonally into 96 half-square triangles for blocks.
Cut 8 strips, 1½" x 42", for middle border.

From the dark gray print:
Cut 6 strips, 4⅞" x 42". Cut the strips into 48 squares, 4⅞" x 4⅞". Cut once diagonally into 96 half-square triangles for blocks.
Cut 8 strips, 2½" x 42", for inner border.

From the light gold print:
Cut 15 strips, 2½" x 42", for blocks.

From the multicolored print:
Cut 15 strips, 2½" x 42", for blocks.
Cut 8 strips, 3½" x 42", for outer border.

DIRECTIONS

1. Join the ivory and dark gray half-square triangles into 96 units as shown.

Make 96.

2. Join the 2½" x 42" multicolored and light gold strips to make 15 strip units as shown. The units should measure 4½" wide when sewn. Cut the units into 240 segments, 2½" wide, and join the segments into 120 four-patch units.

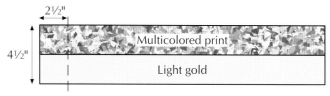

Make 15.

Make 120.

3. Piece 24 Jacob's Ladder blocks as shown.

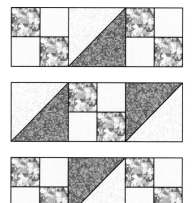

Make 24.

4. Set the blocks together in 6 rows of 4, rotating every other block so that the small gold squares form a diagonal chain across the surface of the quilt as shown in the quilt photo. Join the rows.

NOTE: In the pictured quilt, four-patch units were turned the wrong way in 3 of the blocks. When all blocks are properly placed, the pattern will continue correctly throughout the quilt.

5. Add the inner border, seaming strips as necessary. See "Borders with Straight-Cut Corners" on page 243.

6. Add the middle border as for the inner border.
7. Add the outer border as for the previous borders.
8. Layer with batting and backing; quilt or tie. See page 260 for a quilting suggestion.
9. Bind with straight-grain or bias strips of fabric.

Jacob's Ladder *by Sheila Rae Robinson, 1990, Palmer, Alaska, 60" x 84".*
An exotic floral print updates this classic quilt, which is finished by tying.

Kansas Troubles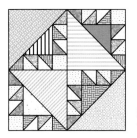

Kansas Troubles
16" block

Dimensions: 74" x 74"

16 blocks, 16", set 4 across and 4 down; 5"-wide border.

Materials: 44"-wide fabric

⅜ yd. *each* of 8 assorted dark blue prints for bias squares

⅝ yd. *each* of 8 assorted light-background prints for bias squares and large triangles

1 fat quarter *each* of 8 assorted medium blue prints for small triangles

2¼ yds. medium blue solid for border

4½ yds. fabric for backing (lengthwise or cross-wise seam)

⅝ yd. fabric for binding

Batting and thread to finish

NOTE: Directions are for cutting 8 groups of 8 identical blocks, which is the most economical way to purchase and use the fabric. If you have a large collection of scraps, don't hesitate to use them for a scrappier look as shown in the photo.

Cutting: All measurements include ¼" seams.

From each of the 8 dark blue prints:
Cut 4 squares, 8" x 8", for bias squares (32 total).

Cut 8 squares, 2⅞" x 2⅞" (64 total). Cut once diagonally into a total of 128 half-square triangles.

From each of the 8 light-background prints:
Cut 4 squares, 8" x 8", for bias squares (32 total). Pair each 8" light print square with an 8" dark print square, right sides up. Cut and piece 2½"-wide bias strips, following the directions for making bias squares on page 16. Cut 8 bias squares, 2½" x 2½", from each pair of squares for a total of 256 bias squares.

From each of the 8 medium blue prints:
Cut 4 squares, 4⅞" x 4⅞" (32 total). Cut once diagonally into 64 half-square triangles.

Cut 4 squares, 8⅞" x 8⅞" (32 total). Cut once diagonally into 64 half-square triangles.

Cut 8 squares, 2½" x 2½" (64 total).

From the *length* of the medium blue solid:
Cut 2 strips, 5½" x 64½", for side borders.

Cut 2 strips, 5½" x 74", for top and bottom borders.

DIRECTIONS

1. Piece 16 Kansas Troubles blocks as shown.

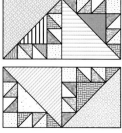

Make 4.

Make 16.

2. Set the blocks together in 4 rows of 4 as shown in the quilt photo; join the rows.
3. Add the medium blue borders. See "Borders with Straight-Cut Corners" on page 243.
4. Layer with batting and backing; quilt or tie. This quilt was divided into several areas of unequal size, then quilted with a different overall pattern (which does not outline the block design) for each area. Suggested patterns are a straight-line grid, Clamshells, or Baptist Fan.

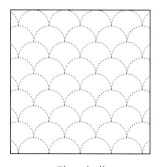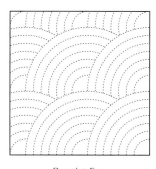

Clamshell

Baptist Fan

5. Bind with straight-grain or bias strips of fabric.

Kansas Troubles *by Nancy J. Martin, 1991, Woodinville, Washington, 74" x 74".*
An assortment of randomly placed blue fabrics gives a soft, pleasing look to this angular
design. Quilted by Sue von Jentzen. (Collection of Martingale & Company)

Lady of the Lake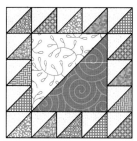

Lady of the Lake
10" block

Dimensions: 42" x 42"

9 blocks, 10", set 3 across and 3 down; 6"-wide border with corner squares.

Materials: 44"-wide fabric

½ yd. purple print for large triangles and corner squares

¼ yd. large-scale light green floral print for large triangles

¾ yd. light green print for small triangles

1 strip, 2⅞" x 25", *each* of 9 different medium-to-dark purple and green prints for small triangles (Nearest cut is ⅛ yd.)

⅞ yd. large-scale multicolored floral print for border

2¾ yds. fabric for backing (lengthwise or crosswise seam)

½ yd. fabric for binding

Batting and thread to finish

Cutting: All measurements include ¼" seams.

From the purple print:
Cut 1 strip, 6⅞" x 42".
Cut 1 strip, 6½" x 42". Cut the strip into 4 squares, 6½" x 6½", for corner squares.

From the large-scale light green floral print:
Cut 1 strip, 6⅞" x 42".

From the *length* of the light green print:
Cut 9 strips, 2⅞" x 25".

From the multicolored floral print:
Cut 4 strips, 6½" x 42", for border.

DIRECTIONS

1. Make ◸: Layer the 6⅞"-wide purple and large-scale light green floral strips, right sides together, to make 1 contrasting strip pair. Cut 5 layered squares, 6⅞" x 6⅞", from the strip pair. Cut the squares once diagonally and chain-piece the resulting triangle pairs to make 10 half-square triangles units. You will have 1 unit left over.

2. Make ◸: Layer the 2⅞"-wide light green and the medium-to-dark purple and green strips, right sides together, to make 9 contrasting strip pairs. Cut 8 squares, 2⅞" x 2⅞", from each strip pair for a total of 72 layered squares. Cut the squares once diagonally and chain-piece the resulting triangle pairs to make 144 half-square triangle units.

3. Piece 9 Lady of the Lake blocks as shown.

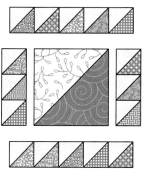

Make 9.

4. Set the blocks together in 3 rows of 3 as shown in the quilt photo; join the rows.

5. Add the multicolored floral border and purple corner squares. See "Borders with Corner Squares" on page 243.

6. Layer with batting and backing; quilt or tie. See page 260 for a quilting suggestion.

7. Bind with straight-grain or bias strips of fabric.

Nimue *by Dee Morrow, 1995, Anchorage, Alaska, 41½" x 41½". Dee has done up the popular Lady of the Lake design in antique-reproduction prints. This small but special nine-block quilt is a great place to try out any of those exciting new fabric lines.*

London Roads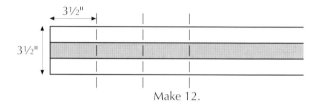

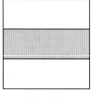

Block A
3" block

Block B
3" block

Block C
3" block

Dimensions: 49" x 61"

221 blocks (111 Block A, 56 Block B, and 54 Block C), 3", set 13 across and 17 down; 1"-wide inner border, 4"-wide outer border.

Materials: 44"-wide fabric

½ yd. *each* of 3 different ivory prints for Block A
⅞ yd. red print for Block A and inner border
1 strip, 2" x 42", *each* of 6 different dark prints (greens, blues, and tans) for Block B (Nearest cut is ⅛ yd.)
1 strip, 2" x 42", *each* of 6 different medium prints (greens, blues, and tans) for Block B (Nearest cut is ⅛ yd.)
⅝ yd. navy blue print for Block C
⅞ yd. dark blue print for outer border
3⅛ yds. fabric for backing (crosswise seam)
½ yd. fabric for binding
Batting and thread to finish

Cutting: All measurements include ¼" seams.

From each of the 3 ivory prints:
Cut 8 strips, 1½" x 42" (24 total).

From the red print:
Cut 17 strips, 1½" x 42", for blocks and inner border.

From the navy blue print:
Cut 5 strips, 3½" x 42". Cut the strips into a total of 54 squares, 3½" x 3½" (Block C).

From the dark blue print:
Cut 6 strips, 4½" x 42", for outer border.

DIRECTIONS

1. Join the 1½"-wide ivory strips and 12 of the 1½"-wide red strips to make 12 strip units as shown. Use just 1 ivory print in each strip unit. Cut 9 segments, each 3½" wide, from each of 11 strip units. Then cut 12 segments, each 3½" wide, from the remaining strip unit. You will have a total of 111 segments (Block A). Use the remaining strip-unit pieces for another project.

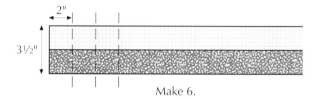

Make 12.

2. Join the 2"-wide assorted dark and medium strips to make 6 strip units as shown. Cut the strip units into a total of 112 segments, each 2" wide.

Make 6.

3. Piece 56 dark/medium Four Patch blocks (Block B), using matching segments in each Four Patch.
4. Set the blocks together in 17 rows of 13 as shown in the quilt photo; join the rows.
5. Add the red inner border, seaming strips as necessary. See "Borders with Straight-Cut Corners" on page 243.
6. Add the dark blue outer border as for the inner border.
7. Layer with batting and backing; quilt or tie. See page 261 for a quilting suggestion.
8. Bind with straight-grain or bias strips of fabric.

London Roads *by Stephanie Burrill Urda, 1995, Anchorage, Alaska, 47" x 59".*
Simple squares and strips and an abundance of prints combine to make this
dynamic crib-size quilt. Try it in jelly-bean colors for an entirely different look.

London Square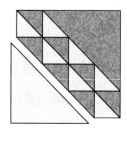

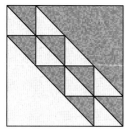

London Square
8" block

Dimensions: 48" x 64"

48 blocks, 8", set 6 across and 8 down; finished without a border.

Materials: 44"-wide fabric

2⅝ yds. tone-on-tone ivory print for blocks
2⅝ yds. red print for blocks
3¼ yds. fabric for backing (crosswise seam)
½ yd. fabric for binding
Batting and thread to finish

Cutting: All measurements include ¼" seams.

From the ivory tone-on-tone print:
 Cut 4 fat quarters, 18" x 22".
 Cut 24 squares, 6⅞" x 6⅞". Cut once diagonally into 48 large half-square triangles.
 Cut 72 squares, 2⅞" x 2⅞". Cut once diagonally into 144 small half-square triangles.

From the red print:
 Cut 4 fat quarters, 18" x 22". Pair each red fat quarter with an ivory fat quarter, right sides up. Cut and piece 2½"-wide bias strips, following the directions for making bias squares on page 14. Cut a total of 192 bias squares, 2½" x 2½".
 Cut 24 squares, 6⅞" x 6⅞". Cut once diagonally into 48 large half-square triangles.
 Cut 72 squares, 2⅞" x 2⅞". Cut once diagonally into 144 small half-square triangles.

DIRECTIONS

1. Piece 48 London Square blocks as shown.

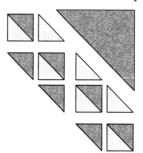

2. Set the blocks together in 8 rows of 6 as shown in the quilt photo, alternating the position of the darks and lights in each block. Join the rows.
3. Layer with batting and backing; quilt or tie. See page 261 for a quilting suggestion.
4. Bind with straight-grain or bias strips of fabric.

Vanilla Ice *by Judy and Tom Morrison, 1991, Anchorage, Alaska, 48" x 64".*
Made from traditional London Square blocks in red and cream prints, this quilt is
utility quilted with perle cotton in a random pattern of leaves and vines.

Lost Ships Signature 🧵

Lost Ships Signature
10" block

Dimensions: 60" x 84"

24 blocks, 10", set 4 across and 6 down with 2"-wide sashing; 5"-wide border.

Materials: 44"-wide fabric

⅜ yd. *each* of 9 assorted dark prints for medium triangles and bias squares
1 fat quarter *each* of 9 light-background prints for small triangles and bias squares
1½ yds. paisley or large print for large triangles
1¼ yds. green print for sashing
1⅜ yds. print for border (cut crosswise)
5⅛ yds. fabric for backing (lengthwise seam)
⅝ yd. fabric for binding
Batting and thread to finish

NOTE: Directions are for cutting 9 groups of 3 identical blocks (you will have 3 extra), which is the most economical way to purchase and use the fabric. If you have a large collection of scraps, don't hesitate to use them for a scrappier look as shown in the photo.

Cutting: All measurements include ¼" seams.

From each of the 9 dark prints:

Cut 3 squares, 8" x 8", for bias squares (27 total).

Cut 2 squares, 6⅞" x 6⅞" (18 total). Cut once diagonally into 36 medium half-square triangles.

From each of the 9 light-background prints:

Cut 3 squares, 8" x 8", for bias squares (27 total). Pair each 8" light print square with an 8" dark print square, right sides up. Cut and piece 2½"-wide bias strips, following the directions for making bias squares on page 16. Cut 8 bias squares, 2½" x 2½", from each pair of squares for a total of 216 bias squares. You will have 13 left over.

Cut 3 squares, 2⅞" x 2⅞" (27 total). Cut once diagonally into 54 small half-square triangles.

From the paisley or large print:

Cut 12 squares, 10⅞" x 10⅞". Cut once diagonally into 24 large half-square triangles.

From the green print:

Cut 58 rectangles, 2½" x 10½", for sashing strips.

From the border print:

Cut 8 strips, 5½" x 42", for border.

DIRECTIONS

1. Piece 24 Lost Ships Signature blocks as shown, using either identical or unmatched bias squares in each block. Reserve the remaining bias squares for the sashing squares.

Make 24.

2. Set the blocks together in 6 rows of 4 with the sashing strips and remaining bias squares as shown in the quilt photo; join the rows. See "Straight Sets" on page 238.
3. Add the print border, seaming strips as necessary. See "Borders with Straight-Cut Corners" on page 243.
4. Layer with batting and backing; quilt or tie. See page 261 for a quilting suggestion.
5. Bind with straight-grain or bias strips of fabric.

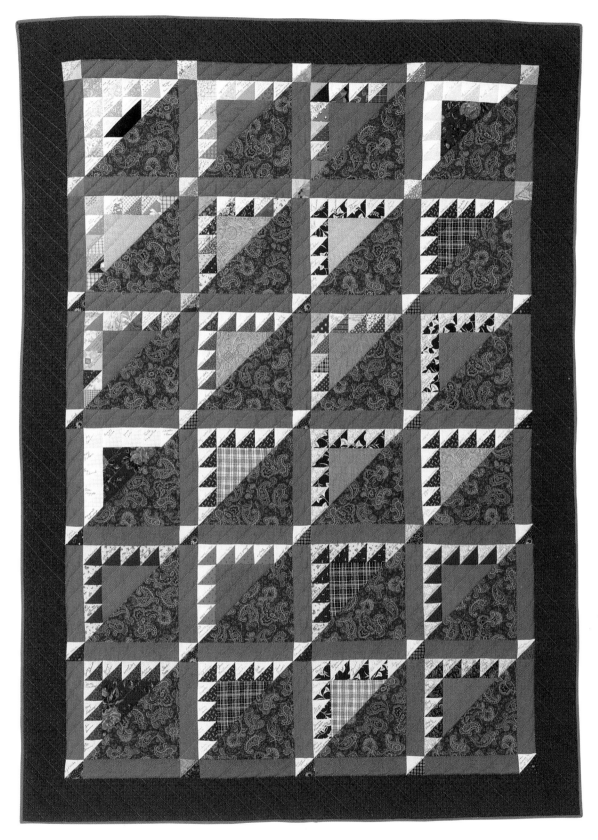

Lost Ships Signature *by Nancy J. Martin, 1990, Woodinville, Washington, 60" x 84". The large-scale paisley print and soft green lattices help to unify the wide range of colors used in the bias squares, many donated by Nancy's students. Each square in this wonderful memory quilt contains a signature of quilting friends and students, collected from both home and abroad. Quilted by Freda Smith.*

Louisiana

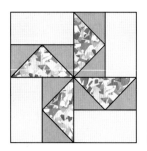

Louisiana
8" block

Dimensions: 28¾" x 38"

6 blocks, 8", set 2 across and 3 down with 1¼"-wide sashing and sashing squares; 4½"-wide border.

Materials: 44"-wide fabric

⅓ yd. red print for blocks and sashing squares
⅓ yd. tan print for blocks
⅞ yd. chili pepper print for blocks and border
⅓ yd. green print for sashing
1⅓ yds. fabric for backing
⅜ yd. fabric for binding
Batting and thread to finish

Cutting: All measurements include ¼" seams.

From the red print:

Cut 2 strips, 2⅞" x 42". Cut the strips into a total of 24 squares, 2⅞" x 2⅞". Cut once diagonally into 48 half-square triangles.

Cut 1 strip, 1¾" x 42". Cut the strip into 12 squares, 1¾" x 1¾", for sashing squares.

From the tan print:

Cut 3 strips, 2½" x 42". Cut the strips into a total of 24 segments, each 4½" wide, to make 2½" x 4½" rectangles.

From the chili pepper print:

Cut 1 strip, 5¼" x 42". Cut the strip into 6 squares, 5¼" x 5¼". Cut twice diagonally into 24 quarter-square triangles.

Cut 4 strips, 5" x 42", for border.

From the green print:

Cut 1 strip, 8½"* x 42". Cut the strip into 17 segments, each 1¾" wide, to make 1¾" x 8½" sashing pieces.

*Your blocks may not measure exactly 8½" square when sewn. Cut this strip a little wider than 8½" and trim the sashing pieces to size after you piece the blocks if you wish.

DIRECTIONS

1. Join the 2⅞" red half-square triangles and the 5¼" chili pepper quarter-square triangles to make 24 units as shown.

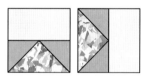

Make 24.

2. Piece 6 Louisiana blocks as shown.

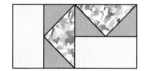

Make 6.

3. Set the blocks together in 3 rows of 2 with the green sashing pieces and red sashing squares as shown in the quilt photo; join the rows. See "Straight Sets" on page 238.
4. Add the chili pepper print border. See "Borders with Straight-Cut Corners" on page 243.
5. Layer with batting and backing; quilt or tie. See page 261 for a quilting suggestion.
6. Bind with straight-grain or bias strips of fabric.

Tabasco *by Judy Dafoe Hopkins, 1994, Anchorage, Alaska, 28¾" x 38". Judy used Tabasco-bottle colors and a chili pepper print for this fiery little quilt. The block choice is particularly appropriate—the famous pepper sauce is made in Avery Island, Louisiana. Quilted with perle cotton.*

Magic Carpet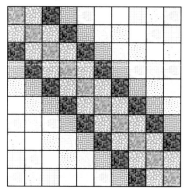

Magic Carpet
15" block

Dimensions: 60" x 81"

20 blocks, 15", set 5 across and 4 down; 3"-wide top and bottom borders.

Materials: 44"-wide fabric

⅝ yd. yellow print for blocks
1⅛ yds. pink or light red print for blocks
1 yd. black print for blocks
⅞ yd. red print for blocks
3½ yds. assorted neutral prints for blocks*
½ yd. black or gray print for borders
3¾ yds. fabric for backing (crosswise seam)
⅝ yd. fabric for binding
Batting and thread to finish
*Try ¼ yd. each of 14 different fabrics.

Cutting: All measurements include ¼" seams.

From the yellow print:
    Cut 10 strips, 2" x 42", for blocks.

From the pink or light red print:
    Cut 18 strips, 2" x 42", for blocks.

From the black print:
    Cut 16 strips, 2" x 42", for blocks.

From the red print:
    Cut 14 strips, 2" x 42", for blocks.

From the assorted neutral prints:
    Cut 42 strips, 2" x 42" (3 strips from each fabric), for blocks.

From the black or gray print:
    Cut 4 strips, 3½" x 42", for seamed top and bottom borders.

DIRECTIONS

1. Join the 2" x 42" strips into strip units as shown. Make 2 each of Units A–E. Each unit uses 10 strips; the units should measure 15½" wide when sewn. Cut each strip unit into 20 segments, 2" wide.

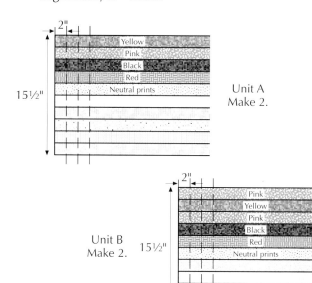

Unit A
Make 2.

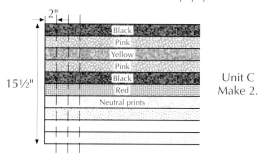

Unit B
Make 2.

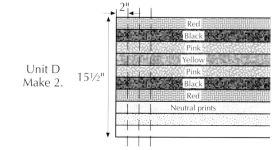

Unit C
Make 2.

Unit D
Make 2.

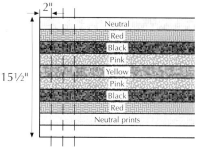

Unit E
Make 2.

2. Join the segments into 20 Magic Carpet blocks. Each block uses 2 segments from each unit.

3. Set the blocks together in 4 rows of 5 as shown in the quilt photo; join the rows.

4. Add the top and bottom borders, seaming strips as necessary. See "Borders with Straight-Cut Corners" on page 243.

5. Layer with batting and backing; quilt or tie. See page 261 for a quilting suggestion.

6. Bind with straight-grain or bias strips of fabric.

Magic Carpet, *maker unknown, c. 1900, Pennsylvania, 60" x 81". This well-worn treasure features several repeating fabrics in the twenty identical blocks. Create a contemporary version quickly and easily by using strip-piecing techniques. (Collection of Nancy J. Martin)*

Market Square

Market Square
16" block

Dimensions: 76" x 76"

16 blocks, 16", set 4 across and 4 down; 6"-wide border.

Materials: 44"-wide fabric

2⅝ yds. assorted purple fabrics
8 fat quarters of assorted light-background fabrics
⅝ yd. red bandanna fabric or 3 bandannas
1¼ yds. assorted large-scale chintz prints for block centers
1½ yds. purple fabric for border
4¾ yds. fabric for backing (lengthwise or crosswise seam)
⅝ yd. fabric for binding
Batting and thread to finish

Cutting: All measurements include ¼" seams.

From the assorted purple fabrics:

Cut 5 fat quarters (18" x 22"). Pair each purple fat quarter with a light-background fat quarter, right sides up. Cut and piece 2½"-wide bias strips, following the directions for making bias squares on page 14. Cut a total of 256 bias squares, 2½" x 2½".

Cut 16 squares, 6⅞" x 6⅞". Cut once diagonally into 32 half-square triangles for block corners.

Cut 96 squares, 2⅞" x 2⅞". Cut once diagonally into 192 half-square triangles.

From the remaining fat quarters of light-background fabrics:

Cut 96 squares, 2⅞" x 2⅞". Cut once diagonally into 192 half-square triangles.

From the red bandanna fabric:

Cut 16 squares, 6⅞" x 6⅞". Cut once diagonally into 32 half-square triangles for block corners.

From the assorted large-scale chintz prints:

Cut 16 squares, 9" x 9", for block centers.

From the purple fabric for border:

Cut 8 strips, 6¼" x 42".

DIRECTIONS

1. Piece 16 Market Square blocks. Use red corner triangles on 8 blocks and purple corner triangles on the other 8 blocks.

Make 16.

2. Set the blocks together into 4 rows of 4 as shown in the quilt photo; join the rows.
3. Add the purple border, seaming strips as necessary. See "Borders with Straight-Cut Corners" on page 243.
4. Layer with batting and backing; quilt or tie. See page 261 for a quilting suggestion.
5. Bind with straight-grain or bias strips of fabric.

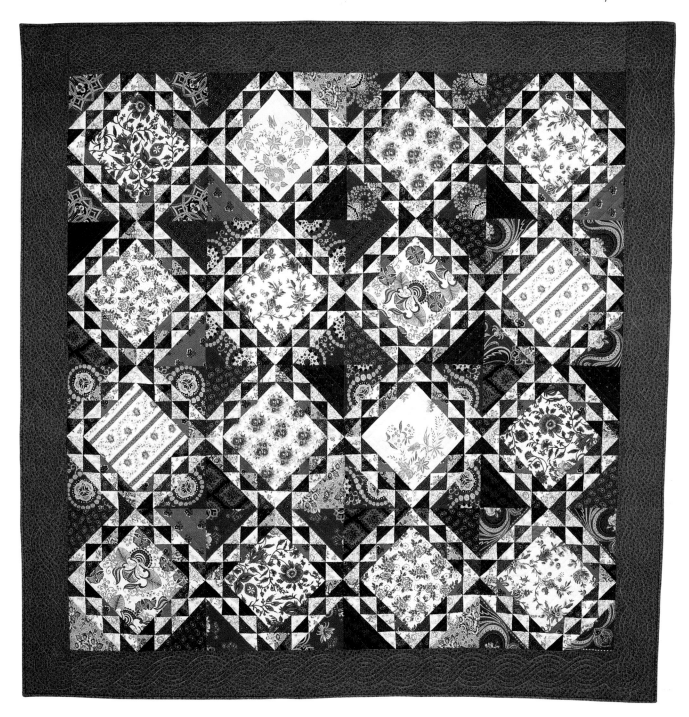

Market Square *by Nancy J. Martin, 1992, Woodinville, Washington, 76" x 76". This quilt was named for the central square, where one finds the town hall, town clock, and open-air markets, in the villages of Holland and Belgium. The fabrics were purchased in The Netherlands and represent the variety of people who congregate in the market square: i.e., purple antique fabrics for the widows who observe the traditional mourning period, and red triangles cut from bandannas for the younger women. The large squares feature both antique and reproduction chintz fabrics used in costumes of the various villages. Quilted by Sue von Jentzen. (Collection of Martingale & Company)*

Memory Wreath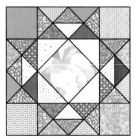

Memory Wreath
12" block

Dimensions: 71½" x 85½"

20 blocks, 12", set 4 across and 5 down with 2"-wide sashing; 1¾"-wide inner border, 5"-wide outer border.

Materials: 44"-wide fabric

12 fat quarters of assorted red fabrics for centers, star tips, and sashing
5 fat quarters of assorted tan fabrics
4 fat quarters of assorted navy blue fabrics
5 fat quarters of assorted green fabrics
¼ yd. plaid fabric for sashing squares
⅝ yd. navy blue fabric for inner border
1⅜ yds. fabric for outer border*
5¼ yds. fabric for backing (lengthwise seam)
⅝ yd. fabric for binding
Batting and thread to finish

*To duplicate the mitered border shown in the quilt photo, purchase 2½ yds. striped fabric.

Cutting: All measurements include ¼" seams

From 2 red and 2 tan fat quarters:
Pair red and tan fat quarters right sides up. Cut and piece 2½"-wide bias strips, following the directions for making bias squares on page 14. Cut a total of 80 bias squares, 2⅝" x 2⅝".

From 4 red and 4 navy blue fat quarters:
Pair red and navy blue fabrics right sides up. Cut and piece 3½"-wide bias strips, following the directions for making bias squares on page 14. Cut a total of 80 bias squares, 3⅞" x 3⅞". Cut these bias squares once diagonally to make 160 of Unit .5, following the directions on page 17.

From the remaining red fat quarters:
Cut 20 squares, 4¾" x 4¾", for centers.
Cut 49 strips, 2½" x 12½", for sashing.

From the remaining tan fat quarters:
Cut 40 squares, 3⅞" x 3⅞". Cut once diagonally into 80 half-square triangles.

From the green fat quarters:
Cut 80 squares, 3½" x 3½", for corners.
Cut 40 squares, 4¼" x 4¼". Cut twice diagonally into 160 quarter-square triangles for outside edges.

From the plaid fabric:
Cut 2 strips, 2½" x 42". Cut into a total of 30 sashing squares, 2½" x 2½".

From the navy blue fabric for inner border:
Cut 8 strips, 2¼" x 42".

From the length of the fabric for outer border:
Cut 2 strips, 5¼" x 74".
Cut 2 strips, 5¼" x 88".

NOTE: Cut 8 strips, 5¼" x 42", if you choose not to use striped fabric.

DIRECTIONS

1. Piece 20 Memory Wreath blocks as shown.

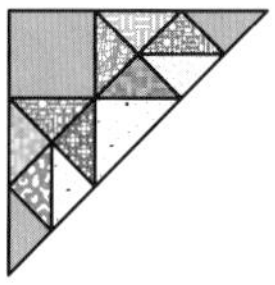

Make 2.

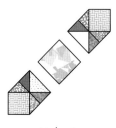

Make 1.

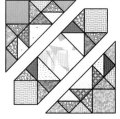

Make 20.

2. Join 4 blocks and 5 sashing strips into a row. Make 5 rows.
3. Join 5 sashing squares and 4 sashing strips. Make 6 of these.
4. Join the rows of blocks with sashing strips as shown in the quilt photo.

5. Join the strips for the inner and outer borders; sew to the quilt top, mitering the corners as shown on page 243.

6. Layer with batting and backing; quilt or tie. See page 262 for a quilting suggestion.

7. Bind with straight-grain or bias strips of fabric.

Memory Wreath *by Nancy J. Martin, 1992, Woodinville, Washington, 71½" x 85½". This scrappy quilt has a traditional color scheme that features a collection of patriotic prints. A dark, swirling paisley border surrounds and calms the interior blocks. Quilted by Hazel Montague. (Collection of Martingale & Company)*

Milky Way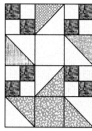

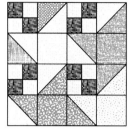

Milky Way
12" block

Right side unit
9" x 12"
Make 5.

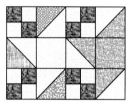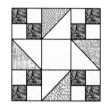

Bottom unit
9" x 12"
Make 5.

Corner unit
9" x 9"
Make 1 for lower right.

Dimensions: 69" x 69"

25 blocks, 12", set 5 across and 5 down with side, bottom, and corner units; finished without a border.

Materials: 44"-wide fabric

10 fat quarters of navy blue prints with light background
10 fat quarters of navy blue prints with dark background
4 fat quarters of purple fabric for four-patch units
1 yd. light blue fabric for four-patch units
4⅜ yds. fabric for backing (lengthwise or crosswise seam)
½ yd. fabric for binding
Batting and thread to finish

Cutting: All measurements include ¼" seams

From the fat quarters of navy blue prints with light background:
Cut 61 squares (total), 3½" x 3½".
Cut 132 squares (total), 3⅞" x 3⅞". Cut once diagonally into 264 half-square triangles.

From the fat quarters of navy blue prints with dark background:
Cut 60 squares (total), 3½" x 3½".
Cut 132 squares (total), 3⅞" x 3⅞". Cut once diagonally into 264 half-square triangles.

From the purple fat quarters:
Cut 30 strips, 2" x 22", for four-patch units.

From the light blue fabric:
Cut 30 strips, 2" x 22", for four-patch units.

DIRECTIONS

1. Make 144 four-patch units to use in the blocks. Sew purple and light blue 2" x 22" strips in pairs. The units should measure 3½" wide when sewn. Press the seams toward the purple fabric. Layer strips with opposing seams and cut each strip into 10 segments, each 2" wide. Sew segments together, using ¼"-wide seam allowances, and press flat.

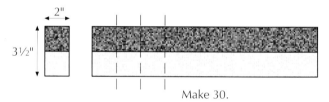

Make 30.

Four-patch units
Make 144.

2. Join navy blue light background triangles and navy blue dark background triangles to make 264 units.

Make 264.

3. Make 25 Milky Way blocks. Take care that fabrics match on adjoining blocks by placing fabrics in position on a design wall before stitching.

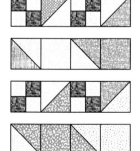

Make 25.

4. Set blocks together in 5 rows of 5 as shown in the quilt photo; join the rows.
5. Stitch 5 side units; join and add to the right side of quilt.

6. Stitch 5 bottom units. Add a corner unit to the right side and join to the quilt top.

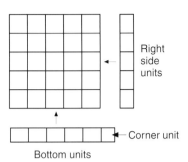

Right side units

Bottom units

Corner unit

7. Layer with batting and backing; quilt or tie. See page 262 for a quilting suggestion.
8. Bind with straight-grain or bias strips of fabric.

Milky Way *by Cleo Nollette, 1992, Seattle, Washington, 69" x 69". This lively scrap quilt is made from a classic collection of indigo-and-white prints, a traditional favorite. Quilted by Hazel Montague. (Collection of Martingale & Company.)*

Mrs. Keller's Nine Patch

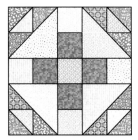

Mrs. Keller's Nine Patch
12½" block

Dimensions: 60" x 85"

24 blocks, 12½", set 4 across and 6 down; 5"-wide border.

Materials: 44"-wide fabric

2 yds. dark green print for blocks and border
1 strip, 3⅜" x 42", *each* of 14 different medium or dark prints (predominantly browns, greens, and golds) for blocks (Nearest cut is ⅛ yd.)
1 strip, 10" x 42", *each* of 5 different light prints for blocks (Nearest cut is ⅓ yd.)
1 strip, 5⅞" x 42", *each* of 8 additional light prints for blocks (Nearest cut is ¼ yd.)
5¼ yds. fabric for backing (lengthwise seam)
⅝ yd. fabric for binding
Batting and thread to finish

Cutting: All measurements include ¼" seams.

From the dark green print:
Cut 8 strips, 5½" x 42", for border.
Cut 8 strips, 3" x 42", for blocks.

From each of the 14 different medium or dark strips:
Cut 11 squares, 3⅜" x 3⅜" (154 total). Cut once diagonally into 308 half-square triangles for blocks. You will have 20 triangles left over.

From each of the 5 different light strips:
Cut 2 strips, 3" x 42" (10 total), for blocks.
Cut 1 strip, 3⅜" x 42" (5 total). Cut the strips into a total of 48 squares, 3⅜" x 3⅜". Cut once diagonally into 96 half-square triangles for blocks.

From each of the 8 additional light strips:
Cut 6 squares, 5⅞" x 5⅞" (48 total). Cut once diagonally into 96 half-square triangles for blocks.

DIRECTIONS

1. Join the 3⅜" light half-square triangles, the 3⅜" medium or dark half-square triangles, and the 5⅞" light half-square triangles to make 96 units as shown. Combine the fabrics at random.

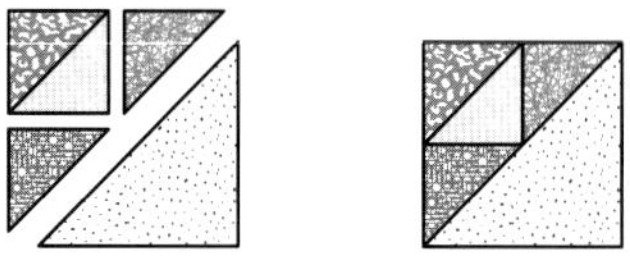

Make 96.

2. Join any 6 of the 3"-wide light print strips and 4 of the 3"-wide dark green strips to make 2 strip units as shown. The strip units should measure 13" wide when sewn. Cut the units into 24 segments, each 3" wide.

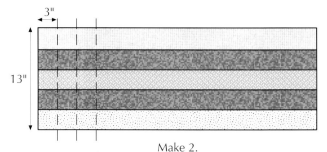

Make 2.

3. Join the remaining 3"-wide light print strips and 3"-wide dark green strips to make 4 strip units as shown. The strip units should measure 5½" wide when sewn. Cut the units into 48 segments, each 3" wide.

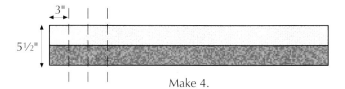

Make 4.

4. Join the pieces made in the previous steps to make 24 Mrs. Keller's Nine Patch blocks.

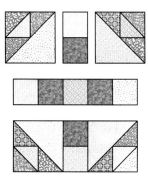

Make 24.

5. Set the blocks together in 6 rows of 4 as shown in the quilt photo; join the rows.

6. Add the dark green border, seaming strips as necessary. See "Borders with Straight-Cut Corners" on page 243.

7. Layer with batting and backing; quilt or tie. See page 262 for a quilting suggestion.

8. Bind with straight-grain or bias strips of fabric.

Not Quite Nine *by Julie Wilkinson Kimberlin, 1993, Anchorage, Alaska, 60" x 85". Julie captured the classic scrap-quilt look by using background fabrics that range from light to medium; the contrast varies from block to block. The small triangles feature a variety of interesting contemporary fabrics, including a rich brown-and-gold rooster print.*

Nine Patch Plaid

The strip-piecing method used in this pattern will yield enough pieces to make 41 or 42 blocks, several more than are needed to make the pictured quilt. The directions are written for 35 blocks; cut more segments and make more blocks if you wish. You could use these blocks to make the quilt one row wider or longer than the one shown. The border fabric requirements given will accommodate a larger quilt.

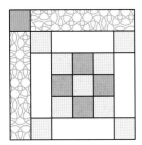

Nine Patch Plaid
9" block

Dimensions: 57½" x 75½"

35 blocks, 9", set 5 across and 7 down with 1½"-wide right and bottom edge sashing; 1"-wide inner border, 4½"-wide outer border.

NOTE: The pictured quilt appears to have sashing with red corner squares, but those pieces are actually part of the block, except for the pieces that finish the right and bottom edges.

Materials: 44"-wide fabric

1⅝ yds. white-on-white print for blocks and inner border
1⅛ yds. medium gray-green print for blocks
¾ yd. red print for blocks and sashing
2⅓ yds. multicolored floral print for blocks, sashing, and outer border
3⅝ yds. fabric for backing (crosswise seam)
⅝ yd. fabric for binding
Batting and thread to finish.

Cutting: All measurements include ¼" seams.

From the white-on-white print:
Cut 8 strips, 5" x 42". Cut 4 of the strips into a total of 70 segments, each 2" wide, to make 2" x 5" rectangles. Leave the remaining 4 strips uncut.
Cut 8 strips, 1½" x 42", for inner border.

From the medium gray-green print:
Cut 18 strips, 2" x 42".

From the red print:
Cut 11 strips, 2" x 42".
Cut 1 square, 2" x 2" (cut from scraps or from the end of one of the strips).

From the multicolored floral print:
Cut 5 strips, 8" x 42". Cut 2 of the strips into a total of 35 segments, each 2" wide, to make 2" x 8" rectangles. Leave the remaining 3 strips uncut.
Cut 8 strips, 5" x 42", for outer border.

DIRECTIONS

1. Join 8 of the 2"-wide gray-green strips and 4 of the 2"-wide red strips to make 4 strip units as shown. Cut the strip units into a total of 70 segments, each 2" wide.

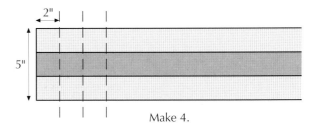

Make 4.

2. Join 4 of the 2"-wide red strips and 2 of the 2"-wide gray-green strips to make 2 strip units as shown. Cut the strip units into a total of 35 segments, each 2" wide.

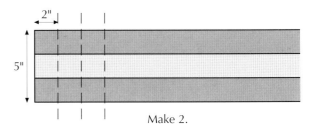

Make 2.

3. Piece 35 red-and-green nine-patch units as shown.

Make 35.

4. Join the remaining 2"-wide gray-green strips and the 5"-wide white-on-white strips to make 4 strip units as shown. Cut the strip units into a total of 70 segments, each 2" wide.

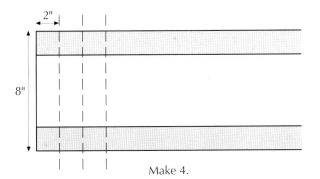

Make 4.

5. Join the remaining 2"-wide red strips and the 8"-wide multicolored floral strips to make 3 strip units as shown. Cut the strip units into a total of 47 segments, each 2" wide. You need 35 of these segments for the blocks. The remaining 12 segments will be used to complete the right and bottom edge sashing.

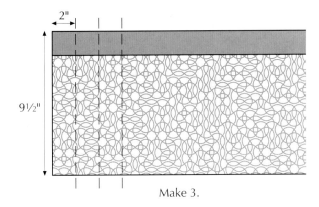

Make 3.

6. Piece 35 Nine Patch Plaid blocks as shown.

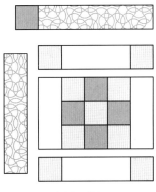

Make 35.

7. Set the blocks together in 7 rows of 5 as shown in the quilt photo; join the rows.
8. Using segments remaining from step 5 and the 2" red square, piece and add the right and bottom edge sashings.
9. Add the white-on-white inner border, seaming strips as necessary. See "Borders with Straight-Cut Corners" on page 243.
10. Add the multicolored floral outer border as for the inner border.
11. Layer with batting and backing; quilt or tie. See page 263 for a quilting suggestion.
12. Bind with straight-grain or bias strips of fabric.

Strawberry Patch *by Janet Strait Gorton, 1994, Anchorage, Alaska, 55½" x 74". The large-scale floral print gives this easy Nine Patch quilt an extraordinary appeal. Janet's version is colored for Christmas but would be a delight to doze under any time of year. Quilted by Mary Miller.*

Nine Patch Strippy

Nine Patch A
4½" block

Nine Patch B
4½" block

Dimensions: 40" x 52"

18 blocks (9 Nine Patch Block A and 9 Nine Patch Block B), 4½", set on point in 3 rows of 6 with border-stripe sashing strips; finished without a border.

Materials: 44"-wide fabric

⅜ yd. assorted dark blue prints for blocks
⅜ yd. assorted white prints for blocks
1 yd. pink print for setting triangles
1¼ yds. border stripe for sashing strips
1¾ yds. fabric for backing
½ yd. fabric for binding
Batting and thread to finish

Cutting: All measurements include ¼" seams.

From the dark blue prints:
   Cut 6 strips, 2" x 42", for blocks.

From the white prints:
   Cut 6 strips, 2" x 42", for blocks.

From the pink print:
   Cut 2 strips, 9¾" x 42". Cut the strips into 8 squares, 9¾" x 9¾". Cut twice diagonally into 32 quarter-square triangles for sides.
   Cut 2 strips, 7" x 42". Cut the strips into 6 squares, 7" x 7". Cut once diagonally into 12 half-square triangles for corners.

From the border stripe:
   Cut 4 lengthwise strips, about 8" wide, depending on the configuration of the border stripe, for sashing strips.

DIRECTIONS

1. Join 4 of the 2" x 42" dark blue strips and 2 of the 2" x 42" white strips to make 2 strip units as shown. The units should measure 5" wide when sewn. Cut the units into 27 segments, each 2" wide.

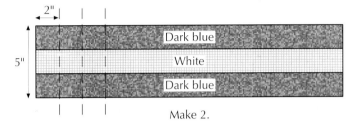

Make 2.

2. Join the remaining 2" x 42" dark blue and white strips to make 2 strip units as shown. The units should measure 5" wide when sewn. Cut the units into 27 segments, each 2" wide.

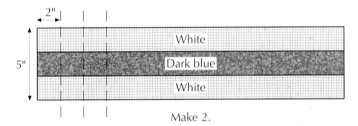

Make 2.

3. Join the segments into 9 Nine Patch Block A and 9 Nine Patch Block B.

4. Set the blocks together, alternating A and B blocks, in 3 rows with the pink side and corner triangles as shown. The side and corner triangles have been cut large enough to allow the Nine Patch blocks to "float"; trim the side triangles ½" beyond the points of the Nine Patch blocks to allow ¼" of float on the tops and bottoms of the strips. Trim and square up the corners and ends if needed; leave more float at the ends of strips. See "Assembling On-Point Quilts" on page 240.

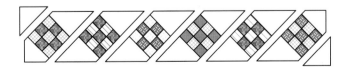

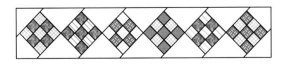

5. Join the rows with the border-stripe sashing strips as shown in the quilt photo.

6. Layer with batting and backing; quilt or tie. See page 263 for a quilting suggestion.

7. Bind with straight-grain or bias strips of fabric.

Nine Patch Strip *by Judy Hopkins, 1991, Anchorage, Alaska, 40" x 52".*
This strippy-style quilt features Nine Patch blocks and a charming, floral border stripe.

Ocean Chain

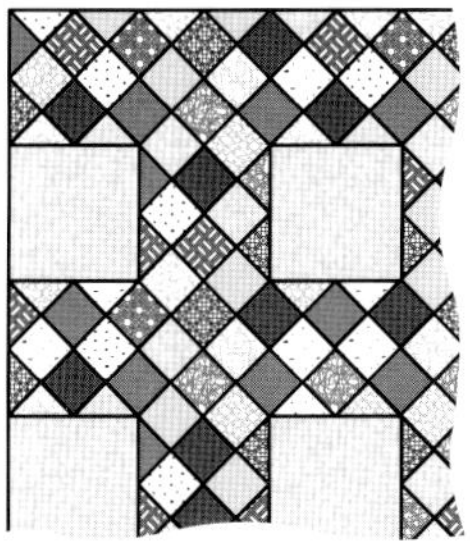

Ocean Chain
Corner of quilt
(shown without borders)

Dimensions: 78" x 96"

Different units joined into diagonal bars; 6"-wide border.

NOTE: The antique quilt shown in the photo was made by attaching pieced lozenge-shaped units to plain squares, a method that requires numerous set-in corners. Our method—joining several different pieced units into diagonal bars—makes it easier to construct the quilt but results in a more random distribution of the fabrics in the "chains."

Materials: 44"-wide fabric

1 strip, 7" x 42", *each* of 24 different light and medium prints for "chains" (Nearest cut is ¼ yd.)*
1 strip, 7" x 42", *each* of 24 different dark prints for "chains" (Nearest cut is ¼ yd.)*
2⅞ yds. red-on-white or pink print for plain squares and border
5⅞ yds. fabric for backing (lengthwise seam)
¾ yd. fabric for binding
Batting and thread to finish
*Use the same fabric more than once if you wish.

Cutting: All measurements include ¼" seams.

From each of the 7"-wide light and medium strips:

Cut 1 strip, 2⅝" x 42" (24 total), for "chains." Cut any 8 of these strips into a total of 114 squares, 2⅝" x 2⅝". Leave the remaining 16 strips uncut.

Cut 2 squares, 4¼" x 4¼" (48 total). Cut twice diagonally into 192 quarter-square triangles for "chains." You will have 4 triangles left over.

From each of the 7"-wide dark strips:

Cut 1 strip, 2⅝" x 42" (24 total), for "chains." Cut any 8 of the strips into 124 squares, 2⅝" x 2⅝". Leave the remaining 16 strips uncut.

Cut 2 squares, 4¼" x 4¼" (48 total). Cut twice diagonally into 192 quarter-square triangles for "chains." You will have 24 triangles left over.

From the red-on-white or pink print:

Cut 15 strips, 6½" x 42". Set aside 8 of the strips for the seamed border. Cut the remaining 7 strips into 42 squares, 6½" x 6½".

DIRECTIONS

1. Using the light and dark quarter-square triangles and the light and dark 2⅝" squares, make Units AA, BB, and CC as shown. Combine the fabrics at random; use as many different combinations as possible.

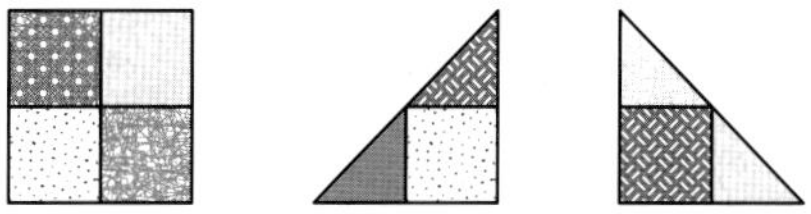

Unit AA Make 15. Unit BB Make 84. Unit CC Make 94.

2. Join 19 each of Units BB and CC to make 19 Unit DD as shown.

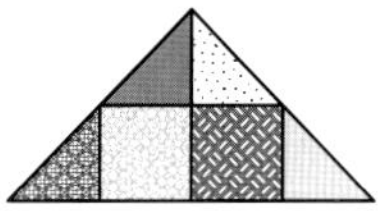

Unit DD
Make 19.

3. Join the uncut 2⅝" light and dark strips to make 8 strip units as shown. Combine the fabrics at random. The strip units should measure 9" wide when sewn. Cut the units into 120 segments, each 2⅝" wide. Join the segments to make 30 Unit A, using many combinations.

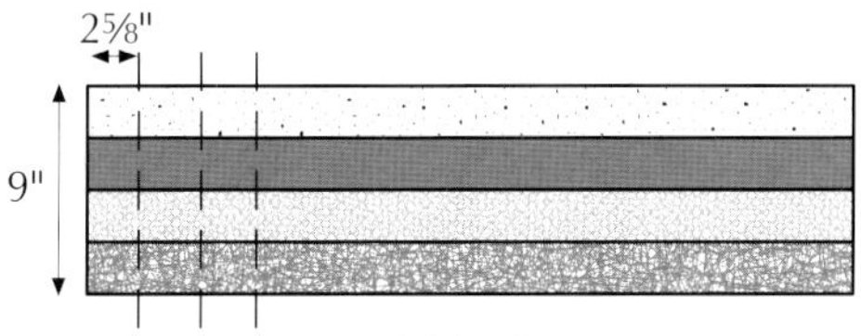

Make 8.

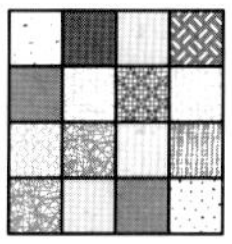

Unit A
Make 30.

4. Using the units you made in steps 1 and 2 and the 6½" red-on-white or pink print squares, make Units B–G as shown. Combine the "chain" fabrics at random.

Unit B
Make 24.
Use 2 Unit BB
and 2 Unit CC
for each.

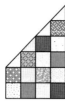
Unit C
Make 12.
Use 1 Unit BB,
1 Unit CC,
and 1 Unit DD
for each.

Unit D
Make 5.
Use 2 Unit CC
and 3 Unit AA
for each.

Unit E
Make 4.
Use 1 Unit BB,
1 Unit CC,
and 1 Unit DD
for each.

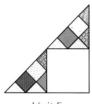
Unit F
Make 1.
Use 2
Unit DD.

Unit G
Make 1.
Use 1 Unit BB
and 1 Unit CC.

5. Set the units together in diagonal rows as shown; join the rows.

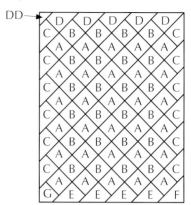

6. Add the red-on-white borders, seaming strips as necessary. See "Borders with Straight-Cut Corners" on page 243.
7. Layer with batting and backing; quilt or tie. See page 263 for a quilting suggestion.
8. Bind with straight-grain or bias strips of fabric.

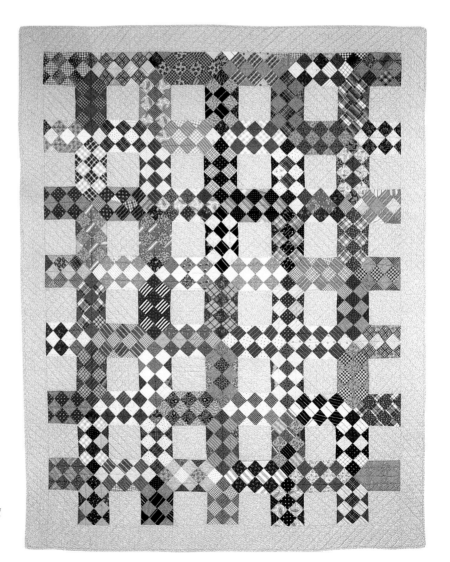

Ocean Chain *variation, maker unknown, c. 1920, Indiana, 67" x 85". The "waves" in this unique variation of the classic Ocean Waves design were made predominantly of squares instead of the more familiar triangles.*
NOTE: The pattern uses units sized more appropriately for rotary cutting and produces a 78" x 96" quilt.
(Collection of Lucy J. Smith)

Ohio Fence

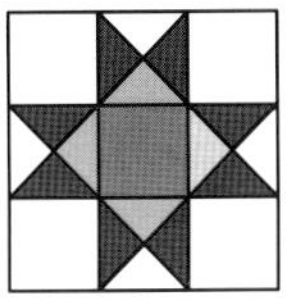

Ohio Star
9" block

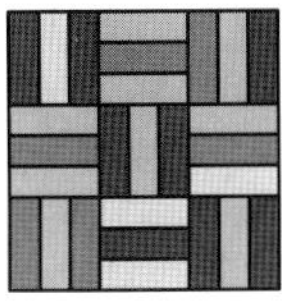

Rail Fence
9" block

Dimensions: 63" x 81"

35 blocks (17 Ohio Star blocks and 18 Rail Fence blocks), 9", set 5 across and 7 down; 1½"-wide inner border, 7½"-wide outer border.

NOTE: The quilt pictured has four different light fabrics for the Ohio Star backgrounds and two different medium fabrics for a "collaged" outer border. The pattern provides for a single light fabric for the Ohio Star backgrounds and a single medium-colored fabric for the outer border.

Materials: 44"-wide fabric

1⅛ yds. dark green solid for blocks and inner border
½ yd. *each* of 3 additional dark green and blue-green solids for blocks
2¼ yds. medium green solid for blocks and outer border
½ yd. *each* of 3 additional medium green and blue-green solids for blocks
1 yd. light green or blue-green solid for blocks
4 yds. fabric for backing (crosswise seam)
⅝ yd. fabric for binding
Batting and thread to finish

Cutting: All measurements include ¼" seams.

From the 1⅛ yds. of dark green solid:
Cut 8 strips, 2" x 42", for inner border.
Cut 1 strip, 4¼" x 42½"*. Cut the strip into 10 squares, 4¼" x 4¼". Cut twice diagonally into 40 quarter-square triangles for Ohio Star blocks.
Cut 2 strips, 3½" x 42". Cut the strips into a total of 17 squares, 3½" x 3½", for Ohio Star blocks.
Cut 4 strips, 1½" x 42", for Rail Fence blocks.
*If your strip does not measure 42½", you will need to cut the last square from leftovers.

From each of the 3 additional dark green and blue-green solids:
Cut 1 strip, 4¼" x 42" (3 total). Cut the strips into 24 squares, 4¼" x 4¼". Cut twice diagonally into 96 quarter-square triangles for Ohio Star blocks.
Cut 7 strips, 1½" x 42" (21 total), for Rail Fence blocks.

From the 2¼ yds. of medium green solid:
Cut 8 strips, 8" x 42", for outer border.
Cut 5 strips, 1½" x 42", for Rail Fence blocks.
Cut 5 squares, 4¼" x 4¼". Cut twice diagonally into 20 quarter-square triangles for Ohio Star blocks.

From each of the 3 additional medium green and blue-green solids:
Cut 6 strips, 1½" x 42" (18 total), for Rail Fence blocks.
Cut 4 squares, 4¼" x 4¼" (12 total). Cut twice diagonally into 48 quarter-square triangles for Ohio Star blocks.

From the light green or blue-green solid:
Cut 7 strips, 3½" x 42". Cut the strips into a total of 68 squares, 3½" x 3½", for Ohio Star blocks.
Cut 2 strips, 4¼" x 42". Cut the strips into a total of 17 squares, 4¼" x 4¼". Cut twice diagonally into 68 quarter-square triangles for Ohio Star blocks.

DIRECTIONS

1. Using the quarter-square triangles and the light and dark squares, piece 17 Ohio Star blocks as shown. Combine the dark and medium fabrics at random.

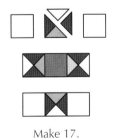

Make 17.

2. Join the 1½"-wide dark and medium strips to make 9 Strip Unit I and 7 Strip Unit II as shown. Combine the fabrics at random. The strip units should measure 3½" wide when sewn. Cut the strip units into 3½"-wide segments. You will need 90 segments from Strip Units I and 72 segments from Strip Units II.

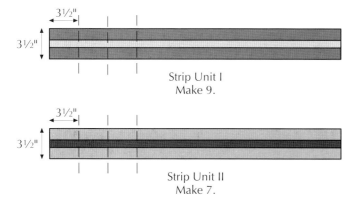

3½"

3½"

Strip Unit I
Make 9.

3½"

3½"

Strip Unit II
Make 7.

3. Join the segments into 18 Rail Fence blocks. Combine the segments at random.
4. Set the blocks together into 7 rows of 5 as shown in the quilt photo, alternating Rail Fence and Ohio Star blocks. Join the rows.
5. Add the dark green inner border, seaming strips as necessary. See "Borders with Straight-Cut Corners" on page 243.
6. Add the medium green outer border as for inner border.
7. Layer with batting and backing; quilt or tie. See page 263 for a quilting suggestion.
8. Bind with straight-grain or bias strips of fabric.

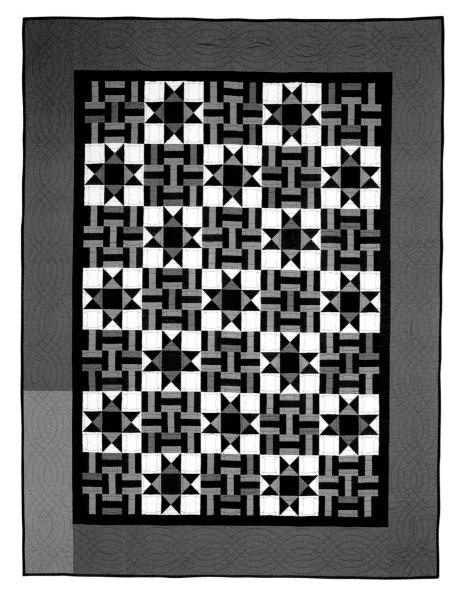

Ohio Fence *by George Taylor, 1993, Anchorage, Alaska, 63" x 81". George jazzed up this simple but striking design by arranging eleven different shades of green and blue-green at random. The two-color outer border is a more obvious expression of his effective mix-and-match approach.*

Ohio Stars

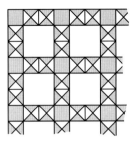

Ohio Stars
Corner of quilt

Dimensions: 66" x 84"

3" and 6" units joined in 2 different bar formats; finished without a border.

Materials: 44"-wide fabric

4⅞ yds. muslin for blocks
3⅝ yds. gold solid for blocks
5¼ yds. fabric for backing (lengthwise seam)
⅝ yd. fabric for binding
Batting and thread to finish

Cutting: All measurements include ¼" seams.

From the muslin:

Cut 11 strips, 6½" x 42". Cut the strips into a total of 63 squares, 6½" x 6½".

Cut 7 strips, 13½" x 42". Cut the strips into a total of 21 squares, 13½" x 13½", for bias squares.

From the gold solid:

Cut 8 strips, 3½" x 42". Cut the strips into a total of 80 squares, 3½" x 3½".

Cut 7 strips, 13½" x 42". Cut the strips into a total of 21 squares, 13½" x 13½", for bias squares. Pair each 13½" gold square with a 13½" muslin square, right sides up. Cut and piece 3½"-wide bias strips, following the directions for making bias squares on page 16. Cut 14 bias squares, 3⅞" x 3⅞", from each pair of squares for a total of 294 bias squares. You will have 10 bias squares left over.

DIRECTIONS

1. Match pairs of 3⅞" bias squares, right sides together, nesting opposing seams. Make 284 Square Two units, following the directions on page 16.

Square Two
Make 284.

2. Join the Square Two units into 142 Square Two pairs as shown.

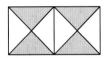

Square Two pairs
Make 142.

3. Combine 70 of the Square Two pairs with the 3½" gold squares to make 10 bars as shown. Each bar contains 7 Square Two pairs and 8 gold squares.

Make 10.

4. Combine the remaining Square Two pairs with the 6½" muslin squares to make 9 bars as shown. Each bar contains 8 Square Two pairs and 7 muslin squares.

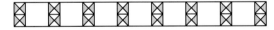

Make 9.

5. Set the bars together as shown in the quilt photo, alternating the narrow and wide bars. Join the rows.

6. Layer with batting and backing; quilt or tie. See page 264 for a quilting suggestion.

7. Bind with straight-grain or bias strips of fabric.

Ohio Star *bar quilt, origin unknown, purchased in Minnesota, 66" x 84".*
The sashing forms the pattern in this crisp and sunny gold-and-muslin quilt. Like
many early quilts, this one is finished without a border. (Collection of Terri Shinn)

Old Favorite

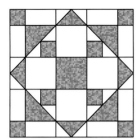

Old Favorite
16" block

Dimensions: 60" x 76"

NOTE: In order to eliminate unnecessary seams, this quilt is constructed in units, which are then joined into rows, rather than into blocks; 6"-wide border.

Materials: 44"-wide fabric

2½ yds. white print for blocks
3¼ yds. dark blue print for blocks and border
3⅞ yds. fabric for backing (crosswise seam)
⅝ yd. fabric for binding
Batting and thread to finish

Cutting: All measurements include ¼" seams.

From the white print:

Cut 13 strips, 4½" x 42". Cut 2 of the strips into 28 rectangles, 2½" x 4½". Cut the remaining strips into 82 squares, 4½" x 4½".

Cut 5 strips, 2⅞" x 42". Cut the strips into 62 squares, 2⅞" x 2⅞". Cut once diagonally into 124 half-square triangles.

Cut 2 strips, 5¼" x 42". Cut the strips into 9 squares, 5¼" x 5¼". Cut twice diagonally into 36 quarter-square triangles. You will have 2 left over.

From the dark blue print:

Cut 3 strips, 4⅞" x 42". Cut the strips into 24 squares, 4⅞" x 4⅞". Cut once diagonally into 48 half-square triangles.

Cut 3 strips, 4½" x 42". Cut the strips into 18 squares, 4½" x 4½", and 10 rectangles, 2½" x 4½".

From the length of the remaining dark blue print:

Cut 2 strips, 2½" x 84". Cut the strips into 52 squares, 2½" x 2½".

Cut 1 strip, 5¼" x 84". Cut the strip into 12 squares, 5¼" x 5¼". Cut twice diagonally into 48 quarter-square triangles.

Cut 4 strips, 7" x 84", for border.

DIRECTIONS

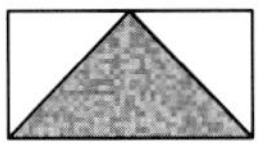

Unit A
Make 14.

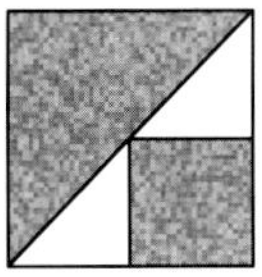

Unit B
Make 48.

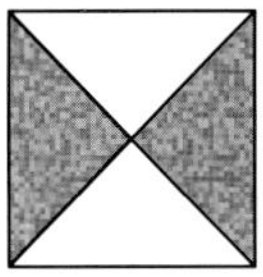

Unit C
Make 17.

1. Using 14 of the dark blue quarter-square triangles and 28 of the small white half-square triangles, piece 14 Unit A.
2. Using the remaining small, white half-square triangles, 48 of the small dark blue squares, and the large dark blue half-square triangles, piece 48 Unit B.
3. Using the remaining dark blue quarter-square triangles and 34 of the white quarter-square triangles, piece 17 Unit C.
4. Using small dark blue squares, dark blue and white rectangles, and Unit A, make 2 Row A as shown.

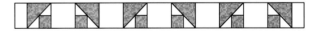

Row A
Make 2.

5. Using large white squares, white rectangles, and Unit B, make 8 Row B as shown.

Row B
Make 8.

6. Using large white and dark blue squares, Unit A, and Unit C, make 4 Row C as shown.

Row C
Make 4.

7. Using the remaining pieces, make 3 Row D as shown.

Row D
Make 3.

8. Join the rows as shown in the full-quilt drawing at right. Rows marked * in the drawing are turned upside down.

9. Add the dark blue border. See "Borders with Straight-Cut Corners" on page 243.

10. Layer with batting and backing; quilt or tie. See page 264 for a quilting suggestion.

11. Bind with straight-grain or bias strips of fabric.

Northern Nites *by Peggy J. Hinchey, 1991, Anchorage, Alaska, 60" x 76". This striking two-fabric quilt features blue and white prints and the traditional Old Favorite block.*

Oregon Trail

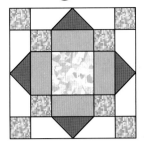

Oregon Trail
12" block

Dimensions: 80" x 80"

25 blocks, 12", set on point with side setting triangles; 6"-wide border.

NOTE: The Oregon Trail block pattern, an original design by Judy Martin, first appeared in Judy Martin's *Ultimate Book of Quilt Block Patterns,*© 1988. Used by permission.

Materials: 44"-wide fabric

½ yd. large-scale blue floral print for block centers
1 yd. medium-scale blue floral print for block corners
1 strip, 2½" x 42", *each* of 25 different light prints for block backgrounds (Nearest cut is ⅛ yd.)*
1 strip, 5¼" x 28", *each* of 5 different dark blue solids or tone-on-tone prints for blocks (Nearest cut is ¼ yd.)
1 strip, 2½" x 19", *each* of 25 different medium blue prints for blocks (Nearest cut is ⅛ yd.)*
1⅛ yds. white-on-white print for setting triangles
1⅝ yds. dark blue print for border
7¼ yds. fabric for backing (2 crosswise seams), or use 2½ yds. of 90"-wide backing fabric
¾ yd. fabric for binding
Batting and thread to finish
*Use the same fabric more than once if you wish.

Cutting: All measurements include ¼" seams.

From the large-scale blue floral print:
Cut 3 strips, 4½" x 42". Cut the strips into a total of 25 squares, 4½" x 4½".

From the medium-scale blue floral print:
Cut 13 strips, 2½" x 42". Cut the strips into a total of 200 squares, 2½" x 2½".

From the 25 light strips:
Work with 1 fabric at a time. From the first fabric, cut 8 rectangles, 2½" x 4⅞". Trim the corners at a 45° angle to make 4 A and 4 B trimmed rectangles as shown. Repeat with the remaining light strips for a total of 200 trimmed rectangles, 100 A and 100 B.

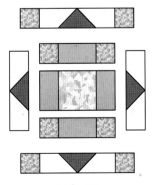

Trim the corners at a 45° angle.

From each of the 5 dark blue solids or tone-on-tone prints:
Cut 5 squares, 5¼" x 5¼" (25 total). Cut twice diagonally into 100 quarter-square triangles.

From each of the 25 medium blue strips:
Cut 4 rectangles, 2½" x 4½" (100 total).

From the white-on-white print:
Cut 3 squares, 18¼" x 18¼". Cut twice diagonally into 12 quarter-square triangles for side setting triangles.
Cut 2 squares, 9⅜" x 9⅜". Cut once diagonally into 4 half-square triangles for corner setting triangles.

From the dark blue print:
Cut 8 strips, 6½" x 42", for border.

DIRECTIONS

1. Piece 25 Oregon Trail blocks as shown. In each block, use just 1 fabric for the medium blue rectangles, 1 fabric for the dark blue quarter-square triangles, and 1 fabric for the light trimmed rectangles.

Make 25.

2. Set the blocks and setting pieces together in diagonal rows as shown in the quilt photo; join the rows. See "Assembling On-Point Quilts" on page 240.

3. Add the dark blue print border, seaming strips as necessary. See "Borders with Straight-Cut Corners" on page 243.

4. Layer with batting and backing; quilt or tie. See page 264 for a quilting suggestion.

5. Bind with straight-grain or bias strips of fabric.

China Blue *by Kathleen Urban Bungart, 1991, Fairbanks, Alaska, 76" x 76".*
Kathleen crafted this original Judy Martin design in soothing blues. Several of the blocks were made by friends; Kathleen provided the focus fabrics, and The 13 Easy Piecers completed the blocks with prints from their personal collections.

Paths and Stiles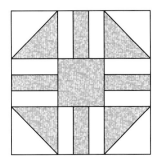

Paths and Stiles
9" block

Dimensions: 80" x 86"

42 blocks, 9", set 7 across and 6 down with 3"-wide sashing strips; 3"-wide inner border, 3"-wide middle border, 2½"-wide outer border.

Materials: 44"-wide fabric

3¾ yds. assorted pink-on-pink prints for blocks and middle border
5½ yds. light print for blocks and inner and outer borders
5¼ yds. fabric for backing (lengthwise seam)
⅝ yd. fabric for binding
Batting and thread to finish

Cutting: All measurements include ¼" seams.

From the assorted pink-on-pink prints:
 Cut 5 fat quarters, 18" x 22", for bias squares.
 Cut 16 strips, 1½" x 42", for blocks.
 Cut 4 strips, 3½" x 42". Cut the strips into 42 squares, 3½" x 3½", for blocks.
 Cut 9 strips, 3½" x 42", for middle border.

From the light print:
 Cut 5 fat quarters, 18" x 22", for bias squares. Pair each light print fat quarter with a pink fat quarter, right sides up. Cut and piece 3"-wide bias strips, following the directions for making bias squares on page 14. Cut a total of 168 bias squares, 3½" x 3½".
 Cut 32 strips, 1½" x 42", for blocks.
 Cut 10 strips, 3½" x 42", for sashing.
 Cut 8 strips, 3½" x 42", for inner border.
 Cut 9 strips, 3" x 42", for outer border.

DIRECTIONS

1. Join the 1½" x 42" pink and light print strips to make 16 strip units as shown. The units should measure 3½" wide when sewn. Cut a total of 168 segments, each 3½" wide, from the strip units.

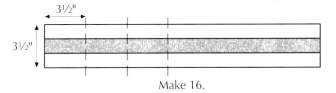

Make 16.

2. Piece 42 Paths and Stiles blocks as shown.

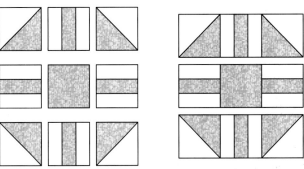

Make 42.

3. Set the blocks together in 6 rows of 7 as shown in the quilt photo. Seam the sashing strips as necessary and join the rows, adding a sashing strip between each row.
4. Add the light print inner border, seaming strips as necessary. See "Borders with Straight-Cut Corners" on page 243.
5. Add the pink-on-pink middle border as for the inner border.
6. Add the light print outer border as for the previous borders.
7. Layer with batting and backing; quilt or tie. See page 264 for a quilting suggestion.
8. Bind with straight-grain or bias strips of fabric.

Paths and Stiles, *maker unknown, c. 1920, Pennsylvania, 80" x 86". A vintage collection of double-pink prints are used for this variation of Paths and Stiles, an early Nancy Cabot pattern. (Collection of Nancy J. Martin)*

Pinwheel Mosaic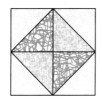

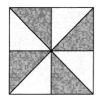

| Block A
6" block | Block B
6" block | Block C
6" block |

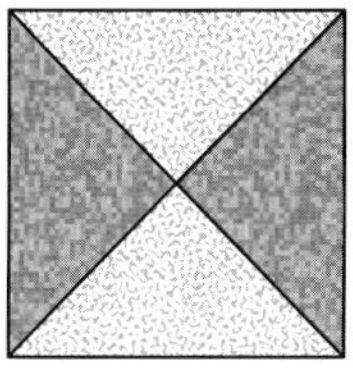

Dimensions: 61½" x 73½"

63 blocks (20 Block A, 31 Block B, and 12 Block C), 6", set 7 across and 9 down with half blocks and quarter blocks; ¾"-wide inner border, 6"-wide outer border.

Materials: 44"-wide fabric

1⅝ yds. brown print for blocks
1 yd. ivory print for blocks
1⅛ yds. beige leaf print for blocks
⅓ yd. red print for blocks
⅓ yd. tan print for blocks
⅓ yd. dark red print for inner border
1⅞ yds. tan plaid for outer border
3⅞ yds. fabric for backing (crosswise seam)
⅝ yd. fabric for binding
Batting and thread to finish

Cutting: All measurements include ¼" seams.

From the brown print:
Cut 4 strips, 3⅞" x 42".
Cut 5 strips, 7¼" x 42". Cut 1 of the strips into 5 squares, 7¼" x 7¼". Cut twice diagonally into 20 quarter-square triangles. You will have 2 triangles left over. Leave the remaining 4 strips uncut.

From the ivory print:
Cut 8 strips, 3⅞" x 42".

From the beige leaf print:
Cut 2 strips, 3⅞" x 42". Cut the strips into a total of 18 squares, 3⅞" x 3⅞". Cut once diagonally into 36 half-square triangles.
Cut 4 strips, 7¼" x 42".

From the red print:
Cut 2 strips, 3⅞" x 42".

From the tan print:
Cut 2 strips, 3⅞" x 42".

From the dark red print:
Cut 6 strips, 1¼" x 42", for inner border.

From the *length* of the tan plaid:
Cut 4 strips, 6½" wide, for outer border.

DIRECTIONS

1. Make ◺: Layer the 3⅞"-wide brown strips and 4 of the 3⅞"-wide ivory strips, right sides together, to make 4 contrasting strip pairs. Cut 10 squares, 3⅞" x 3⅞", from each strip pair for a total of 40 layered squares. Cut the squares once diagonally and chain-piece the resulting triangle pairs to make 80 half-square triangle units.
2. Piece 20 Block A as shown af left.
3. Make ◺: Layer the 7¼"-wide brown strips and the 7¼"-wide beige leaf strips, right sides together, to make 4 contrasting strip pairs. Cut 4 squares, 7¼" x 7¼", from each strip pair for a total of 16 layered squares. Cut the squares once diagonally and chain-piece the resulting triangle pairs to make 32 half-square triangles.
4. Cut the half-square triangle units you made in step 3 once diagonally as shown; join the resulting pieces to make 32 Block B as shown at left. You will have 1 block left over.

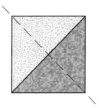

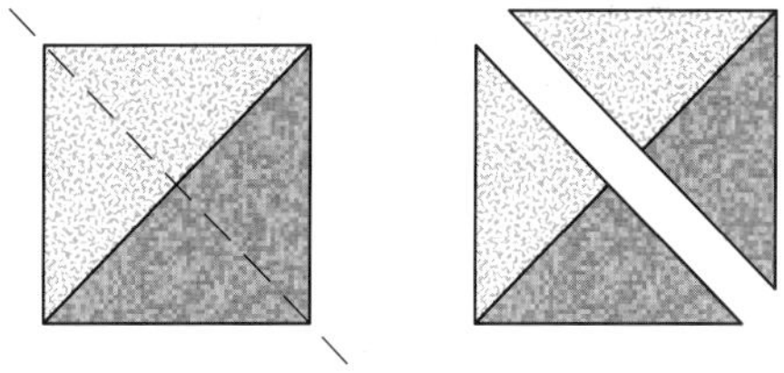

5. Make ◺: Layer the 3⅞"-wide red strips and 2 of the 3⅞"-wide ivory strips, right sides together, to make 2 contrasting strip pairs. Cut 10 squares, 3⅞" x 3⅞", from each strip pair for a total of 20 layered squares. Cut the squares once diagonally and chain-piece the resulting triangle pairs to make 40 half-square triangle units.
6. Make ◺: Layer the 3⅞"-wide tan strips and the remaining 3⅞"-wide ivory strips, right sides together, to make 2 contrasting strip pairs. Cut 10 squares, 3⅞" x 3⅞", from each strip pair for a total of 20 layered squares. Cut the squares once diagonally and chain-piece the resulting triangle pairs to make 40 half-square triangle units.

7. Piece 12 Block C as shown on page 161. Then piece 10 Half Block D and 4 Half Block E as shown below. You will have 2 ivory/red units and 2 ivory/tan units left over for the quarter blocks used in the quilt corners.

 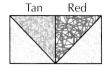

Half Block D
Make 10.

Half Block E
Make 4.

8. Join the 7¼" brown quarter-square triangles and the 3⅞" beige leaf half-square triangles to make 18 Half Block F as shown.

Half Block F
Make 18.

9. Set the blocks and the half and quarter blocks together in 9 rows of 7 as shown in the quilt photo; join the rows.

10. Add the dark red inner border, seaming the strips as necessary. See "Borders with Straight-Cut Corners" on page 243.

11. Add the tan plaid outer border as for inner border.

12. Layer with batting and backing; quilt or tie. See page 262 for a quilting suggestion.

13. Bind with straight-grain or bias strips of fabric.

Spin Doctor *by Judy Dafoe Hopkins, 1994, Anchorage, Alaska, 61" x 73". Judy converted the traditional Mosaic 9 pattern to a bar format, which reduced the number of seams. The windowpane-check border quietly reflects the colors of the quilt. Quilted by Peggy Hinchey. (Collection of Robert Pittman)*

Pinwheel Star

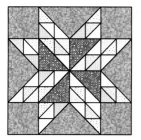

Pinwheel Star
16" block

Dimensions: 54" x 54"

9 blocks, 16", set as a bar quilt with 3 stars across and 3 down; 3"-wide border.

Materials: 44"-wide fabric

8 fat quarters of coordinating fabric for bias squares
½ yd. blue fabric for pinwheels
3 yds. star print for setting pieces and border
3½ yds. fabric for backing (lengthwise or crosswise seam)
½ yd. fabric for binding
Batting and thread to finish

Cutting: All measurements include ¼" seams.

From each fat quarter of coordinating fabric:

Cut 14 squares, 2⅞" x 2⅞" (112 total). Cut once diagonally into 224 half-square triangles. You will have 8 left over.

Pair the remainder of the fat quarters into sets of contrasting fabrics. Cut each pair of fabrics into 2½"-wide bias strips, following the directions for making bias squares on page 14. From this pieced fabric, cut 108 bias squares, 2½" x 2½".

From the blue fabric:

Cut 3 strips 4⅞" x 42". Cut the strips into a total of 18 squares, 4⅞" x 4⅞". Cut once diagonally into 36 triangles for Unit 1.

From the star print fabric:

Cut 4 lengthwise strips, 3¼" x 55", for border.
Cut 12 squares, 6⅛" x 6⅛", for Unit II.
Cut 4 squares, 4½" x 4½", for Unit III.
Cut 8 rectangles, 4½" x 8½", for Unit IV.
Cut 4 squares, 8½" x 8½", for Unit V.
Cut 3 squares, 9¼" x 9¼". Cut twice diagonally into 12 triangles for Unit VI.

DIRECTIONS

NOTE: To avoid seams through the large areas of background fabric, this quilt is constructed in units as a bar quilt. See pages 241–42.

Make all units and join the completed units into rows. The stars and pinwheels will emerge after the quilt is set together. The units are identified below:

1. Piece 9 of Unit I, using large blue triangles, bias squares, and small triangles cut from coordinating fabric.

Unit I
Make 9.

2. Piece 12 of Unit II, using the piecing diagram below as a guide.

Unit II
Make 12.

3. Piece 12 of Unit VI, using the piecing diagram below as a guide.

Unit VI
Make 12.

4. Set the completed units into rows. Join the rows as shown.

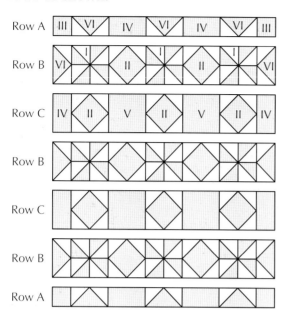

5. Add the star print border, seaming strips as necessary. See "Borders with Straight-Cut Corners" on page 243.
6. Layer with batting and backing; quilt or tie. See page 264 for a quilting suggestion.
7. Bind with straight-grain or bias strips of fabric.

Pinwheel Star *by Cleo Nollette, 1992, Seattle, Washington, 54" x 54". The stunning background and border fabric inspired this star quilt with a unique setting. This bar quilt was quilted in-the-ditch with occasional outline quilting to highlight the moon motifs. Quilted by Donna K. Gundlach.*

Pot of Flowers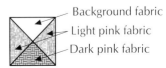

Pot of Flowers
12½" block

Dimensions: 65½" x 65½"

9 blocks, 12½", set on point with alternate blocks and setting pieces; 1¾"-wide inner border, 4½"-wide outer border.

Materials: 44"-wide fabric

2¼ yds. pink-print background fabric
4 fat quarters of light pink fabric for flowers
4 fat quarters of dark pink fabric for flowers
5 fat quarters of lavender fabric for pots
1 fat quarter of yellow print for flower centers
1 yd. green fabric for stems, leaves, and inner border
1¼ yds. pink fabric for outer border
4¼ yds. fabric for backing (lengthwise or crosswise seam)
½ yd. fabric for binding
Batting and thread to finish

Cutting: All measurements include ¼" seams.

From the pink-print background fabric:
Cut 4 squares, 9" x 9".

From the light pink fat quarters:
Cut 8 squares, 9" x 9". Pair 4 light pink squares with 4 pink-print background squares, right sides up. Cut and piece 3"-wide bias strips, following the directions for making bias squares on page 16. From this pieced fabric, cut 27 bias squares, 3⅜" x 3⅜".

From the dark pink fat quarters:
Cut 4 squares, 9" x 9". Pair each 9" dark pink square with a 9" light pink square, right sides up. Cut and piece 3"-wide bias strips. From this pieced fabric, cut 27 bias squares, 3⅜" x 3⅜".

From the remaining pink-print background fabric:
Cut 4 squares, 13" x 13", for alternate blocks.
Cut 2 squares, 19" x 19". Cut twice diagonally into 8 quarter-square triangles for side setting triangles.
Cut 2 squares, 9¾" x 9¾". Cut once diagonally into 4 half-square triangles for corner setting triangles.
Cut 27 squares, 3" x 3", for blocks.
Cut 18 rectangles, 3" x 5½", for blocks.
Cut 5 squares, 6⅞" x 6⅞". Cut once diagonally into 10 half-square triangles for blocks.
Cut 18 rectangles, 2" x 5", for blocks.
Cut 5 squares, 3⅞" x 3⅞". Cut once diagonally into 10 half-square triangles for blocks.

From each lavender fat quarter:
Cut 1 square, 6⅞" x 6⅞" (5 total). Cut once diagonally into 10 half-square triangles for pots.
Cut 2 squares, 2⅜" x 2⅜" (10 total). Cut once diagonally into 20 half-square triangles for base of pot.

From the yellow fat quarter:
Cut 27 squares, 3" x 3".

From the green fabric:
Cut 8 strips, 2¼" x 42", for inner border.
Cut 27 bias strips, 1¼" x 6", for stems.
Cut remaining fabric into leaves, following the appliqué directions on page 22. Use the template on page 166.

From the pink fabric for outer border:
Cut 8 strips, 4¾" x 42".

DIRECTIONS

1. Pair bias squares of each coloration with right sides together and seam allowances pressed in opposite directions. Make 54 Square Two units, following the directions on page 16.

Background fabric
Light pink fabric
Dark pink fabric

Make 54.

2. Piece 9 Pot of Flowers blocks as shown. Use 2 matching Square Two units for each of the 3 flowers. Vary the flower colors in each pot.

NOTE: You will have one extra set of lavender pieces for the pot.

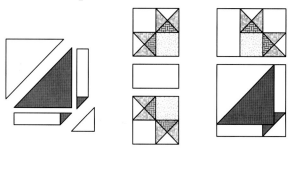

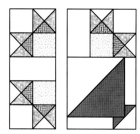

Make 9.

3. To make stems, fold the 1¼" x 6" strips in thirds; baste. Appliqué 3 stems and 4 leaves to each block, following the directions on page 22. Open previously sewn seams to insert the raw edges of the stem pieces. Resew these seams after the appliqué is completed.

4. Set the blocks and setting pieces together into diagonal rows as shown; join the rows. See "Assembling On-Point Quilts" on page 240.

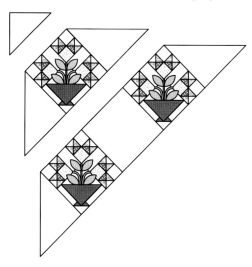

5. Add the green inner border, seaming strips as necessary. See "Borders with Straight-Cut Corners" on page 243.
6. Add the pink outer border, seaming strips as necessary. Miter the corners. See "Borders with Mitered Corners" on page 243.
7. Layer with batting and backing; quilt or tie. See page 265 for a quilting suggestion.
8. Bind with straight-grain or bias strips of fabric.

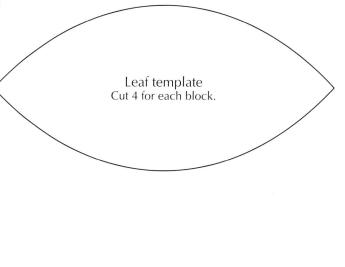

Leaf template
Cut 4 for each block.

Pot of Flowers *by Nancy J. Martin, 1992, Woodinville, Washington, 65½" x 65½". Square Two units comprise the lily-like flowers in this charming pastel quilt. Alternate blocks of background fabric feature feathered wreaths quilted by Alvina Nelson. The inner green border and appliqué leaves and stems offer an effective contrast to the other pastel fabrics. (Collection of Martingale & Company)*

Puss in the Corner I

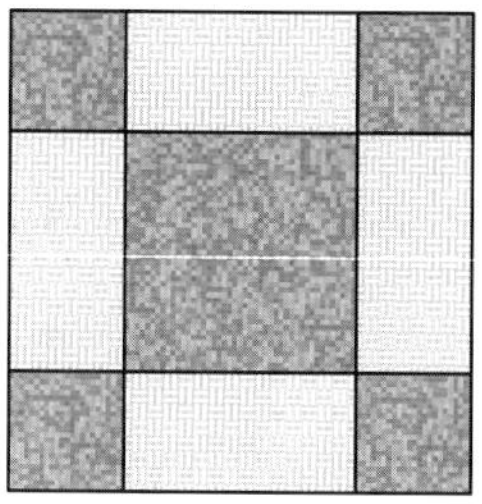

Puss in the Corner
7½" block

Dimensions: 89" x 96½"

110 blocks (55 Puss in the Corner blocks and 55 alternate blocks), 7½", set 11 across and 10 down; 7"-wide border.

Materials: 44"-wide fabric

2 yds. assorted light background fabrics for Puss in the Corner blocks
2 yds. total brown, tan, and navy blue fabrics
2½ yds. beige fabric for alternate blocks
2¼ yds. beige fabric for border
8¼ yds. coordinating fabric for backing (2 crosswise seams)
¾ yd. fabric for binding
Batting and thread to finish

Cutting: All measurements include ¼" seams.

From the assorted light background fabrics:
Cut 14 strips, 2¼" x 42".
Cut 7 strips, 4½" x 42".

From the brown, tan, and navy blue fabrics:
Cut 14 strips, 2¼" x 42".
Cut 7 strips, 4½" x 42".

From the beige fabric for alternate blocks:
Cut 11 strips, 8" x 42". Cut the strips into a total of 55 squares, 8" x 8".

From the beige fabric for border:
Cut 10 strips, 7¼" x 42".

Directions

1. Join 2 of the 2¼" x 42" light background strips with 1 of the 4½" x 42" brown, tan, or navy blue strips; make 7 strip units as shown. The units should measure 8" wide when sewn. Cut the units into a total of 55 segments, each 4½" wide.

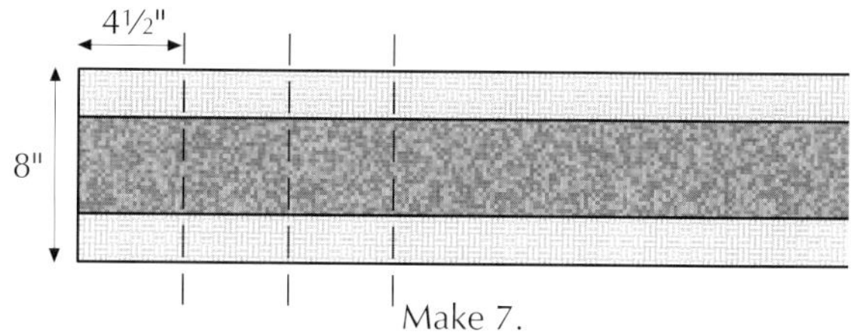

Make 7.

2. Join a 4½" x 42" light background strip with 2 of the 2¼" x 42" brown, tan, or navy blue strips; make 7 strip units as shown. The units should measure 8" wide when sewn. Cut the units into a total of 110 segments, each 2¼" wide.

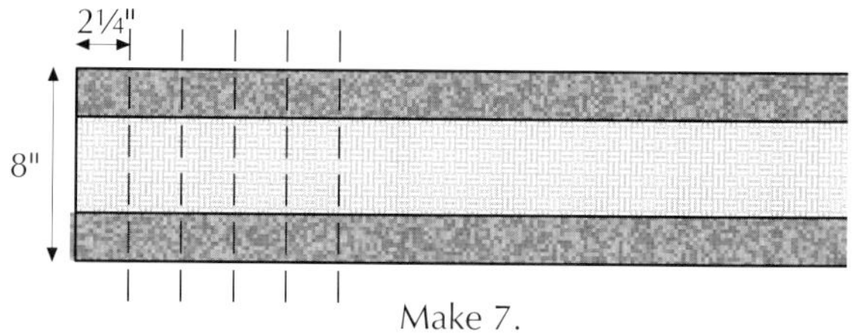

Make 7.

3. Join the segments to piece 55 Puss in the Corner blocks.

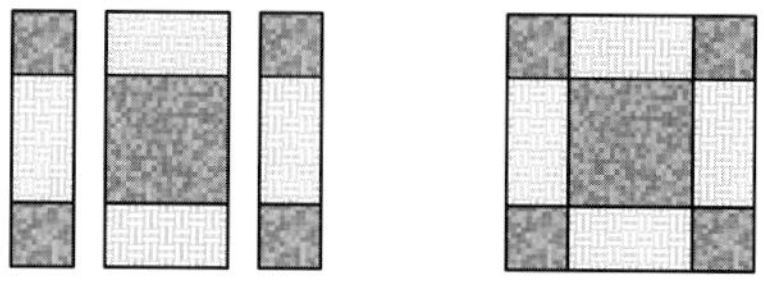

Make 55.

4. Set the blocks together in 10 rows of 11, alternating Puss in the Corner blocks and 8" beige squares. Join the rows.
5. Add the beige border, seaming strips as necessary. See "Borders with Straight-Cut Corners" on page 243.
6. Layer with batting and backing; quilt or tie. See page 264 for a quilting suggestion.
7. Bind with straight-grain or bias strips of fabric.

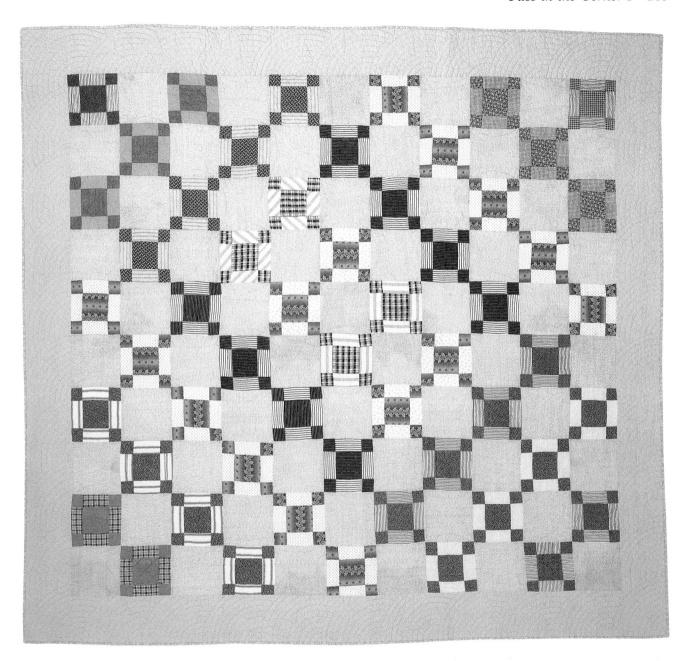

Puss in the Corner I, *origin unknown, c. 1890, 89" x 96½". The soft browns, beiges, and indigos of this antique quilt create a tranquil composition, just right for a soothing bedcover. Lavish quilting by Hazel Montague contributes to the overall design. (Collection of Martingale & Company)*

Puss in the Corner II

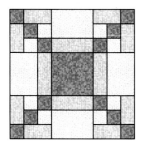

Puss in the Corner
13½" block

Dimensions: 62" x 78"

12 blocks, 13½", set 3 across and 4 down with 3"-wide sashing; 4½"-wide border with corner squares.

Materials: 44"-wide fabric

4 yds. mauve print for blocks, sashing, and border
1⅛ yds. raspberry print for blocks, sashing squares, and corner squares
1⅛ yds. light blue print for blocks
4 yds. fabric for backing (crosswise seam)
⅝ yd. fabric for binding
Batting and thread to finish

Cutting: All measurements include ¼" seams.

From the mauve print:

Cut 7 strips, 2" x 42", for blocks.

Cut 6 strips, 3½" x 42", for blocks. Cut 3 of the strips into 48 rectangles, 2" x 3½". Leave 3 strips uncut.

From the *length* of the remaining fabric, cut 2 strips, 5" x 75", and 2 strips, 5" x 68", for border.

From the remaining piece of fabric, cut 31 rectangles, 3½" x 14", for sashing.

From the raspberry print:

Cut 8 strips, 2" x 42", for blocks.

Cut 2 strips, 5" x 42". Cut the strips into 16 squares, 5" x 5", for block centers and corner squares.

Cut 2 strips, 3½" x 42". Cut the strips into 20 squares, 3½" x 3½", for sashing squares.

From the light blue print:

Cut 7 strips, 3½" x 42", for blocks.
Cut 5 strips, 2" x 42", for blocks.

DIRECTIONS

1. Join 5 of the 2"-wide raspberry strips to the 2"-wide light blue strips to make 5 strip units as shown. The strip units should measure 3½" wide when sewn. Cut the units into 96 segments, each 2" wide.

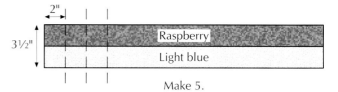

Make 5.

2. Join the segments into 48 four-patch units. Join the 2" x 3½" mauve rectangles to the four-patch units. Make sure the raspberry corners of the four-patch units are oriented as shown.

Make 48.

3. Join the 3 uncut 3½" x 42" mauve strips to the 3 remaining 2"-wide raspberry strips to make 3 strip units as shown. The units should measure 5" wide when sewn. Cut the units into 48 segments, each 2" wide.

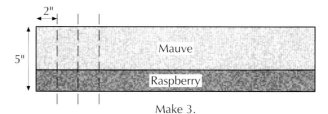

Make 3.

4. Join the segments to the four-patch units.

5. Join the 3½"-wide light blue strips to the 2"-wide mauve strips to make 7 strip units as shown. The units should measure 5" wide when sewn. Cut the units into 48 segments, each 5" wide.

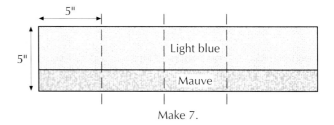

Make 7.

6. Using the units made in steps 4 and 5 and the 5" raspberry squares, piece 12 Puss in the Corner blocks as shown.

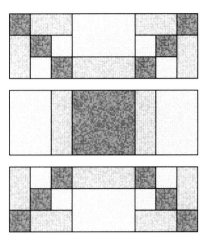

Make 12.

7. Set the blocks together in 4 rows of 3 with the sashing pieces and sashing squares as shown in the quilt photo; join the rows.
8. Add the mauve border with corner squares. See "Borders with Corner Squares" on page 243.
9. Layer with batting and backing; quilt or tie. See page 266 for a quilting suggestion.
10. Bind with straight-grain or bias strips of fabric.

Judy's Choice *by Catherine Shultz, 1991, Anchorage, Alaska, 62" x 78". This mauve-and-blue Puss in the Corner variation is machine quilted along the raspberry chains.*

Rail Fence

Rail Fence
4½" block

Nine Patch
4½" block

Dimensions: 54" x 63"

120 blocks (112 Rail Fence blocks and 8 Nine Patch blocks), 4½", set 10 across and 12 down; 1½"-wide inner border, 3"-wide outer border with corner squares.

Materials: 44"-wide fabric

2¾ yds. assorted red, purple, and gold prints for blocks
½ yd. bright purple print for inner border
⅞ yd. hot pink print for outer border
¼ yd. red print for border corners
3½ yds. fabric for backing (crosswise seam)
½ yd. fabric for binding
Batting and thread to finish

Cutting: All measurements include ¼" seams.

From the assorted red, purple, and gold prints:
   Cut 48 strips, 2" x 42", for blocks. Cut each strip in half to yield 96 strips, 2" x 22".

From the bright purple print:
   Cut 8 strips, 2" x 42", for inner border.

From the hot pink print:
   Cut 8 strips, 3½" x 42", for outer border.

From the red print:
   Cut 4 squares, 5" x 5", for border corners.

DIRECTIONS

1. Join the 2" x 22" strips at random to make 32 strip units as shown. The units should measure 5" wide when sewn. Cut 28 units into a total of 112 segments, each 5" wide, to make 112 Rail Fence blocks.

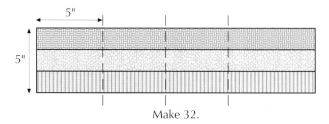

Make 32.

2. From the remaining strip units, cut 24 segments, each 2" wide. Join these segments at random into 8 Nine Patch blocks.

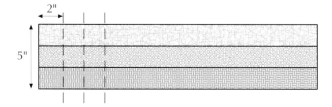

3. Set the blocks together in 12 rows of 10 as shown in the quilt photo, distributing the Nine Patch blocks at random. Join the rows.

4. Add the borders, seaming the bright purple and hot pink strips as necessary to make strips long enough to border the quilt. Join the purple and hot pink strips into 4 stripped border pieces, staggering the seams. Measure the length and the width of the quilt at the center. Cut 2 of the stripped border pieces to the lengthwise measurement and join to the sides of the quilt. Cut the 2 remaining stripped border pieces to the original crosswise measurement, join the red corner squares to the ends of the strips, and stitch to the top and bottom. See "Borders with Corner Squares" on page 243.

5. Layer with batting and backing; quilt or tie. The quilt shown in the photo is finished with the Mennonite Tack (page 247), using perle cotton. See page 266 for a quilting suggestion.

6. Bind with straight-grain or bias strips of fabric.

Sunset Strip *by Judy Dafoe Hopkins, 1991, Anchorage, Alaska, 54" x 63".*
Traditional Rail Fence blocks in hot pinks, reds, and purples are joined by a
few Nine Patch blocks. The quilt is finished with the Mennonite Tack.

The Railroad

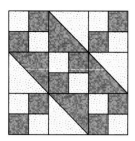

The Railroad
12" block

Dimensions: 72" x 84"

42 blocks (21 Railroad blocks and 21 alternate blocks), 12", set 6 across and 7 down; finished without a border.

Materials: 44"-wide fabric

1 strip, 5" x 42", *each* of 21 different light prints for Railroad blocks (Nearest cut is ¼ yd.)*

1 strip, 5" x 42", *each* of 21 different dark prints (predominantly brown and black with some red, some navy blue) for Railroad blocks (Nearest cut is ¼ yd.)*

2½ yds. red print for alternate blocks

5¼ yds. fabric for backing (lengthwise seam)

¾ yd. fabric for binding

Batting and thread to finish

*Use the same fabric more than once if you wish.

Cutting: All measurements include ¼" seams.

From each of the light and dark strips:

Cut 2 squares, 4⅞" x 4⅞", for a total of 42 light and 42 dark squares. Cut once diagonally into 84 light and 84 dark half-square triangles for Railroad blocks.

Cut 1 strip, 2½" x approximately 27", for a total of 42 strips for Railroad blocks.

From the red print:

Cut 7 strips, 12½" x 42". Cut the strips into a total of 21 squares, 12½" x 12½", for alternate blocks.

DIRECTIONS

1. Join one of the 2½"-wide light strips and one of the 2½"-wide dark strips to make a strip unit as shown. Pick a fabric combination that you find pleasing. The strip unit should measure 4½" wide when sewn. Cut the strip unit into 10 segments, each 2½" wide. Join the segments to make 5 four-patch units as shown.

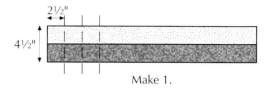

Make 1.

Make 5.

2. Using the same fabric combination as in step 1, join 4 light half-square triangles and 4 dark half-square triangles to make 4 half-square triangle units as shown.

Make 4.

3. Join the four-patch units and the half-square triangle units to make a Railroad block as shown.

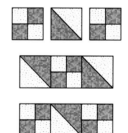

Make 21.

4. Repeat steps 1–3 with the remaining light and dark strips and half-square triangles. You will have a total of 21 Railroad blocks.

5. Set the Railroad blocks together in 7 rows of 6, alternating Railroad blocks and 12½" red squares as shown in the quilt photo. Join the rows.

6. Layer with batting and backing; quilt or tie. See page 266 for a quilting suggestion.

7. Bind with straight-grain or bias strips of fabric.

The Railroad, *origin unknown, c. 1900, 72" x 84". Purchased as a top in Anchorage, Alaska, and quilted in 1993 by Debby Coates, this graphic, classic quilt sports an interesting assortment of subdued turn-of-the-century prints, enlivened by cheery red alternate blocks. (Collection of Debby Coates)*

Ribbon Quilt

Ribbon
6" x 54"

Dimensions: 42" x 54"

7 vertical "ribbons," 6" x 54"; finished without a border.

NOTE: Bias squares are not used in this quilt, although it might appear logical to use them at first glance. Bias squares, if used, would have to be cut to an unusual size—2.62". A standard cutting size is possible with the quarter-square triangles required, and the straight grain is maintained on the outside edges of the ribbons.

Materials: 44"-wide fabric

1½ yds. pink print for background
1½ yds. dusty rose print for "ribbons"
⅔ yd. maroon print for small accent triangles
2¾ yds. fabric for backing (crosswise seam)
½ yd. fabric for binding
Batting and thread to finish

Cutting: All measurements include ¼" seams.

From the pink print:
  Cut 11 strips, 4¼" x 42". Cut the strips into 93 squares, 4¼" x 4¼". Cut twice diagonally into 372 quarter-square triangles.
  Cut 1 strip, 2⅜" x 42". Cut the strip into 7 squares, 2⅜" x 2⅜". Cut once diagonally into 14 half-square triangles.

From the dusty rose print:
  Cut 6 strips, 7¼" x 42". Cut the strips into 30 squares, 7¼" x 7¼". Cut twice diagonally into 120 quarter-square triangles.
  Cut 1 strip, 3⅞" x 42". Cut the strip into 7 squares, 3⅞" x 3⅞". Cut once diagonally into 14 half-square triangles.

From the maroon print:
  Cut 4 strips, 4¼" x 42". Cut the strips into 30 squares, 4¼" x 4¼". Cut twice diagonally into 120 quarter-square triangles.
  Cut 1 strip, 2⅜" x 42". Cut the strip into 7 squares, 2⅜" x 2⅜". Cut once diagonally into 14 half-square triangles.

DIRECTIONS

Unit A
Make 119.

Unit B
Make 7.

Unit C
Make 7.

1. Using the pink and maroon quarter-square triangles, piece 119 Unit A.
2. Using the remaining pink and maroon quarter-square triangles and the small pink and maroon half-square triangles, piece 7 Unit B and 7 Unit C.
3. Set the pieced units together into rows with the dusty rose triangles to make 7 Row A and 7 Row B. Start and end Row A with a dusty rose half-square triangle; start and end Row B with Units B and C.

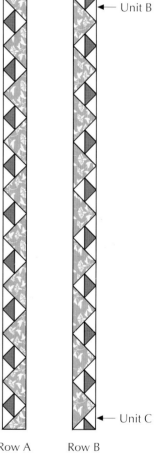

← Unit B

← Unit C

Row A
Make 7.

Row B
Make 7.

4. Join the rows, alternating A and B.
5. Layer with batting and backing; quilt or tie. See page 266 for a quilting suggestion.
6. Bind with straight-grain or bias strips of fabric.

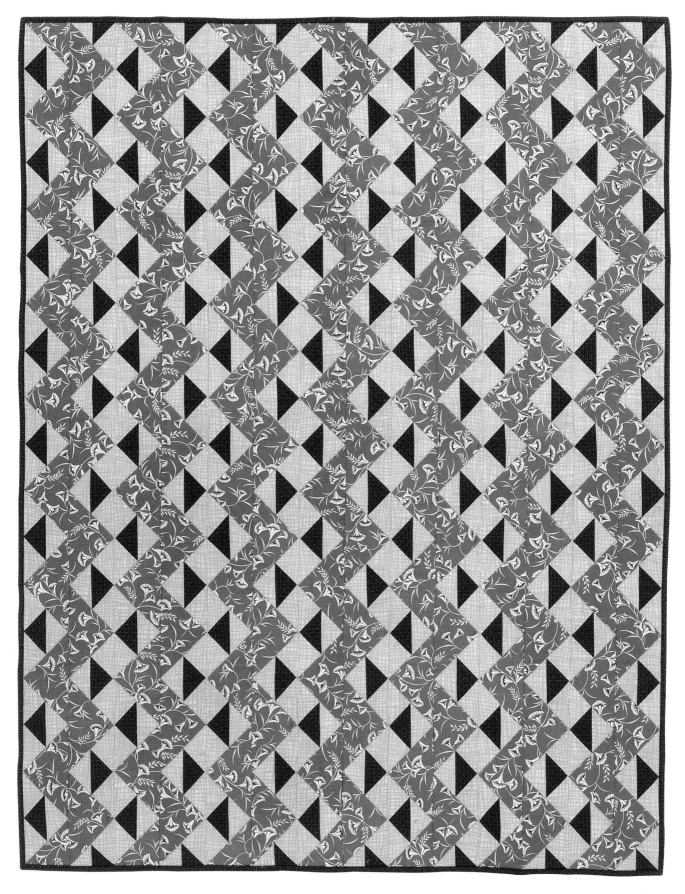

Cathy's Quilt *by George Taylor, 1991, Anchorage, Alaska, 42" x 54". A Streak of Lightning with a difference, this quilt is based on the traditional Ribbon block. (Collection of Catherine Shultz)*

Rolling Pinwheel

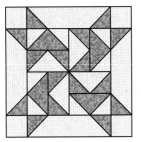

Rolling Pinwheel
9" block

Dimensions: 55¾" x 55¾"

13 blocks (9 Rolling Pinwheel blocks and 4 alternate blocks), 9", set on point with 1¾"-wide float; 1½"-wide inner border, 5½"-wide outer border.

Materials: 44"-wide fabric

2 yds. pink print for background
⅞ yd. blue-green print for blocks and inner border
1⅛ yds. multicolored floral print for outer border
3½ yds. fabric for backing (lengthwise or crosswise seam)
½ yd. fabric for binding
Batting and thread to finish

Cutting: All measurements include ¼" seams.

From the pink print:

Cut 2 strips, 2" x 42". Cut the strips into a total of 36 squares, 2" x 2".

Cut 3 strips, 2⅜" x 42". Cut the strips into a total of 36 squares, 2⅜" x 2⅜". Cut once diagonally into 72 half-square triangles.

Cut 1 strip, 4¼" x 42". Cut the strip into 9 squares, 4¼" x 4¼". Cut twice diagonally into 36 quarter-square triangles.

Cut 2 strips, 7¼" x 42". Cut the strips into a total of 36 segments, each 2" wide, to make 2" x 7¼" rectangles. Trim the corners of the rectangle at a 45° angle as shown.

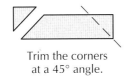

Trim the corners
at a 45° angle.

Cut 1 strip, 9½" x 42". Cut the strip into 4 squares, 9½" x 9½", for alternate blocks.

Cut 1 strip, 19" x 42". Cut the strip into 2 squares, 19" x 19". Cut twice diagonally into 8 quarter-square triangles for side setting triangles. These are cut extra large to allow for "float."

Cut 2 squares, 9¾" x 9¾". Cut once diagonally into 4 half-square triangles for corner setting triangles. These pieces are cut extra large to allow for float.

From the blue-green print:

Cut 5 strips, 2⅜" x 42". Cut the strips into a total of 72 squares, 2⅜" x 2⅜". Cut once diagonally into 144 half-square triangles.

Cut 1 strip, 4¼" x 42". Cut the strip into 9 squares, 4¼" x 4¼". Cut twice diagonally into 36 quarter-square triangles.

Cut 5 strips, 2" x 42", for inner border.

From the multicolored floral print:

Cut 6 strips, 6" x 42", for outer border.

DIRECTIONS

1. Join 2⅜" half-square triangles and 4¼" quarter-square triangles to make 36 units with pink corners and 36 units with blue-green corners as shown.

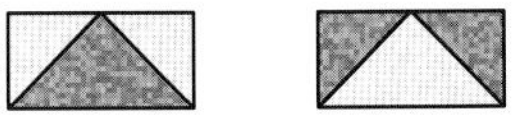

Make 36.   Make 36.

2. Join the units you made in step 1 to make 36 units as shown.

Make 36.

3. Join 72 blue-green half-square triangles to the 36 trimmed pink rectangles.

Make 36.

4. Piece 9 Rolling Pinwheel blocks as shown.

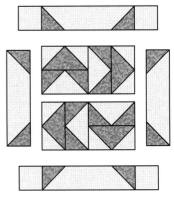

Make 9.

5. Set the Rolling Pinwheel blocks and the pink alternate blocks and setting pieces together in diagonal rows as shown in the quilt photo; join the rows. Trim the outside edges and square up the corners of the quilt as necessary, leaving 2" of fabric outside the block corners to allow the blocks to float. See "Assembling On-Point Quilts" on page 240.

6. Add the blue-green inner border, seaming strips as necessary. See "Borders with Straight-Cut Corners" on page 243.

7. Add the multicolored floral outer border as for the inner border.

8. Layer with batting and backing; quilt or tie. See page 266 for a quilting suggestion.

9. Bind with straight-grain or bias strips of fabric.

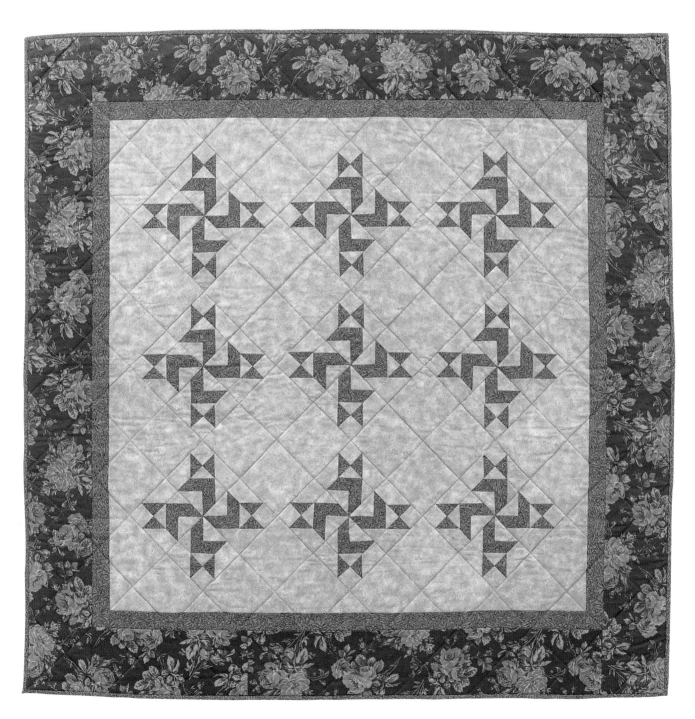

Spinning in Time *by Jennifer Roseland, 1995, Anchorage, Alaska, 55" x 55". This delicate design demanded high-contrast, small-scale prints. The large-scale print used in the borders picks up the colors in the quilt and provides a pleasing textural counterpoint.*

Rosebud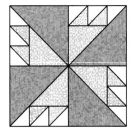

Rosebud
9" block

Dimensions: 60" x 73"

20 blocks, 9", set on point with alternate blocks; 4½"-wide border.

Materials: 44"-wide fabric

3¾ yds. light-background print for blocks and border
1 fat quarter each of 5 assorted rose and pink prints for blocks
1 yd. assorted green prints for large triangles
3¾ yds. fabric for backing (crosswise seam)
½ yd. fabric for binding
Batting and thread to finish

NOTE: Directions are for cutting 5 groups of 4 identical blocks, which is the most economical way to purchase and use the fabric. If you have a large collection of scraps, don't hesitate to use them for a scrappier look as shown in the photo.

Cutting: All measurements include ¼" seams.

From the light-background print:

Cut 20 squares, 7" x 7", for bias squares.
Cut 12 squares, 9½" x 9½", for alternate blocks.
Cut 4 squares, 14" x 14". Cut twice diagonally into 16 quarter-square triangles for side setting triangles. You will have 2 triangles left over.
Cut 2 squares, 7¼" x 7¼". Cut once diagonally into 4 half-square triangles for corner setting triangles.
Cut 8 strips, 5" x 42", for border.

From each of the 5 rose and pink prints:

Cut 4 squares, 7" x 7", for bias squares (20 total). Pair each 7" rose or pink print square with a 7" light-background print square, right sides up. Cut and piece 2"-wide strips, following the directions for making bias squares on page 16. Cut 8 bias squares, 2" x 2", from each pair of squares for a total of 160 bias squares.
Cut 8 squares, 3⅞" x 3⅞" (40 total). Cut once diagonally into 80 half-square triangles.

From the assorted green prints:

Cut 40 squares, 5⅜" x 5⅜". Cut once diagonally into 80 half-square triangles.

DIRECTIONS

1. Piece 20 Rosebud blocks as shown.

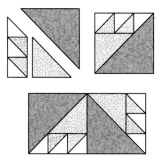

Make 20.

2. Set the Rosebud blocks into diagonal rows with the alternate blocks and side and corner setting triangles; join the rows. See "Assembling On-Point Quilts" on page 240.
3. Add the light-background print border, seaming strips as necessary. See "Borders with Straight-Cut Corners" on page 243.
4. Layer with batting and backing; quilt or tie. See page 267 for a quilting suggestion.
5. Bind with straight-grain or bias strips of fabric.

Kristy's Quilt *by Alice Graves, 1991, Girdwood, Alaska, 60" x 73". Five similar rose prints were used for the Rosebud blocks; the alternate blocks are quilted with a rose-and-leaf design. Quilted by Alice and Jim Graves. (Collection of Kristy Stevens)*

Scot's Plaid

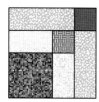

Scot's Plaid
10" block

Dimensions: 62½" x 82½"

48 blocks, 10", set 6 across and 8 down with 2½"-wide sashing on left and bottom edges; finished without a border.

Materials: 44"-wide fabric

½ yd. dark green print for blocks

¼ yd. *each* of 6 different dark green and blue-green prints for blocks

1 strip, 5½" x 42", *each* of 8 different light and medium gold and tan prints for blocks (Nearest cut is ¼ yd.)

2⅛ yds. medium brown print for blocks and sashing

4 yds. fabric for backing (crosswise seam)

⅝ yd. fabric for binding

Batting and thread to finish

Cutting: All measurements include ¼" seams.

From the ½ yard of dark green print:

Cut 1 strip, 5½" x 42". Cut the strip into 6 squares, 5½" x 5½", for blocks.

Cut 3 strips, 3" x 42", for blocks.

Cut 1 square, 3" x 3", for sashing.

From each of the 6 dark green and blue-green prints:

Cut 1 strip, 5½" x 42 (6 total). Cut these strips into 42 squares, 5½" x 5½", for blocks. You will have a total of 48 squares, including the 5½" dark green squares you cut earlier.

Cut 1 strip, 3" x 42", for blocks. You will have a total of 9 strips, including the 3"-wide dark green strips you cut earlier.

From the light and medium gold and tan strips:

Cut any 4 of the strips into 3"-wide segments, to make 48 rectangles, 3" x 5½", for blocks. Leave the remaining 4 strips uncut.

From the medium brown print:

Cut 9 strips, 8" x 42", for blocks and sashing. Cut 4 of the strips into 3"-wide segments, to make 48 rectangles, 3" x 8". Leave the remaining 5 strips uncut.

DIRECTIONS

1. Join the 3" x 5½" light and medium gold and tan rectangles to the 5½" dark green and blue-green squares to make 48 units as shown. Combine the fabrics at random.

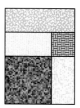

Make 48.

2. Join any 4 of the 3"-wide dark green and blue-green strips to the 4 uncut 5½"-wide light and medium gold and tan strips to make 4 strip units as shown. The strip units should measure 8" wide when sewn. Cut the units into 48 segments, each 3" wide.

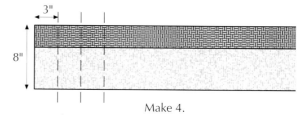

Make 4.

3. Join the segments you cut in step 2 to the units you made in step 1 to make 24 each of the units shown below. Combine the fabrics at random.

Make 24.   Make 24.

4. Join the 3" x 8" medium brown rectangles to the units you made in step 3 to make 48 units as shown, rotating the units as needed.

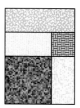

Make 48.

5. Join the remaining 3"-wide dark green and blue-green strips to the uncut 8" medium brown strips to make 5 strip units as shown. The strip units should measure 10½" wide when sewn. Cut the units into 62 segments, each 3" wide.

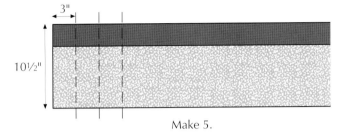

Make 5.

6. Join 48 of the segments you cut in step 5 to the units in step 4 to make 48 Scot's Plaid blocks.

7. Set the blocks together in 8 rows of 6 as shown in the quilt photo, adding 1 of the segments from step 5 to the left side of each row. Join the rows.

8. Join the remaining segments from step 5 and the 3" dark green square to make a sashing strip to add to the bottom of the quilt as shown.

9. Layer with batting and backing; quilt or tie. See page 267 for a quilting suggestion.

10. Bind with straight-grain or bias strips of fabric.

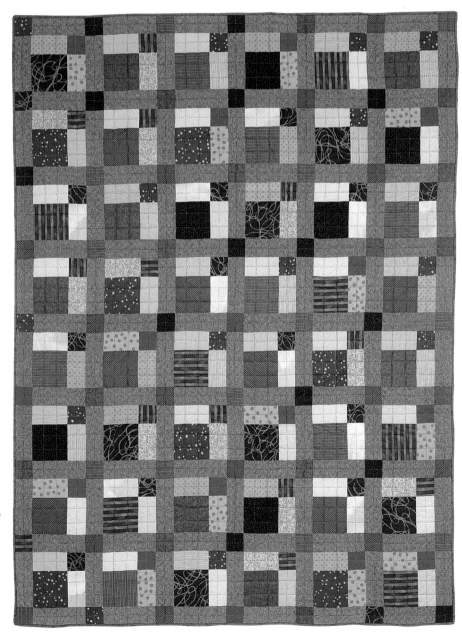

John Doe *by Dee Morrow, 1993, Anchorage, Alaska, 62½" x 82½". Challenged to make a quilt that would appeal to men and boys, Dee used the traditional Scot's Plaid pattern and an eclectic selection of green, blue, and brown prints. Perle-cotton quilting echoes the pieced plaid design.*

Scrap Angles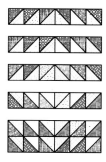

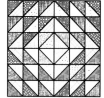

Scrap Angles
12" block

Dimensions: 52½" x 72½"

24 blocks, 12", set 4 across and 6 down; finished without a border.

Materials: 44"-wide fabric

1 fat quarter each of 9 assorted light prints for blocks

1 fat quarter each of 13 assorted medium prints for blocks

1 fat quarter each of 10 assorted dark prints for blocks

3¼ yds. fabric for backing (crosswise seam)

½ yd. fabric for binding

Batting and thread to finish

DIRECTIONS

1. Pair fat quarters as indicated below, right sides up. Cut and piece 2½"-wide bias strips, following the directions for making bias squares on page 14. Cut 2½" x 2½" bias squares as indicated. You will have extra bias squares to play with.

Pairs of Fat Quarters	No. of Bias Squares to Cut
3 light print + 3 light print	180
3 light print + 3 medium print	180
3 medium print + 3 medium print	180
4 medium print + 4 dark print	240
3 dark print + 3 dark print	180

2. Piece 24 Scrap Angles blocks as shown. Beginning at the block center, arrange the bias squares in each block from light to medium to dark.

Make 24.

3. Set the blocks together in 6 rows of 4 as shown in the quilt photo; join the rows.

4. Using leftover medium/dark bias squares, join 36 bias squares to make each of the side borders. Add one border to each of the long sides.

5. Layer with batting and backing; quilt or tie. See page 267 for a quilting suggestion.

6. Bind with straight-grain or bias strips of fabric.

Scrap Angles *by Paulette Peters, 1988, Elkhorn, Nebraska, 52½" x 72½". Made as a color study, this wonderful scrap quilt incorporates a wide variety of prints. (Photo courtesy of Myron Miller, ©1990)*

Shaded Nine Patch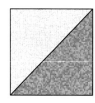

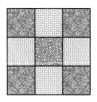 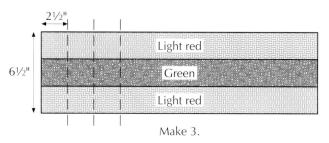

Nine Patch A
6" block

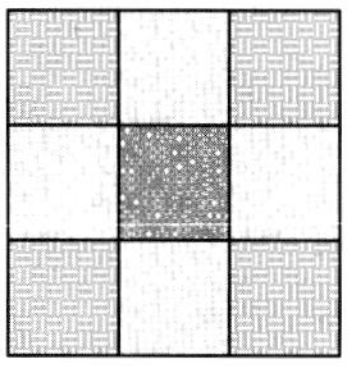

Nine Patch B
6" block

Block C
6" block

Dimensions: 76" x 76"

100 blocks (40 Nine Patch A and 10 Nine Patch B blocks and 50 half-square triangle blocks), 6", set 10 across and 10 down; 2"-wide inner border; 6"-wide outer border.

Materials: 44"-wide fabric

1¼ yds. assorted light red prints for Nine Patch blocks

⅞ yd. assorted dark brown and gray prints for Nine Patch blocks

⅓ yd. light print for Nine Patch blocks

1⅞ yds. green print for Nine Patch blocks and outer border

1 yd. pink print for half-square triangle blocks

1 yd. gray solid for half-square triangle blocks

⅝ yd. yellow print for inner border

4¾ yds. fabric for backing (lengthwise or cross-wise seam)

⅝ yd. fabric for binding

Batting and thread to finish

Cutting: All measurements include ¼" seams.

From the assorted light red prints:
Cut 16 strips, 2½" x 42", for Nine Patch blocks.

From the assorted dark brown and gray prints:
Cut 12 strips, 2½" x 42", for Nine Patch blocks.

From the light print:
Cut 4 strips, 2½" x 42", for Nine Patch blocks.

From the green print:
Cut 4 strips, 2½" x 42", for Nine Patch blocks.
Cut 8 strips, 6½" x 42", for outer border.

From the pink print:
Cut 5 strips, 6⅞" x 42". Cut the strips into 25 squares, 6⅞" x 6⅞". Cut once diagonally into 50 half-square triangles for alternate blocks.

From the gray solid:
Cut 5 strips, 6⅞" x 42". Cut the strips into 25 squares, 6⅞" x 6⅞". Cut once diagonally into 50 half-square triangles for alternate blocks.

From the yellow print:
Cut 8 strips, 2½" x 42", for inner border.

DIRECTIONS

1. Join 6 of the assorted light red strips and 3 of the green strips to make 3 strip units. The units should measure 6½" wide when sewn. Cut the units into 40 segments, each 2½" wide.

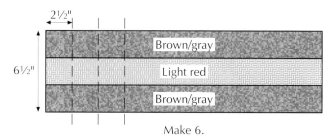

2½"

6½"

Light red

Green

Light red

Make 3.

2. Join the dark brown and gray strips and 6 of the assorted light red strips to make 6 strip units. The units should measure 6½" wide when sewn. Cut the units into 80 segments, each 2½" wide.

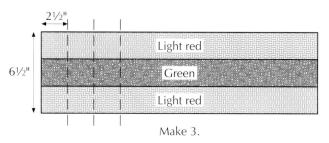

2½"

6½"

Brown/gray

Light red

Brown/gray

Make 6.

3. Join the segments into 40 Nine Patch A.
4. Join 2 of the light print strips and the remaining green strip to make 1 strip unit. The unit should measure 6½" wide when sewn. Cut the unit into 10 segments, each 2½" wide.

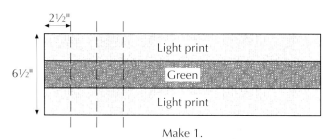

2½"

6½"

Light print

Green

Light print

Make 1.

5. Join the remaining light red and light print strips into 2 strip units. The units should measure 6½" wide when sewn. Cut the units into 20 segments, each 2½" wide.

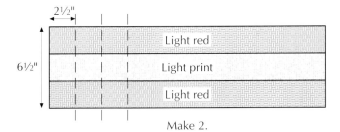

Make 2.

6. Join the segments into 10 Nine Patch B.

7. Join pink and gray triangles into 50 Block C.
8. Set the blocks together in 10 rows of 10 as shown in the quilt photo, alternating Nine Patch and half-square triangle blocks. Join the rows.
9. Add the yellow print inner border, seaming strips as necessary. See "Borders with Straight-Cut Corners" on page 243.
10. Add the green print outer border as for inner border.
11. Layer with batting and backing; quilt or tie. See page 267 for a quilting suggestion.
12. Bind with straight-grain or bias strips of fabric.

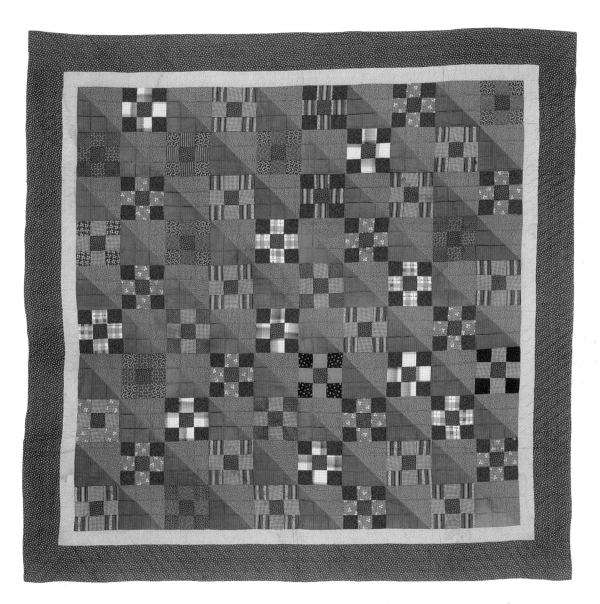

Shaded Nine Patch, *maker unknown, c. 1920, Pennsylvania, 76" x 76". The green center squares in these simple Nine Patch blocks, which are made from many dark fabric scraps, unify the quilt. The alternate blocks of pink and gray triangles also tie the quilt together and create a feeling of movement. (Collection of Nancy J. Martin)*

Shaded Pinwheel

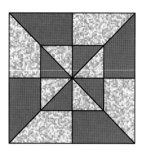

Shaded Pinwheel
10" block

Dimensions: 45" x 55"

12 blocks, 10", set 3 across and 4 down; 7½"-wide border.

Materials: 44"-wide fabric

⅞ yd. coral print for blocks
2 yds. tone-on-tone black print for blocks and border
3 yds. fabric for backing (crosswise seam)
½ yd. fabric for binding
Batting and thread to finish

Cutting: All measurements include ¼" seams.

From the coral print:

Cut 2 strips, 3⅜" x 42". Cut the strips into a total of 24 squares, 3⅜" x 3⅜". Cut once diagonally into 48 half-square triangles.

Cut 7 strips, 3" x 42". Cut the strips into a total of 48 segments, each 5⅞" long, to make 3" x 5⅞" rectangles. Trim one corner of each rectangle at a 45° angle exactly as shown.
02 Shaded

Trim the corner
at a 45° angle.

From the tone-on-tone black print:

Cut 7 strips, 3" x 42". Cut the strips into a total of 48 segments, each 5⅞" long, to make 3" x 5⅞" rectangles. Trim one corner of each rectangle at a 45° angle as shown. Note that you are trimming a different corner than you did from the coral rectangles!

Trim the corner
at a 45° angle.

From the *length* of the remaining black print:

Cut 5 strips, 8" x 42", for border.
Cut 2 strips, 3⅜" wide. Cut the strips into a total of 24 squares, 3⅜" x 3⅜". Cut once diagonally into 48 half-square triangles.

DIRECTIONS

1. Join the 3⅜" black triangles to the trimmed coral rectangles to make 48 units.

Make 48.

2. Join the 3⅜" coral triangles to the trimmed black rectangles to make 48 units.

Make 48.

3. Join the units you made in steps 1 and 2 to make 48 Shaded Pinwheel segments.

Make 48.

4. Using the Shaded Pinwheel segments you made in step 3, piece 12 Shaded Pinwheel blocks as shown.
5. Set the blocks together in 4 rows of 3 as shown in the quilt photo; join the rows.
6. Add the black print border, seaming strips as necessary. See "Borders with Straight-Cut Corners" on page 243.
7. Layer with batting and backing; quilt or tie. See page 267 for a quilting suggestion.
8. Bind with straight-grain or bias strips of fabric.

Shaded Pinwheel *by Clara M. Limberg, 1995, Anchorage, Alaska, 43½" x 53½".*
Clara's eye-catching quilt combines a tone-on-tone black with a distinctive large-scale
coral print. Bull's-eye quilting provides a nice relief from the strong construction lines.

Snowball Strip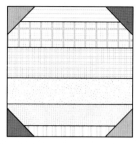

Snowball Strip
7½" block

Dimensions: 68" x 98"

96 blocks, 7½", set 8 across and 12 down; 4"-wide border.

Materials: 44"-wide fabric

⅛ to ¼ yd. *each* of 20 different light blue and beige prints and plaids for blocks*
½ yd. blue solid for block corners
½ yd. rust solid for block corners
1¼ yds. blue-and-white plaid for border
5⅞ yds. fabric for backing (lengthwise seam)
¾ yd. fabric for ⅜"-wide binding
Batting and thread to finish
ScrapMaster cutting guide (optional)

*If the fabric is cut evenly from the bolt and there is minimal shrinkage when you prewash, ⅛ yd. will be adequate. You can use a multitude of scrap strips 8½" or longer and of various widths instead of purchased yardage.

Cutting: All measurements include ¼" seams.

From each of the 20 light prints and plaids:
   Cut 1 strip, 2½" x 42".
   Cut 1 strip, 2¼" x 42".
   Cut 1 strip, 2" x 42".
   Cut 1 strip, 1¾" x 42".
   Cut 2 strips, 1½" x 42".

From the blue solid:
   Cut 5 strips, 2⅝" x 42". Cut the strips into a total of 77 squares, 2⅝" x 2⅝". Cut once diagonally into 154 half-square triangles for block corners.

From the rust solid:
   Cut 5 strips, 2⅝" x 42". Cut the strips into a total of 77 squares, 2⅝" x 2⅝". Cut once diagonally into 154 half-square triangles for block corners.

From the blue-and-white plaid:
   Cut 9 strips, 4½" x 42", for border.

DIRECTIONS

1. Join the assorted light strips to make 20 strip units as shown. Each strip unit should contain 6 strips: two 1½"-wide strips, one 1¾"-wide strip, one 2"-wide strip, one 2¼"-wide strip, and one 2½"-wide strip. Use many different fabric combinations and vary the placement of the strips according to width so that each strip unit looks different.

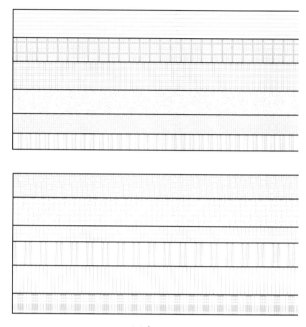

Make 20.

2. Cut 5 squares, 8" x 8", from 19 of the strip units and 1 square from the remaining strip unit for a total of 96 squares. (The strip units may measure as much as 9" wide, raw edge to raw edge, when sewn. I allowed for extra width, as strip units sewn from many strips often don't end up as wide as we expect!)

3. Using the trimming template on page 191 or the 1⅞" "edge" markings on the ScrapMaster cutting guide, trim all 4 corners from 60 of the squares. See "Trimming Templates" on page 12. Add 2⅝" blue and rust corner triangles to make 30 Unit A and 30 Unit B as shown. Note that the strips all run horizontally and that the

placement of the blues and rusts differs between Unit A and Unit B.

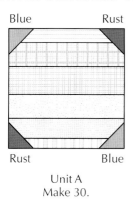

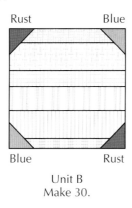

Unit A
Make 30.

Unit B
Make 30.

4. Trim 2 corners from 16 of the squares and add blue and rust corner triangles to make 6 Unit C and 10 Unit D for the outside edges of the quilt as shown. Note that the strips all run horizontally.

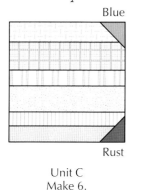

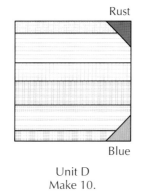

Unit C
Make 6.

Unit D
Make 10.

5. Trim 2 corners from 16 of the squares and add blue and rust corner triangles to make 6 Unit E and 10 Unit F for the outside edges of the quilt as shown. Note that the strips all run vertically.

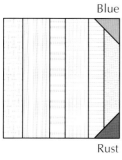

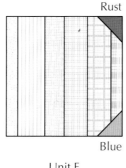

Unit E
Make 6.

Unit F
Make 10.

6. Trim 1 corner from each of the remaining 4 squares and add blue and rust corner triangles to make 2 Unit G and 2 Unit H for the corners of the quilt as shown. Note that the strips all run vertically.

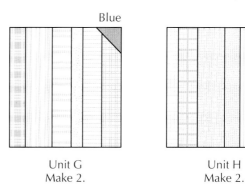

Unit G
Make 2.

Unit H
Make 2.

7. Set the blocks together in 12 rows of 8 as shown in the quilt photo, rotating the blocks as necessary to make the horizontal/vertical strip pattern. Join the rows.

8. Add the blue-and-white plaid border, seaming strips as necessary. See "Borders with Straight-Cut Corners" on page 243.

9. Layer with batting and backing; quilt or tie. See page 268 for a quilting suggestion.

10. Bind with straight-grain or bias strips of fabric.

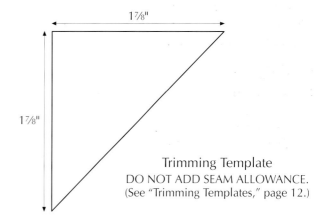

Trimming Template
DO NOT ADD SEAM ALLOWANCE.
(See "Trimming Templates," page 12.)

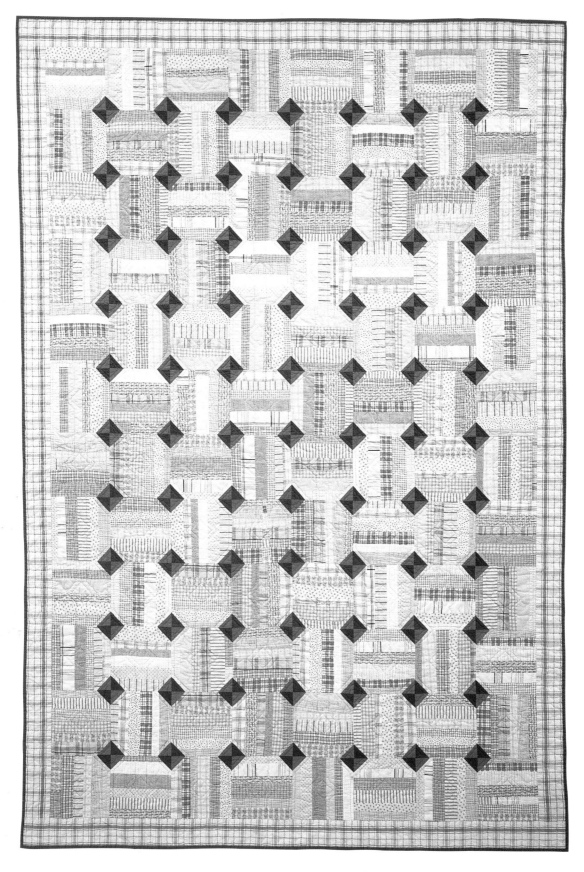

Snowball Strip *by Judy Dafoe Hopkins, 1995, Anchorage, Alaska, 66½" x 97". Blue and rust diamonds float on a scrappy concoction of light print strips, primarily plaids and stripes. This design would be great with black and white diamonds and hot, bright prints! Quilted with perle cotton.*

Snowbows

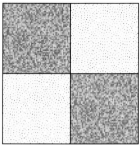 

Four Patch
6" block

Snowball
6" block

Dimensions: 71" x 83"

99 blocks (49 Four Patch blocks and 50 Snowball blocks), 6", set 9 across and 11 down with half and quarter blocks to complete the outside edges; 5½"-wide border.

Materials: 44"-wide fabric

3½ yds. red print for blocks and border
1½ yds. tan print for blocks
1½ yds. gray print for blocks
5⅛ yds. fabric for backing (lengthwise seam)
¾ yd. fabric for binding
Batting and thread to finish

Cutting: All measurements include ¼" seams.

From the red print:

Cut 8 strips, 6" x 42", for border.

Cut 11 strips, 6½" x 42". Cut 9 of the strips into a total of 50 squares, 6½" x 6½", for Snowball blocks. Cut the remaining 2 strips into a total of 18 segments, each 3½" wide, to make 3½" x 6½" rectangles for half blocks.

Cut 4 squares, 3½" x 3½", for quarter blocks.

From the tan print:

Cut 11 strips, 3½" x 42", for Four Patch blocks.

Cut 4 strips, 2⅜" x 42". Cut the strips into a total of 60 squares, 2⅜" x 2⅜". Cut once diagonally into 120 half-square triangles for Snowball blocks.

From the gray print:

Cut 11 strips, 3½" x 42", for Four Patch blocks.

Cut 4 strips, 2⅜" x 42". Cut the strips into a total of 60 squares, 2⅜" x 2⅜". Cut once diagonally into 120 half-square triangles for Snowball blocks.

DIRECTIONS

1. Using the trimming template on page 194, trim all 4 corners from each 6½" red square. See "Trimming Templates" on page 12. Trim 2 corners from each 3½" x 6½" red rectangle and 1 corner from each 3½" red square as shown.

2. Join tan and gray half-square triangles to the trimmed corners of the large and small squares and the rectangles as shown. Follow the color-placement notes on the diagrams carefully: T = Tan; G = Gray.

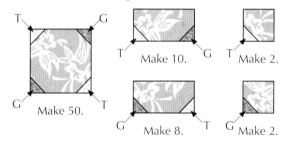

3. Join the 3½"-wide tan and gray strips to make 11 strip units as shown. The strip units should measure 6½" wide when sewn. Cut the units into 120 segments, each 3½" wide.

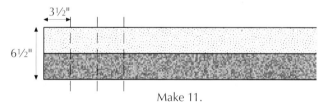

Make 11.

4. Join 98 of the 3½"-wide segments to make 49 Four Patch blocks. The remaining 22 segments are half blocks.

5. Set Four Patch blocks and Snowball blocks together in 11 rows of 9 as shown in the quilt photo, alternating the blocks. Tan half-square triangles must be adjacent to tan squares, and gray half-square triangles adjacent to gray squares, to form the pattern of tan and gray bow ties. Note that the half and quarter blocks are joined to the outside edges of the quilt to complete the Bow Tie pattern. Join the rows.

6. Add the red print border, seaming strips as necessary. See "Borders with Straight-Cut Corners" on page 243.

7. Layer with batting and backing; quilt or tie. See page 268 for a quilting suggestion.
8. Bind with straight-grain or bias strips of fabric.

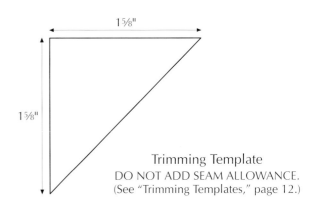

Trimming Template
DO NOT ADD SEAM ALLOWANCE.
(See "Trimming Templates," page 12.)

Snowbows *by Judy Dafoe Hopkins, 1993, Anchorage, Alaska, 71" x 83". Judy suffered severe "Bow Tie burnout" after she finished her 1990 book,* Fit To Be Tied, *but when she realized that Four Patch and Snowball blocks combine nicely to make Bow Ties, she couldn't resist doing it "just one more time!" Quilted by Julie Kimberlin. (Collection of Julie Wilkinson Kimberlin)*

Split Nine Patch

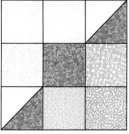 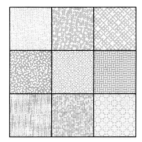

Split Nine Patch
6¾" block

Nine Patch
6¾" block

Dimensions: 72" x 72"

100 blocks (92 Split Nine Patch blocks and 8 Nine Patch blocks), 6¾", set 10 across and 10 down; 2¼"-wide pieced border.

Materials: 44"-wide fabric

1⅓ yds. black print for blocks

1 strip, 2¾" x 42", *each* of 23 different light prints for blocks and pieced border (Nearest cut is ⅛ yd.)*

1 strip, 6½" x 42", *each* of 8 or more light prints for blocks (Nearest cut is ¼ yd.)*

1 strip, 2¾" x 42", *each* of 25 different medium green prints for blocks (Nearest cut is ⅛ yd.)*

4½ yds. fabric for backing (lengthwise or crosswise seam)

⅝ yd. fabric for binding

Batting and thread to finish

*Use the same fabric more than once if you wish.

Cutting: All measurements include ¼" seams.

From the black print:
Cut 8 strips, 3⅛" x 42".
Cut 7 strips, 2¾" x 42".

From each of the 6½" x 42" light print strips:
Cut 1 strip, 3⅛" x 42" (8 total).
Cut 1 strip, 2¾" x 42" (8 total).

You now have a total of 31 assorted light strips, 2¾" x 42". From each of any 24 of these strips, cut 3 rectangles, 2¾" x 6", for a total of 72 rectangles for the pieced border. Leave the remaining 7 strips uncut.

From each of any 12 medium green print strips:
Cut 2 squares, 2¾" x 2¾", for a total of 24 loose squares. Leave the remaining 13 strips uncut.

DIRECTIONS

1. Make ◹: Layer the 3⅛"-wide black and light strips, right sides together, to make 8 contrasting strip pairs. Cut 12 squares, 3⅛" x 3⅛", from each strip pair for a total of 96 layered squares. Cut 92 of the squares once diagonally and chain-piece the resulting triangle pairs to make 184 half-square triangle units.

2. Set aside 7 of the long (2¾" x 42") green strips, all different fabrics. Join the remaining 18 green strips to make 9 all-green strip units. Sew long strips to long strips and short strips to short strips, combining the fabrics at random. Cut the strip units into a total of 116 segments, each 2¾" wide.

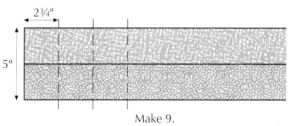

2¾"

5"

Make 9.

3. Add a loose 2¾" green square to one end of each of 24 segments cut in step 2. Use as many different fabric combinations as possible. Join these all-green, 3-square segments to make 8 Nine Patch blocks as shown above.

4. Join the long (2¾" x 42") black, light print, and green strips to make 7 strip units. Cut the strip units into a total of 92 segments, each 2¾" wide.

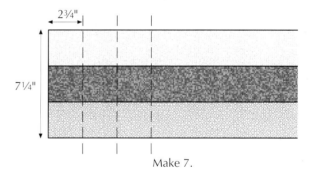

2¾"

7¼"

Make 7.

5. Join the short (2¾" x approximately 24") light strips to make 12 all-light strip units. Combine fabrics at random. Cut strip units into a total of 92 segments, each 2¾" wide.

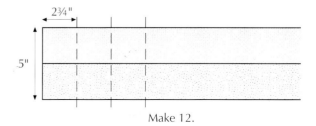

2¾"

5"

Make 12.

6. Using the half-square triangle units made in step 1 and the strip units made in step 5, piece 92 Split Nine Patch blocks as shown.

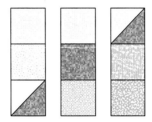

Make 92.

7. Set the blocks together in 10 rows of 10 as shown in the quilt photo. Note that the Nine Patch blocks appear 1 block in from each end of the second and ninth rows, and 4 blocks in from each end of the fourth and seventh rows. Join the rows.

8. Join the 2¾" x 6" light rectangles to make 4 pieced border strips, each at least 72" long, combining the fabrics at random. Cut some of the rectangles down to 2¾" x 2¾" squares as in the pictured quilt if you wish. Add the pieced border strips, trimming the strips as necessary. See "Borders with Straight-Cut Corners" on page 243.

9. Layer with batting and backing; quilt or tie. See page 268 for a quilting suggestion.

10. Bind with straight-grain or bias strips of fabric.

Split Nine Patch *by Holly Rebekah Layton, 1995, Anchorage, Alaska, 69" x 70". This Split Nine Patch setting is commonly associated with quilters of the Perkiomen Valley in Pennsylvania. Holly used a myriad of scraps for her "period piece" and crafted the narrow border from the leftovers.*

Split Rail Fence

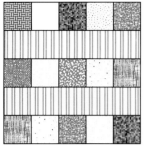

Block A
10" block

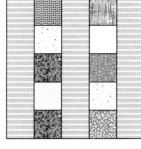

Block B
10" block

Dimensions: 56" x 76"

35 blocks (18 Block A and 17 Block B), 10", set 5 across and 7 down; 3"-wide border.

Materials: 44"-wide fabric

¼ yd. *each* of 6 different dark blue prints for blocks
¼ yd. *each* of 4 different light prints for blocks
¾ yd. Stripe A for Block A
1 yd. Stripe B for Block B
⅞ yd. Stripe C for border
3⅝ yds. fabric for backing (crosswise seam)
⅝ yd. fabric for binding
Batting and thread to finish

Cutting: All measurements include ¼" seams.

From each of the dark blue prints:
Cut 3 strips, 2½" x 42" (18 total), for blocks.

From each of the light prints:
Cut 3 strips, 2½" x 42" (12 total), for blocks.

From Stripe A:
Cut 9 strips, 2½" x 42". Cut the strips into a total of 36 segments, each 10½" wide, to make 2½" x 10½" rectangles for Block A.

From Stripe B:
Cut 13 strips, 2½" x 42". Cut the strips into a total of 51 segments, each 10½" wide, to make 2½" x 10½" rectangles for Block B.

From Stripe C:
Cut 8 strips, 3½" x 42", for border.

DIRECTIONS

1. Join the 2½"-wide dark blue and light strips to make 6 strip units as shown. Combine the fabrics at random. The strip units should measure 10½" wide when sewn. Cut the units into a total of 88 segments, each 2½" wide.

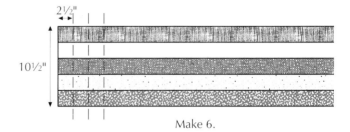

2½"

10½"

Make 6.

2. Join 54 of the 2½"-wide segments with the Stripe A rectangles to make 18 Block A.

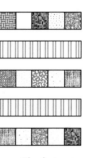

Block A
Make 18.

3. Join the remaining 2½"-wide segments with the Stripe B rectangles to make 17 Block B.

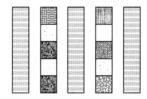

Block B
Make 17.

4. Set the blocks together in 7 rows of 5 as shown in the quilt photo, alternating Block A and Block B. Join the rows.
5. Add the Stripe C border, seaming strips as necessary. See "Borders with Straight-Cut Corners" on page 243.
6. Layer with batting and backing; quilt or tie. See page 268 for a quilting suggestion.
7. Bind with straight-grain or bias strips of fabric.

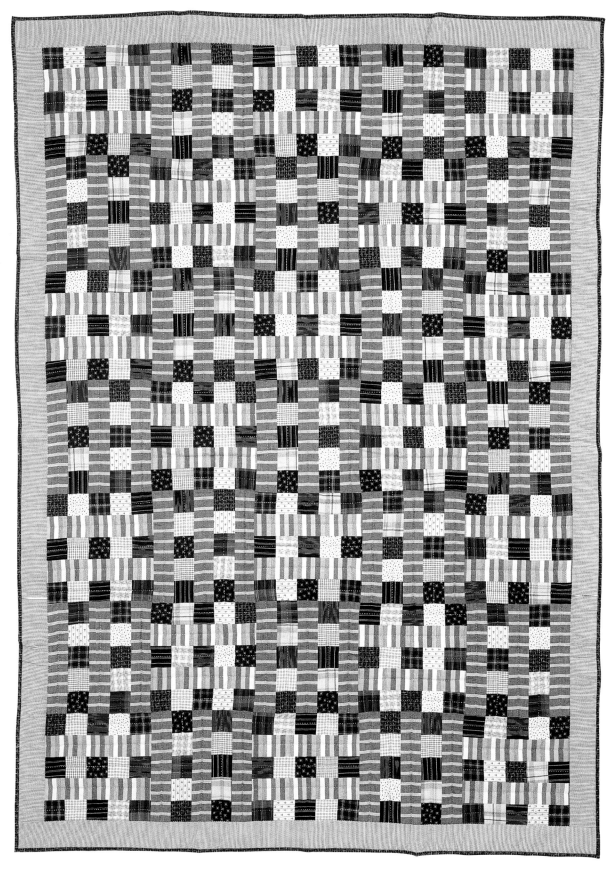

Split Rail Fence *by Judy Dafoe Hopkins, 1992, Anchorage, Alaska, 56" x 76". Judy got carried away with striped chambrays! The antique quilt that inspired her was done in slightly more subdued solids—red and white squares set against mint green strips. This easy quilt would be effective in a number of fabric and color combinations. (Collection of Darien and Jeff Reece)*

Spools

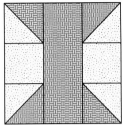

Spools
6" block

Dimensions: 66" x 78"

143 blocks, 6", set 11 across and 13 down; finished without a border.

Materials: 44"-wide fabric

4¾ yds. assorted light-background prints for blocks
5⅛ yds. assorted dark prints in navy, brown, blue, and black for blocks
4⅛ yds. fabric for backing (crosswise seam)
⅝ yd. fabric for binding
Batting and thread to finish

Cutting: All measurements include ¼" seams.

From the assorted light-background prints:
 Cut 72 squares, 8" x 8", for bias squares.
 Cut 286 squares, 2½" x 2½", matching 4 squares to each 8" square.

From the assorted dark prints:
 Cut 72 squares, 8" x 8", for bias squares. Pair each 8" dark print square with an 8" light print square, right sides up. Cut and piece 2½"-wide bias strips, following the directions for making bias squares on page 16. Cut 8 bias squares, 2½" x 2½", from each pair of squares for a total of 572 bias squares.
 Cut 143 rectangles, 2½" x 6½", matching 2 rectangles to each 8" square.

DIRECTIONS

1. Piece 143 Spool blocks as shown.

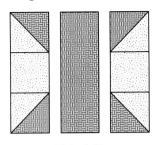

Make 143.

2. Set the blocks together in 13 rows of 11, alternating the spools vertically and horizontally across the row as shown in the quilt photo; join the rows.
3. Layer with batting and backing; quilt or tie. See page 268 for a quilting suggestion.
4. Bind with straight-grain or bias strips of fabric.

Spools, *maker unknown, c. 1900, New York, 66" x 78". The Spool pattern is a perennial favorite of quiltmakers. This spirited version combines plaids, homespuns, and shirtings with the dark calico prints of the period. (Collection of Nancy J. Martin)*

Square in a Square

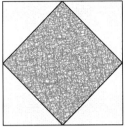
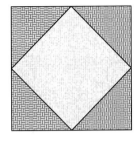

Block A
7¾" block

Block B
7¾" block

Dimensions: 72" x 94"

83 blocks (28 Block A and 55 Block B), 7¾", set on point and "floated" with large setting triangles, which create the border.

Materials: 44"-wide fabric

1½ yds. assorted light and medium blue prints for blocks
1½ yds. assorted light and medium brown prints for blocks
1½ yds. assorted dark blue prints for blocks
1½ yds. assorted dark brown prints for blocks
2 yds. navy blue print for setting triangles
5¾ yds. fabric for backing (lengthwise seam)
⅝ yd. fabric for binding
Batting and thread to finish

Cutting: All measurements include ¼" seams.

From the assorted light and medium blue prints:
Cut 28 squares, 6" x 6", for block centers.
Cut 28 squares, 4¾" x 4¾". Cut once diagonally into 56 half-square triangles for block corners.

From the assorted light and medium brown prints:
Cut 27 squares, 6" x 6", for block centers.
Cut 28 squares, 4¾" x 4¾". Cut once diagonally into 56 half-square triangles for block corners.

From the assorted dark blue prints:
Cut 14 squares, 6" x 6", for block centers.
Cut 55 squares, 4¾" x 4¾". Cut once diagonally into 110 half-square triangles for block corners.

From the dark brown prints:
Cut 14 squares, 6" x 6", for block centers.
Cut 55 squares, 4¾" x 4¾". Cut once diagonally into 110 half-square triangles for block corners.

From the navy blue print:
Cut 6 squares, 18" x 18". Cut twice diagonally into 24 quarter-square triangles for sides.
Cut 2 squares, 12½" x 12½". Cut once diagonally into 4 half-square triangles for corners.

DIRECTIONS

1. Piece 28 Block A and 55 Block B as shown. Use a single fabric for all the corner pieces in each block.

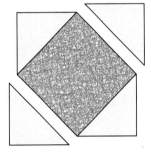
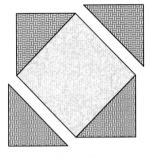

Make 28.

Make 55.

2. Set the blocks together in diagonal rows with the navy blue corner and side triangles as shown in the quilt photo; join the rows. Trim and square up the outside edges after the quilt top has been assembled. The oversized side and corner setting triangles create the border on this quilt. See "Assembling On-Point Quilts" on page 240.
3. Layer with batting and backing; quilt or tie. See page 268 for a quilting suggestion.
4. Bind with straight-grain or bias strips of fabric.

Square within a Square *by Jeanie Smith, 1989, Anchorage, Alaska, 72" x 94".*
Stars appear and disappear in this blue, brown, and purple quilt; the large-scale print
used for the binding adds more sparkle. (Collection of Ramona Chinn)

Square on Square

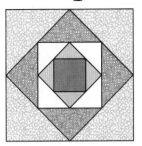

Square on Square
9" block

Dimensions: 75" x 89"

20 blocks, 9", set 4 across and 5 down with 3"-wide strip-pieced sashing strips and Pinwheel sashing squares; 6"-wide inner border, 9"-wide outer border.

Materials: 44"-wide fabric

1⅛ yds. blue print for blocks and sashing squares

1½ yds. medium blue-gray solid for blocks and sashing

2⅛ yds. light blue solid for sashing, sashing squares, and inner border

2½ yds. blue-green solid for outer border

4" x 26" rectangle *each* of 7 different light, medium, and dark blue solids for blocks (Nearest cut is ⅛ yd.)*

5½ yds. fabric for backing (lengthwise seam)

¾ yd. fabric for binding

Batting and thread to finish

*Try 1 light, 3 mediums, and 3 darks.

Cutting: All measurements include ¼" seams.

From the blue print:

Cut 6 strips, 5⅜" x 42". Cut the strips into a total of 40 squares, 5⅜" x 5⅜". Cut once diagonally into 80 half-square triangles for blocks (A).

Cut 2 strips, 2⅜" x 42". Cut the strips into a total of 24 squares, 2⅜" x 2⅜". Cut once diagonally into 48 half-square triangles for sashing squares.

From the medium blue-gray solid:

Cut 4 strips, 5¾" x 42". Cut the strips into a total of 20 squares, 5¾" x 5¾". Cut twice diagonally into 80 quarter-square triangles for blocks (B).

Cut 18 strips, 1½" x 42", for sashing. Cut 2 of these strips into 8 segments, each 9½" wide, to make 1½" x 9½" rectangles (see step 2, optional). Leave the remaining 16 strips uncut (for sashing).

From the light blue solid:

Cut 8 strips, 6½" x 42", for inner border.

Cut 2 strips, 2⅜" x 42". Cut these strips into 24 squares, 2⅜" x 2⅜". Cut once diagonally into 48 half-square triangles for sashing squares.

Cut 8 strips, 1½" x 42", for sashing.

Cut 1 rectangle, 4" x 26". Set aside with the other 4" x 26" rectangles.

From the blue-green solid:

Cut 8 strips, 9½" x 42", for outer border.

Cut 2 rectangles, 4" x 26". Set aside with the other 4" x 26" rectangles.

From each of the 4" x 26" pieces of assorted blue solids (10 total):

Cut 4 squares, 3⅛" x 3⅛" (40 total). Cut once diagonally into 80 half-square triangles for blocks (C).

Cut 2 squares, 3½" x 3½" (20 total). Cut twice diagonally into 80 quarter-square triangles for blocks (D).

Cut 2 squares, 2¾" x 2¾" (20 total) (E).

DIRECTIONS

1. Using pieces A–E, piece 20 Square on Square blocks as shown. Note in the quilt photo that the blue print triangles (A) and the medium blue-gray triangles (B) appear in the same position in every block, but each block uses a different combination of fabrics for pieces C, D, and E.

Make 20.

2. *Optional:* Note in the quilt photo that the 4 blocks along the top edge of the quilt and the 4 blocks along the bottom have extra medium blue-gray strips along their outside edges. You can either include or eliminate these strips. If you wish to include them, join a 1½" x 9½" medium blue-gray rectangle to one side of each of 8 of the Square on Square blocks.

3. Using the 2⅜" blue print and light blue solid half-square triangles, piece 12 Pinwheel blocks.

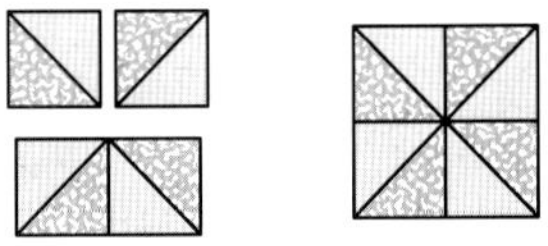

Make 12.

4. Join the 1½"-wide medium blue-gray and light blue strips to make 8 strip units as shown. The strip units should measure 3½" wide when sewn. From the strip units, cut a total of 25 segments, each 9½" wide, for sashing. If you have opted to include the extra strips on the top and bottom blocks, cut 6 sashing segments, each 10½" wide, to use in the top and bottom rows. Otherwise, cut 6 more segments, each 9½" wide.

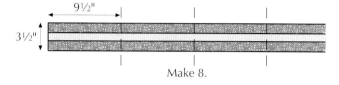

Make 8.

5. Set the blocks together in 5 rows of 4 with the sashing strips and the Pinwheel sashing squares as shown in the quilt photo; join the rows. See "Straight Sets" on page 238.
6. Add the light blue inner border, seaming strips as necessary. See "Borders with Straight-Cut Corners" on page 243.
7. Add the blue-green outer border as for the inner border.
8. Layer with batting and backing; quilt or tie. See page 269 for a quilting suggestion.
9. Bind with straight-grain or bias strips of fabric.

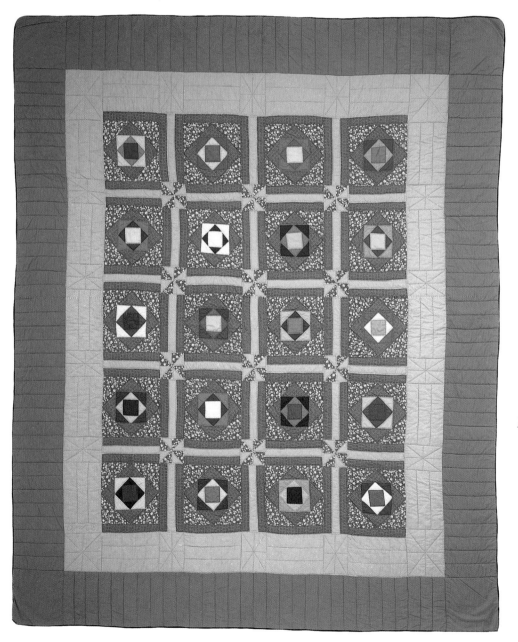

Just Blues Scrap *by Elinor Czarnecki, 1987, Cudahy, Wisconsin, 75" x 89". Inspired by a photo in a 1981* Country Living *magazine, Elinor made this quilt from scraps of two 4' x 15' wall hangings commissioned for a church. The subtle Pinwheel sashing squares add a fresh twist.*

Squares and Ladders

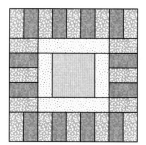

Squares and Ladders
13½" block

Dimensions: 64½" x 84"

12 blocks, 13½", set 3 across and 4 down with 6"-wide sashing and sashing squares; finished without a border.

Materials: 44"-wide fabric

2⅝ yds. light print for blocks and sashing pieces
½ yd. *each* of 3 different red-orange prints for blocks (Fabrics 1, 2, and 3)
⅝ yd. *each* of 3 different dark blue prints for blocks and sashing squares (Fabrics 4, 5, and 6)
5⅛ yds. fabric for backing (lengthwise seam)
⅝ yd. fabric for binding
Batting and thread to finish

NOTE: For this project, you must have at least 42 usable inches of fabric after preshrinking. If the fabric is less than 44" wide on the bolt, you may need ⅜ yd. more of the light print and ⅛ yd. more of each of the red-orange and dark blue prints. Paste a snip of Fabrics 1–6 to a card and number the snips. Use this for reference during the cutting and assembly process.

Cutting: All measurements include ¼" seams.

From the light print:
Cut 8 strips, 2" x 42". Cut 3 of the strips into a total of 24 segments, each 5" wide, to make 2" x 5" rectangles. Cut the remaining strips into a total of 24 segments, each 8" wide, to make 2" x 8" rectangles.

Cut 11 strips, 6½" x 42". Cut the strips into a total of 31 segments, each 14" wide, to make 6½" x 14" rectangles for sashing pieces.

From the 3 red-orange prints:
Cut an 11" x 18" piece from one end of each fabric as shown. From each of these small pieces, cut 4 squares, 5" x 5", for a total of 12 squares.

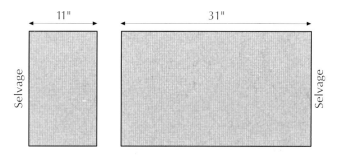

From each of the remaining 18" x 31" pieces, cut 8 strips, 2" x 31". Cut each strip in half for a total of 48 strips, 2" x 15½".

From the 3 dark blue prints:
Cut 1 strip, 6½" x 42", from each fabric for a total of 3 strips. Cut the strips into a total of 18 squares, 6½" x 6½", for sashing squares.

Cut an 11" x 16" piece from one end of each of the remaining 16" x 42" pieces, similar to the piece cut from the red-orange prints as shown above. Cut 1 square, 6½" x 6½", from each of 2 of these small pieces for sashing squares.

From each of the remaining 16" x 31" pieces, cut 6 strips, 2" x 31". Cut each strip in half for a total of 36 strips, 2" x 15½".

DIRECTIONS

1. Join the 2" x 5" and 2" x 8" light rectangles to the 5" red-orange squares to make 12 units as shown.

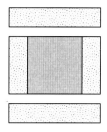

Make 12.

2. Refer to your numbered fabric snips. Join 2" x 15½" strips of Fabric 1 and Fabric 4 to make 1 Strip Unit A and 1 Strip Unit B as shown. Strip Unit A uses 3 red-orange strips and 2 dark blue strips. Strip Unit B uses 5 red-orange strips and 4 dark blue strips. Cut each strip unit into 4 segments, each 3½" wide, for a total of 4 short segments and 4 long segments.

3. Repeat step 2, using Fabric 2 and Fabric 5 strips.
4. Repeat step 2, using Fabric 3 and Fabric 6 strips.
5. Repeat step 2, using Fabric 1 and Fabric 5 strips.
6. Repeat step 2, using Fabric 2 and Fabric 6 strips.
7. Repeat step 2, using Fabric 3 and Fabric 4 strips.
8. Piece 12 Squares and Ladders blocks as shown on page 205, matching the red-orange and dark blue strip-unit segments in each block.
9. Set the blocks together in 4 rows of 3 with the light print sashing strips and assorted dark blue sashing squares as shown in the quilt photo; join the rows. See "Straight Sets" on page 238.
10. Layer with batting and backing; quilt or tie. See page 269 for a quilting suggestion.
11. Bind with straight-grain or bias strips of fabric.

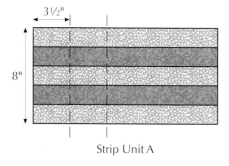

Strip Unit A

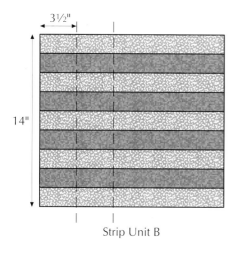

Strip Unit B

Don't Bug Me *by Dee Morrow, 1994, Anchorage, Alaska, 62" x 82". Dee is definitely not afraid of orange—or bugs! Oversized sashing cut from a light-hearted, bug-infested pictorial print anchors the sturdy squares and ladders. Quilted by Bobbi Moore.*

Squares and Points

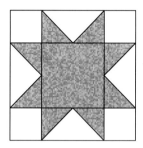

Squares and Points
8" block

Dimensions: 80" x 88"

90 blocks (45 Squares and Points blocks and 45 alternate blocks), 8", set 9 across and 10 down with half blocks and quarter blocks; finished without a border.

Materials: 44"-wide fabric

1 strip, 6½" x 33", *each* of 15 different gold and/or navy blue prints for blocks (Nearest cut is ¼ yd.)
⅝ yd. light gold print for half blocks
5¼ yds. ivory solid for background
7¼ yds. fabric for backing (2 crosswise seams), or use 2⅔ yds. of 90"-wide backing fabric
¾ yd. fabric for binding
Batting and thread to finish

Cutting: All measurements include ¼" seams.

From each of the 15 gold and/or navy blue strips:

Cut 3 squares, 4½" x 4½", (45 total).

From each of the remaining 6½" x 19½" pieces, cut 2 strips, 2⅞" x 19½", for a total of 30 strips. Cut 6 squares, 2⅞" x 2⅞", from each strip for a total of 180 squares. Cut once diagonally into 360 half-square triangles.

From the light gold print:

Cut 4 strips, 2⅞" x 42". Cut 2 of the strips into a total of 19 squares, 2⅞" x 2⅞". Cut once diagonally into 38 half-square triangles. Leave the remaining 2 strips uncut.

Cut 3 strips, 2½" x 42". From one end of a strip, cut 2 squares, 2½" x 2½". Cut the remaining strips into a total of 19 segments, each 4½" wide, to make 2½" x 4½" rectangles.

From the ivory solid:

Cut 2 strips, 2⅞" x 42".

Cut 14 strips, 2½" x 42". Cut the strips into a total of 220 squares, 2½" x 2½".

Cut 1 strip, 4½" x 42". From this strip, cut 2 squares, 4½" x 4½", and 1 rectangle, 4½" x 8½".

Cut 7 strips, 5¼" x 42". Cut the strips into a total of 50 squares, 5¼" x 5¼". Cut twice diagonally into 200 quarter-square triangles. You will have 1 triangle left over.

Cut 12 strips, 8½" x 42". From each of 11 strips, cut 4 squares, 8½" x 8½", and 1 rectangle, 4½" x 8½", for a total of 44 squares (alternate blocks) and 11 rectangles. From the remaining strip, cut 1 square, 8½" x 8½", and 7 rectangles, 4½" x 8½".

DIRECTIONS

1. Join the gold and/or navy blue squares and half-square triangles with 5¼" ivory quarter-square triangles and 2½" ivory squares to make 45 Squares and Points blocks as shown. Use just 1 gold or navy blue fabric in each block.

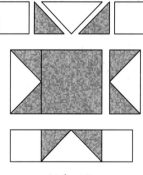

Make 45.

2. Make 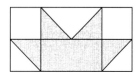: Layer the 2⅞"-wide light gold and ivory strips, right sides together, to make 2 contrasting strip pairs. Cut 11 squares, 2⅞" x 2⅞", from each strip pair for a total of 22 layered squares. Cut the squares once diagonally and chain-piece the resulting triangle pairs to make 44 half-square triangle units. You will have 2 triangle units left over.

3. Piece 19 light gold and ivory half blocks and 2 light gold and ivory quarter blocks as shown.

Make 19.   Make 2.

4. Set the blocks together in 10 rows of 9 with the 8½" ivory alternate blocks, the half and quarter blocks, the 4½" x 8½" ivory rectangles, and the 4½" ivory squares as shown in the quilt photo. Note that the pieced quarter blocks appear in just 2 of the quilt corners; the other 2 corners have plain ivory squares. Join the rows.

5. Layer with batting and backing; quilt or tie. See page 269 for a quilting suggestion.

6. Bind with straight-grain or bias strips of fabric.

Squares and Points *by Sarah Kaufman, 1993, Shaw Island, Washington, 76" x 84". Sara is a "salvage quilter" par excellence. For this star-spangled quilt, she combined contemporary prints, authentic batiks, and years-old treasures from a remarkable scrap bag that predates The Beatles!*

Squares and Strips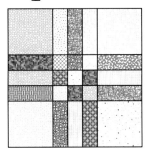

Squares and Strips
13½" block

Dimensions: 62½" x 79"

12 blocks, 13½", set 3 across and 4 down with 3"-wide sashing strips and corner squares; 5"-wide border.

Materials: 44"-wide fabric

⅓ yd. *each* of 3 different bright prints in warm colors (red, red-orange, orange, red-violet, hot pink), for blocks

¼ yd. *each* of 5 additional bright prints in warm colors for blocks

⅛ yd. *each* of 8 different bright prints in cool colors (green, blue-green, blue, blue-violet, purple) for blocks

1¼ yds. bright turquoise print for sashing strips

¼ yd. bright red print for sashing squares

1⅓ yds. bright multicolored print for border

4⅛ yds. fabric for backing (crosswise seam)

⅝ yd. fabric for binding

Batting and thread to finish

Cutting: All measurements include ¼" seams.

From each of the 3 bright prints in warm colors (the ⅓-yard pieces):

Cut 1 strip, 5" x 42" (3 total). Cut these strips into a total of 18 squares, 5" x 5", for blocks.

Cut 2 strips, 2" x 42" (6 total), for blocks.

From each of the 5 additional bright prints in warm colors (the ¼-yard pieces):

Cut 1 strip, 5" x 42" (5 total). Cut these strips into a total of 30 squares, 5" x 5", for blocks. You will have a total of 48 warm squares, including those you cut above.

Cut 1 strip, 2" x 42" (5 total), for blocks. You will have a total of 11 warm color strips, including those you cut above.

From each of the 8 bright prints in cool colors:

Cut 2 strips, 2" x 42" (16 total), for blocks.

From the turquoise print:

Cut 3 strips, 14" x 42". Cut these strips into segments, each 3½" wide, to make 31 rectangles, 3½" x 14", for sashing strips.

From the red print:

Cut 2 strips, 3½" x 42". Cut these strips into a total of 20 squares, 3½" x 3½", for sashing squares.

From the multicolored print:

Cut 8 strips, 5½" x 42", for border.

DIRECTIONS

1. Join any 4 of the 2"-wide warm strips and any 2 of the 2"-wide cool strips to make 2 strip units as shown. The strip units should measure 5" wide when sewn. Cut the units into 24 segments, each 2" wide.

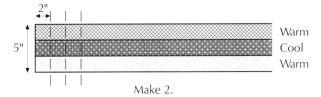

Make 2.

2. Join the remaining 2"-wide warm and cool strips to make 7 strip units as shown. The strip units should measure 5" wide when sewn. Cut 1 of the strip units into 12 segments, each 2" wide. Cut the remaining 6 strip units into a total of 48 segments, each 5" wide.

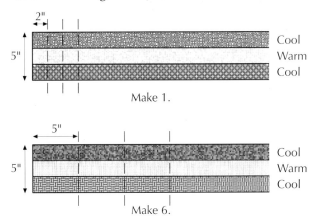

Make 1.

Make 6.

3. Join the 24 warm-cool-warm 2"-wide segments and the 12 cool-warm-cool 2"-wide segments to make 12 nine-patch units with warm corners as shown.

Make 12.

4. Join the nine-patch units, the 5" warm squares, and the 5"-wide cool-warm-cool segments to make 12 Squares and Strips blocks.

5. Set the blocks together in 4 rows of 3 with the sashing strips and sashing squares as shown in the quilt photo; join the rows. See "Straight Sets" on page 238.

6. Add the multicolored print border, seaming strips as necessary. See "Borders with Straight-Cut Corners" on page 243.

7. Layer with batting and backing; quilt or tie. See page 269 for a quilting suggestion.

8. Bind with straight-grain or bias strips of fabric.

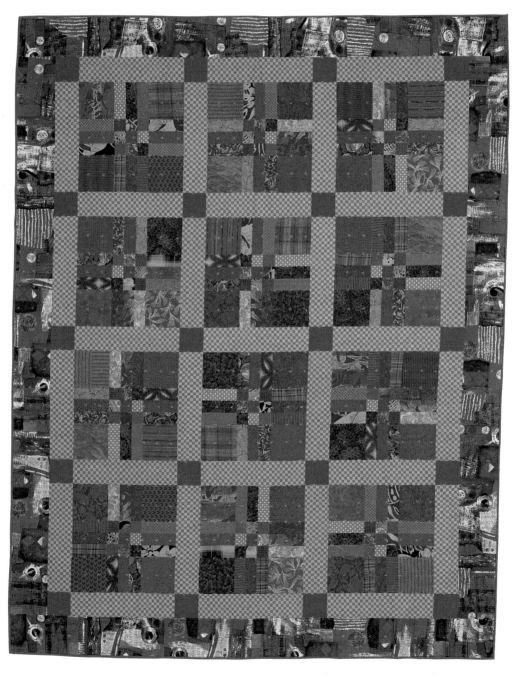

Jujubes *by Judy Dafoe Hopkins, 1992, Anchorage, Alaska, 62½" x 79". Judy updated an unnamed traditional block by using bright, contemporary jewel-toned prints. Quilted by Sarah Kaufman. (Collection of Sarah Pasma Kaufman)*

Stardancer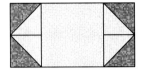

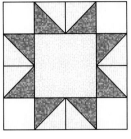

Stardancer
8" block

Lattice Section A

Lattice Section B

Lattice Section C

Dimensions: 92" x 104"

48 blocks, 8", set 6 across and 8 down with pieced lattices that form 49 stars in lattice; 6"-wide pieced border.

Materials: 44"-wide fabric

2¾ yds. dark blue print for star tips and pieced border

8 fat quarters of contrasting prints (browns, golds, reds, and greens) for pieced lattice

5 yds. assorted tan prints for bias squares and pieced border

1¼ yds. assorted light prints for block corners

1½ yds. assorted light blue prints for star centers and pieced border

2¼ yds. assorted large-scale prints for pieced lattice

⅝ yd. *each* of brown, gold, light red, and dark red prints for pieced border

8¼ yds. fabric for backing (2 crosswise seams)

¾ yd. fabric for binding

Batting and thread to finish

Cutting: All measurements include ¼" seams.

From the dark blue print:
Cut 7 fat quarters, 18" x 22".

From the assorted tan prints:
Cut 15 fat quarters, 18" x 22". Pair each tan print fat quarter with a dark blue print fat quarter or a contrasting print fat quarter, right sides up.

Cut and piece 2½"-wide bias strips, following the directions for making bias squares on page 14. Cut a total of 384 tan/dark blue bias squares, 2½" x 2½". Cut a total of 452 tan/contrasting print bias squares, 2½" x 2½".

From the assorted light prints:
Cut 224 squares, 2½" x 2½".

From the assorted light blue prints:
Cut 48 squares, 4½" x 4½".

From the large-scale prints:
Cut 147 squares, 4½" x 4½", for pieced lattice.

For the pieced border:
Cut 9 strips, 2" x 42", from each of the light blue, dark blue, brown, gold, light red, and dark red prints (54 total).

Cut 18 strips, 2" x 42", from tan prints.

Cut 2 light red squares, 5⅛" x 5⅛". Cut once diagonally into 4 half-square triangles for corner units.

Cut 2 dark red squares, 5⅛" x 5⅛". Cut once diagonally into 4 half-square triangles for corner units.

DIRECTIONS

1. Piece 48 Sawtooth Star blocks as shown, using light blue fabric for the star centers and dark blue fabric for the star tips.

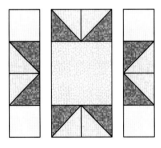

Make 48.

2. Piece 98 Lattice Section A, 16 Lattice Section B, and 14 Lattice Section C, using the bias squares cut from the assorted tan and contrasting (brown, gold, red, and green) prints.

3. Join 6 Stardancer blocks with 7 Lattice Section A and 2 Lattice Section B to make each of 8 rows.

Make 8.

4. Join 7 large-scale print squares with 6 Lattice Section B units and 2 Lattice Section C to make each of 7 rows.

Make 7.

5. Join the rows, alternating rows of Sawtooth Star blocks and lattice rows.

6. The pieced border has a three-dimensional look achieved by the fabric placement in the chevron units. Make 9 dark strip units; cut a total of 86 segments, each 2½" wide, at a 45° angle. Make 9 light strip units; cut a total of 86 segments, each 2½" wide, at a 45° angle.

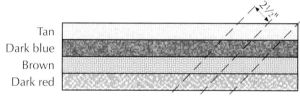

Tan
Dark blue
Brown
Dark red

Make 9.

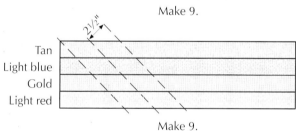

Tan
Light blue
Gold
Light red

Make 9.

7. Alternating light and dark segments, join 23 light segments and 23 dark segments to make each of the side borders. Alternating light and dark segments, join 20 light segments and 20 dark segments to make each of the top and bottom borders.

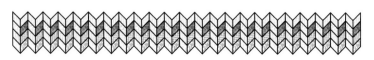

Side border
Make 2.

Top and bottom borders
Make 2.

8. Trim the border strips ¼" from the points.

9. Make 4 corner units as shown.

Corner unit
Make 4.

10. Add the side borders. Add a corner unit to each end of the remaining pieced borders and attach to the top and bottom.

11. Layer with batting and backing; quilt or tie. See page 269 for a quilting suggestion.

12. Bind with straight-grain or bias strips of fabric.

SuzAnn Hull Quilt *by Byrd Tribble, 1988, Coral Gables, Florida, 92" x 104". Byrd added some of her own fabrics and those contributed by friends to a carton of scraps that SuzAnn Hull was about to donate to a thrift shop. The carton contained some wonderful batiks as well as Indian and European cottons. The pieced border was Byrd's addition to the original Stardancer© quilt, designed by Marsha McCloskey.*

Stars in the Sashing

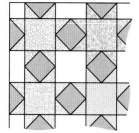

Stars in the Sashing
Corner of quilt

Dimensions: 68" x 85"

Different pieced and plain units joined in 3 different bar formats; finished without a border.

NOTE: We have simplified the cutting and piecing of this quilt by substituting Sawtooth Stars for the eight-pointed stars in the original quilt. The overall appearance of the quilt made from this pattern will be similar to that of the pictured quilt.

Materials: 44"-wide fabric

1 piece, 6½" x 12", *each* of 80 different prints for stars*
1½ yds. yellow solid for background
1⅝ yds. purple solid for background
5¼ yds. fabric for backing (lengthwise seam)
¾ yd. fabric for binding
Batting and thread to finish

* Use a fabric more than once if you wish. If purchasing fabric, ⅜ yd. each of 14 different prints will yield 84 pieces, 6½" x 12".

Cutting: All measurements include ¼" seams.

From each of the 80 different prints:
    Cut 1 square, 4¾" x 4¾" (80 total), for star center.
    Cut 4 squares, 3" x 3" (320 total). Cut once diagonally into 8 half-square triangles for star points (640 total).

From the yellow solid:
    Cut 10 strips, 4¾" x 42". Cut 8 of the strips into a total of 63 squares, 4¾" x 4¾". Cut the remaining 2 strips into 2⅝"-wide segments, to make 32 rectangles, 2⅝" x 4¾", for background.
    Cut 4 squares, 2⅝" x 2⅝", for corners.

From the purple solid:
    Cut 13 strips, 3½" x 42". Cut the strips into a total of 142 squares, 3½" x 3½", for background.

Cut 2 strips, 5½" x 42". Cut the strips into a total of 9 squares, 5½" x 5½". Cut twice diagonally into 36 quarter-square triangles for background.

DIRECTIONS

Important: Three different bar formats combine to form the overall pattern of this quilt. To ensure that the star points will be the same fabric as the star centers throughout the quilt, lay out the pieces for several bars—or for the entire quilt—before you start to sew!

1. Join 3" print half-square triangles to the 3½" purple squares to make 142 Unit I. Join the remaining 3" print half-square triangles to the 5½" purple quarter-square triangles to make 36 Unit II as shown. Arrange the printed fabrics so that complete, single-fabric stars will form when the quilt is assembled as noted above.

Unit I
Make 142.

Unit II
Make 36.

2. Join the units and the yellow squares and rectangles to make 1 top bar, 1 bottom bar, 10 Bar A, and 9 Bar B as shown. The top and bottom bars include the 2⅝" yellow squares. Lay out several bars, matching the prints in the star points with the prints in the star centers, before you sew.

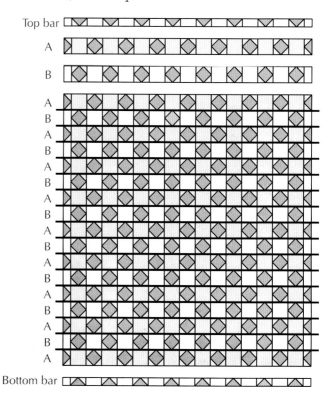

Top bar
A
B
A
B
A
B
A
B
A
B
A
B
A
B
A
B
A
B
A
Bottom bar

3. Join the bars.
4. If desired, trim the corners of the quilt at a 45° angle as shown in the quilt photo.

5. Layer with batting and backing; quilt or tie. See page 270 for a quilting suggestion.
6. Bind with straight-grain or bias strips of fabric.

Stars of Youth *by Lavonne DeBoer, 1937, Harrison, South Dakota, 80" x 98". This is a true scrap quilt. Lavonne made the stars from scraps of clothing before she was eighteen years old; after she married, her mother-in-law helped her complete the quilt. Quilted by Nellie and Lavonne DeBoer. NOTE: The pattern substitutes easier-to-make Sawtooth Stars for Lavonne's eight-pointed stars and produces a 68" x 85" quilt.*

Stars in Strips

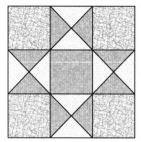

Ohio Star
10½" block

Dimensions: 77" x 89"*

18 Ohio Star blocks, 10½", set on point in 3 strips of 6 stars each; star strips separated by 8"-wide vertical bars; finished without a border.

*Finished size will vary with size of setting triangles and trimming.

Materials: 44"-wide fabric

1 yd. light-medium background print for star corners
1 yd. medium blue print for stars
⅞ yd. medium gray print for stars
½ yd. tan print for stars
1⅝ yds. light background print for stars
2⅝ yds. light gray print for setting triangles
2⅝ yds. gray chintz print for bars
5½ yds. fabric for backing (lengthwise seam)
¾ yd. fabric for binding
Batting and thread to finish

Cutting: All measurements include ¼" seams.

From the light-medium background print:

Cut 8 strips, 4" x 42". Cut the strips into a total of 72 squares, 4" x 4", for star corners.

From the medium blue print:

Cut 1 strip, 4" x 42". Cut the strip into 9 squares, 4" x 4", for star centers.

Cut 2 strips, 13½" x 42". Cut the strips into 5 squares, 13½" x 13½", for bias squares.

From the medium gray print:

Cut 6 squares, 4" x 4", for star centers.
Cut 4 squares, 13½" x 13½", for bias squares.

From the tan print:

Cut 3 squares, 4" x 4", for star centers.
Cut 2 squares, 13½" x 13½", for bias squares.

From the light background print:

Cut 4 strips, 13½" x 42". Cut the strips into a total of 10 squares, 13½" x 13½", for bias squares. Pair each 13½" light background square with a 13½" medium blue square, right sides up. Cut and piece 3¾"-wide bias strips, following the directions for making bias squares on page 00. Cut 8 bias squares, 4⅜" x 4⅜", from each pair of squares for a total of 72 bias squares.

From the light gray print:

Cut 8 squares, 16¼" x 16¼". Cut twice diagonally into 32 quarter-square triangles for side setting triangles. You will have 2 triangles left over.

Cut 2 strips, 13" x 42". Cut the strips into 6 squares, 13" x 13". Cut once diagonally into 12 half-square triangles for corner setting triangles.

From the gray chintz print:

Cut 4 lengthwise strips, 8½" x at least 92", for bars.

DIRECTIONS

1. Match pairs of the 4⅜" bias squares, right sides together, nesting opposing seams. Make a total of 72 Square Two units, following the directions on page 16. You will have 36 light-and-blue, 24 light-and-gray, and 12 light-and-tan Square Two units.

Square Two

2. Join the Square Two units with the 4" light-medium background print squares and the 4" blue, gray, and tan squares to make 9 blue, 6 gray, and 3 tan Ohio Star blocks as shown.

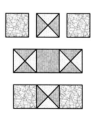

Make 18.

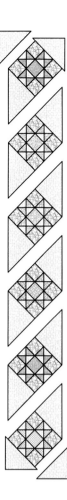

3. Set the blocks together with the light gray setting triangles to make 3 strips as shown. The corner triangles were cut large, to allow some latitude in the finished length of the quilt. Trim the sides of the pieced strips as necessary, leaving a generous ¼" beyond the corners of the star blocks. Trim the tops and bottoms of the strips a generous ¼" or more beyond the corners of the top and bottom blocks.

4. Cut the 8½"-wide chintz strips to the same length as the star strips and set the chintz and the star strips together as shown in the quilt photo.

5. Layer with batting and backing; quilt or tie. See page 270 for a quilting suggestion.

6. Bind with straight-grain or bias strips of fabric.

Stars in the Mist *by Judy Dafoe Hopkins, 1992, Anchorage, Alaska, 75" x 89". A long-time admirer of chintz strippy quilts, Judy indulged her fondness for neutral colors and minimal contrast by using a collection of soft, muted grays, blue-grays, and tans. Quilted by Beatrice Miller.*

State Fair

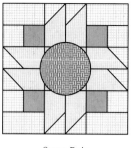 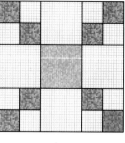

State Fair
9" block

Chain
9" block

Dimensions: 60" x 78"

35 blocks (18 State Fair blocks and 17 Chain blocks), 9", set 5 across and 7 down; 2"-wide pieced inner border, 1½"-wide pieced middle border, 4"-wide pieced outer border.

Materials: 44"-wide fabric

¼ yd. brown print A for Chain block centers
½ yd. brown print B for Chain block
1 square, 4¼" x 4¼", each of 18 different dark prints for appliquéd circles
1 strip, 3⅞" x 21", each of 18 different gold and orange prints for State Fair blocks (Nearest cut is ⅛ yd.)
⅓ yd. green print for State Fair blocks
2⅛ yds. red plaid for background
1 strip, 2½" x 42", each of 7 different red prints and plaids for pieced inner border (Nearest cut is ⅛ yd.)
1 strip, 4½" x 42", each of 8 more red prints and plaids for pieced outer border (Nearest cut is ¼ yd.)*
1 strip, 2" x 42", each of 7 different green prints and plaids for pieced middle border (Nearest cut is ⅛ yd.)
3¾ yds. fabric for backing (crosswise seam)
⅝ yd. fabric for binding
Freezer paper
Batting and thread to finish
*Repeat some of the fabrics used for the inner border if you wish.

Cutting: All measurements include ¼" seams.

From brown print A:
Cut 2 strips, 3½" x 42".

From brown print B:
Cut 7 strips, 2" x 42".

From each of the 18 gold and orange strips:
Cut 1 square, 3½" x 3½" (18 total).
Cut each of the remaining pieces into 8 segments, each 2" wide, to make 2" x 3⅞" rectangles, for a total of 144 rectangles. Trim the corners of the rectangles at a 45° angle as shown.

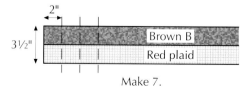

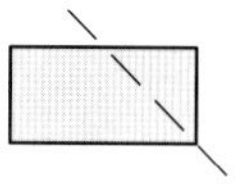

From the green print:
Cut 4 strips, 2" x 42".

From the red plaid:
Cut 11 strips, 2" x 42".
Cut 5 strips, 2⅜" x 42". Cut the strips into a total of 72 squares, 2⅜" x 2⅜". Cut once diagonally into 144 half-square triangles.
Cut 11 strips, 3½" x 42". Cut 4 of the strips into a total of 72 segments, each 2" wide, to make 2" x 3½" rectangles. Cut 3 of the strips into a total of 34 squares, 3½" x 3½". Leave the remaining 4 strips uncut.

DIRECTIONS

1. Join 3½"-wide brown A strips and 3½"-wide red plaid strips to make 2 strip units as shown. Cut the strip units into a total of 17 segments, each 3½" wide.

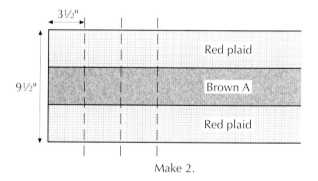

Make 2.

2. Join 2"-wide brown B strips and 2"-wide red plaid strips to make 7 strip units as shown. Cut the strip units into a total of 136 segments, each 2" wide. Join the segments to make 68 four-patch units as shown.

Make 7. 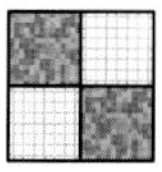   Make 68.

3. Join the four-patch units, the segments you cut in step 1, and the 3½" red plaid squares to make 17 Chain blocks as shown on page 218.

4. Join 2"-wide green strips and 2"-wide red plaid strips to make 4 strip units as shown. Cut the strip units into a total of 72 segments, each 2" wide. Add 2" x 3½" red plaid rectangles to each segment to make 72 units as shown.

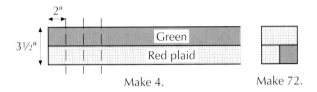

Make 4.　　　　Make 72.

5. Join 2⅜" red plaid triangles to the trimmed gold and orange rectangles as shown. Join these units to make 72 pairs as shown. Use just 1 gold or orange fabric in each pair.

Make 144.　　Make 72.

6. Using the units you made in steps 4 and 5 and the 3½" gold or orange squares, piece 18 State Fair blocks as shown. Match the gold or orange fabrics in each block.

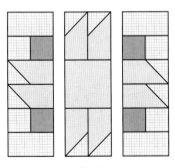

Make 18.

7. Use the template below to make 18 freezer-paper circles. Pin the paper patches, plastic-coated side up, to the wrong sides of the 4¼" dark squares. Cut out circles, adding a ¼"-wide seam allowance. Turn and press the seam allowances over the edges of the paper patches and appliqué a circle to the center of each State Fair block as shown in the quilt photo. See "Appliqué" on page 22.

8. Set the blocks together in 7 rows of 5 as shown in the quilt photo, alternating State Fair and Chain blocks. Join the rows.

9. Cut the assorted 2½" x 42" red strips into various lengths and join them to make 4 pieced border strips, combining the fabrics at random. Repeat with the 2"-wide green strips and the 4½"-wide red strips. Add the borders as shown in the quilt photo, trimming the strips as necessary. See "Borders with Straight-Cut Corners" on page 243.

10. Layer with batting and backing; quilt or tie. See page 270 for a quilting suggestion.

11. Bind with straight-grain or bias strips of fabric.

Appliqué Circle Template
Cut freezer-paper circles this size; add seam allowance when cutting fabric. (See "Appliqué" on page 22.)

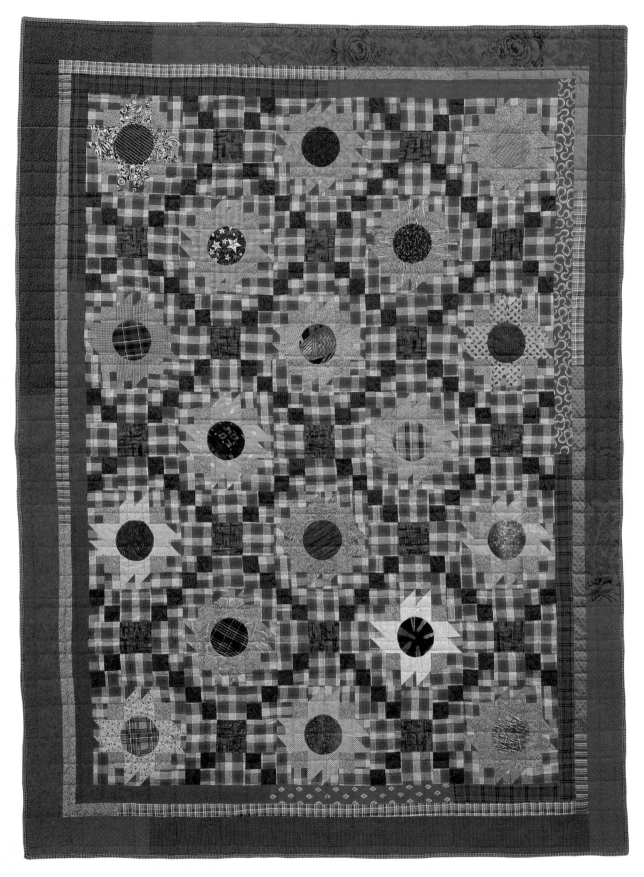

Aunt Goldie's Prize-Winning Quilt by Terri Shinn, 1995, Snohomish, Washington, 58" x 77½".
Classic State Fair blocks, transformed into riotous sunflowers, are separated by alternate blocks that
form a chain. Challenged to use just one fabric for the background of this quilt, Terri predictably opted
for the unusual—a large-scale red-and-beige plaid. Note the collaged border treatment.

Streak of Lightning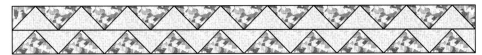

Streak of Lightning
6" x 60"

Dimensions: 60" x 84"

9 horizontal "streaks," 6" x 60", set together with 3"-wide sashing strips; finished without a border.

Materials: 44"-wide fabric

3⅔ yds. multicolored print for background
¼ yd. *each* of 9 different fabrics for "streaks"
5⅛ yds. fabric for backing (lengthwise seam)
⅝ yd. fabric for binding
Batting and thread to finish

Cutting: All measurements include ¼" seams.

From the multicolored print:
    Cut 9 strips, 7¼" x 42". Cut the strips into 43 squares, 7¼" x 7¼". Cut twice diagonally into 172 quarter-square triangles.

From the *length* of the remaining multicolored print:
    Cut 10 strips, 3½" x 63", for sashing strips.
    Cut 1 strip, 3⅞" x 38". Cut the strip into 9 squares, 3⅞" x 3⅞". Cut once diagonally into 18 half-square triangles.

From each of the 9 different "streak" fabrics:
    Cut 1 strip, 7¼" x 42" (9 total). Cut each strip into 5 squares, 7¼" x 7¼". Cut twice diagonally into 20 quarter-square triangles (180 total).
    From the remaining piece of each strip, cut 1 square, 3⅞" x 3⅞". Cut once diagonally into 2 half-square triangles (18 total).

DIRECTIONS

1. Piece 9 Row A/Row B sets. In each A/B set, combine a single streak fabric with the multicolored background fabric. Start and end each row with small half-square triangles as shown.
2. Join the A/B sets into streaks.
3. Measure the length of the streaks and cut the 10 multicolored sashing strips to that length.
4. Set the streaks together, adding a sashing strip between each streak and at the top and bottom of the quilt as shown in the photo.
5. Layer with batting and backing; quilt or tie. See page 271 for a quilting suggestion.
6. Bind with straight-grain or bias strips of fabric.

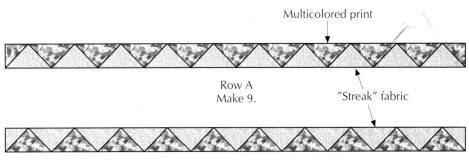

Multicolored print

Row A
Make 9.

"Streak" fabric

Row B
Make 9.

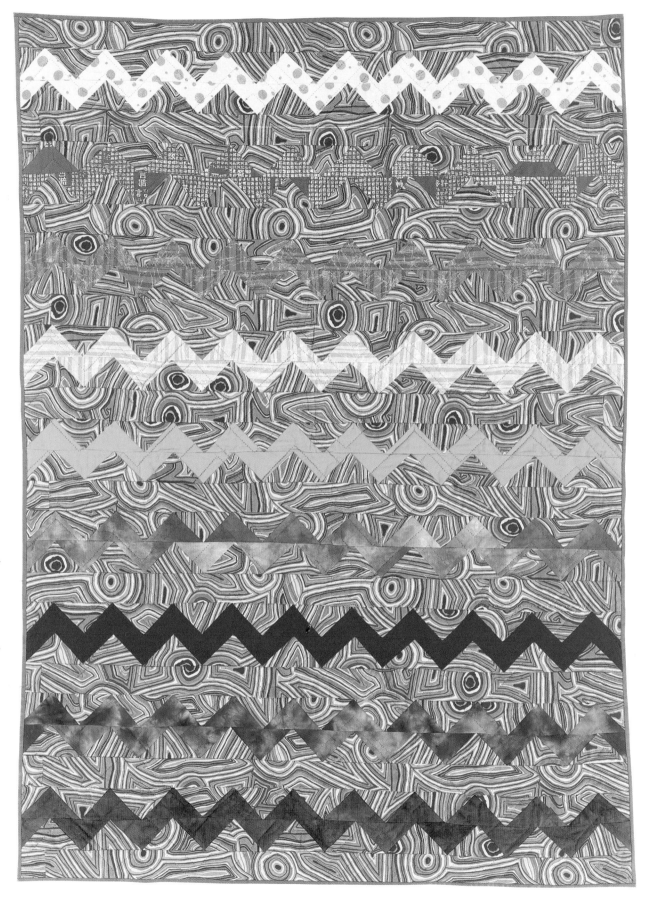

Hot Flashes *by Ella Bosse, 1991, Anchorage, Alaska, 60" x 84". Contemporary, fluorescent fabrics bring the traditional Streak of Lightning pattern into the nineties.*

String Square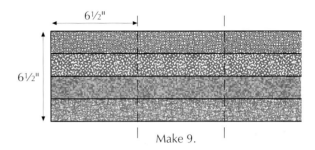

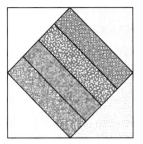

String Square
8½" block

Dimensions: 64" x 89½"

54 blocks, 8½", set 6 across and 9 down; 1½"-wide inner border, 5"-wide outer border.

Materials: 44"-wide fabric

⅛ yd. *each* of 18 different medium and/or dark blue and blue-green prints for blocks
⅓ yd. *each* of 7 different light and/or light-medium blue and blue-green prints for block corners
½ yd. aqua print for inner border
1⅓ yds. multicolored print for outer border
5⅜ yds. fabric for backing (lengthwise seam)
¾ yd. fabric for binding
Batting and thread to finish

Cutting: All measurements include ¼" seams.

From each of the 18 medium and/or dark blue and blue-green prints:
  Cut 2 strips, 2" x 42" (36 total).

From each of the 7 light and/or light-medium blue and blue-green prints:
  Cut 2 strips, 5⅛" x 42" (14 total). Cut 8 squares, 5⅛" x 5⅛", from each of 13 of the strips and 4 squares, 5⅛" x 5⅛", from the last strip for a total of 108 squares. Cut once diagonally into 215 half-square triangles.

From the aqua print:
  Cut 7 strips, 2" x 42", for inner border.

From the multicolored print:
  Cut 8 strips, 5½" x 42", for outer border.

DIRECTIONS

1. Join the 2"-wide medium and/or dark blue and blue-green strips to make 9 strips units as shown. Combine the fabrics at random. Cut the strip units into a total of 54 segments, each 6½" wide.

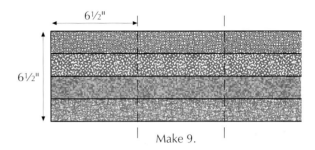

Make 9.

2. Piece 54 String Square blocks as shown, combining the light and/or light-medium blue and blue-green half-square triangles at random.

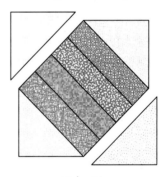

Make 54.

3. Set the blocks together in 9 rows of 6 as shown in the quilt photo. Note that the direction of the strips alternates from block to block. Join the rows.
4. Add the aqua inner border, seaming strips as necessary. See "Borders with Straight-Cut Corners" on page 243.
5. Add the multicolored print outer border as for inner border.
6. Layer with batting and backing; quilt or tie. See page 271 for a quilting suggestion.
7. Bind with straight-grain or bias strips of fabric.

Cosmic Ocean *by Gail Engblom, 1995, Anchorage, Alaska, 62" x 84". Add luscious contemporary batiks to a simple, old pattern and you get a blockbuster quilt—this one is big enough for a twin-size bed. Gail quilted it with perle cotton in a simple overall design.*

Summer Winds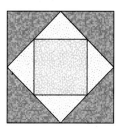

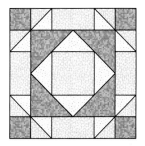

Summer Winds
10½" block

Dimensions: 83½" x 104½"

35 blocks (18 Summer Winds blocks and 17 alternate blocks), 10½", set 5 across and 7 down; 7"-wide inner border, 8½"-wide outer border.

Materials: 44"-wide fabric

1 strip, 4" x 25", *each* of 18 different orange and rust prints for blocks (Nearest cut is ⅛ yd.)

1 strip, 4¾" x 17", *each* of 18 different light blue prints for blocks (Nearest cut is ¼ yd.)

1 strip, 4⅜" x 20", *each* of 18 different medium and dark blue prints for blocks (Nearest cut is ¼ yd.)

3½ yds. dark blue stripe for alternate blocks and inner border

2⅝ yds. tone-on-tone navy blue print for outer border

7⅝ yds. fabric for backing (2 crosswise seams), or use 3⅛ yds. of 90"-wide backing fabric

¾ yd. fabric for binding

Batting and thread to finish

Cutting: All measurements include ¼" seams.

From each of the 18 orange and rust strips:

Cut 1 square, 4" x 4", and 4 rectangles, 2¼" x 4", for a total of 18 squares and 72 rectangles.

From each of the remaining pieces, cut 1 strip, 2⅝" x 12" (18 total).

From each of the 18 light blue strips:

Cut 1 square, 4¾" x 4¾" (18 total). Cut twice diagonally into 72 quarter-square triangles.

From each of the remaining pieces, cut 1 strip, 2⅝" x 12" (18 total).

From each of the 18 medium and dark blue strips:

Cut 2 squares, 4⅜" x 4⅜" (36 total). Cut once diagonally into 72 half-square triangles.

Cut 4 squares, 2¼" x 2¼" (72 total).

From the dark blue stripe:

Cut 3 strips, 7½" x 42", for inner border (top and bottom)

From the *length* of the remaining piece of dark blue stripe, cut 2 strips, 7½" x 90", for inner border (sides)

From the remaining piece of dark blue stripe, cut 17 squares, 11" x 11", for alternate blocks.

From the *length* of the tone-on-tone navy blue print:

Cut 4 strips, 9" wide, for outer border.

DIRECTIONS

1. Make ◩: Layer the 2⅝"-wide orange and rust strips and the 2⅝"-wide light blue strips, right sides together, to make 18 contrasting strip pairs. Cut 4 squares, 2⅝" x 2⅝", from each strip pair for a total of 72 layered squares. Cut the squares once diagonally and chain-piece the resulting triangle pairs to make 144 half-square triangle units.

2. Using the same fabric combinations you used in step 1, join the 4¾" light blue quarter-square triangles to the 4" orange and rust squares to make 18 units as shown.

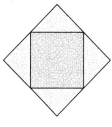

Make 18.

3. Join the 4⅜" medium or dark blue half-square triangles to the units you made in step 2 to make 18 units as shown.

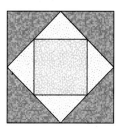

Make 18.

4. Piece 18 Summer Winds blocks as shown. Use just 1 orange, 1 light blue, and 1 medium or dark blue fabric in each block.

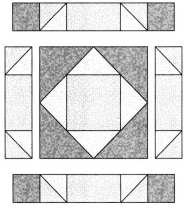

Make 18.

5. Set the blocks together in 7 rows of 5 with the striped alternate blocks as shown in the quilt photo; join the rows.
6. Add the dark blue striped inner border, seaming strips as necessary. Add the top and bottom borders first, then the sides. See "Borders with Straight-Cut Corners" on page 243.
7. Add the navy blue outer border. Add the side borders first, then the top and bottom.
8. Layer with batting and backing; quilt or tie. See page 271 for a quilting suggestion.
9. Bind with straight-grain or bias strips of fabric.

Carried Away *by Judy Dafoe Hopkins, 1994, Anchorage, Alaska, 82¼" x 103¾". There's nothing like a good stripe to add some life to a collection of scrappy blocks. Can you spot the block with the mismatched patch? Quilted by the Willing Workers Quilting Club.*

Three and Six

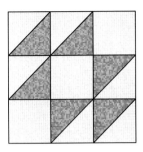

Three and Six
6" block

Dimensions: 68" x 76½"

128 blocks (72 Three and Six blocks and 56 alternate blocks), 6", set on point, 8 across and 9 down; finished without a border.

Materials: 44"-wide fabric

⅜ yd. *each* of 9 different light and medium prints (ivories, tans, grays, blues, light reds) for bias squares and blocks
13" x 13" piece *each* of 18 different dark prints (reds, browns, blues, and blacks) for bias squares (Nearest cut is fat quarter.)
2⅝ yds. light-background print for alternate blocks and setting triangles
4⅜ yds. fabric for backing (crosswise seam)
⅝ yd. fabric for binding
Batting and thread to finish

Cutting: All measurements include ¼" seams.

From each of the 9 light and medium prints:

Cut 2 squares, 13" x 13" (18 total), for bias squares. Pair each 13" light and medium square with a 13" dark print square. Cut and piece 2½"-wide bias strips, following the directions for making bias squares on page 16. Cut 24 bias squares, 2½" x 2½", from each pair of squares for a total of 432 bias squares.

Cut 24 squares, 2½" x 2½", for a total of 216 small squares for blocks.

From the light-background print:

Cut 10 strips, 6½" x 42". Cut these strips into a total of 56 squares, 6½" x 6½", for alternate blocks.

Cut 2 strips, 9¾" x 42". Cut these strips into a total of 8 squares, 9¾" x 9¾". Cut twice diagonally into 32 quarter-square triangles for side setting triangles. You will have 2 triangles left over.

Cut 2 squares, 5⅛" x 5⅛". Cut once diagonally into 4 half-square triangles for corner setting triangles.

DIRECTIONS

1. Join the bias squares with the 2½" light or medium print squares to make 72 Three and Six blocks.

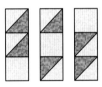

Make 72.

2. Set the blocks together in diagonal rows with the light print alternate blocks and side and corner triangles as shown in the quilt photo; join the rows. Trim and square up the outside edges after the rows are sewn if needed. See "Assembling On-Point Quilts" on page 240.
3. Layer with batting and backing; quilt or tie. See page 271 for a quilting suggestion.
4. Bind with straight-grain or bias strips of fabric.

Three and Six, *origin unknown, 64" x 72". The maker's generous and unrestrained use of broad stripes, sometimes cut straight and sometimes off-grain, adds zest to this scrappy antique.*
NOTE: The pattern uses slightly larger blocks and produces a 68" x 76½" quilt. (Collection of Ella Bosse)

Tin Man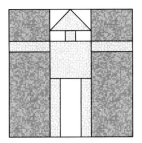

Tin Man
6" block

Dimensions: 40" x 40"

16 blocks, 6", set 4 across and 4 down with 2"-wide sashing; 2"-wide inner border, 3"-wide outer border.

NOTE: The quilt pictured is made from 9" Tin Man blocks and finishes to 60" x 60". The pattern is written for a more usable, wall-sized quilt.

Materials: 44"-wide fabric

3½" x 13" scrap *each* of 16 different red and rust prints for blocks (Nearest cut is ⅛ yd.)

3" x 13" scrap *each* of 16 different medium and dark blue prints for blocks (Nearest cut is ⅛ yd.)

6½" x 42" strip of light-background print for blocks (Nearest cut is ¼ yd.)

⅔ yd. tan or gold print for sashing strips and inner border

½ yd. dark blue print for outer border

1¼ yds. fabric for backing

⅜ yd. fabric for binding

Batting and thread to finish

Cutting: All measurements include ¼" seams.

From each of the red and rust prints:

Cut 1 square, 3¼" x 3¼". Cut twice diagonally into 4 quarter-square triangles. Use 1 of these triangles for the Tin Man's head (A). You will have 3 left over for another project.

Cut 1 square, 1" x 1", for neck (B).

Cut 2 rectangles, 1" x 2½", for arms (C).

Cut 1 rectangle, 2¼" x 2½", for body (D).

Cut 2 rectangles, 1" x 3¼", for legs (E).

From each of the medium and dark blue prints:

Cut 2 rectangles, 2" x 2½" (F).

Cut 2 rectangles, 2½" x 4½" (G).

From the light-background print:

Cut 1 strip, 1⅞" x 42". Cut this strip into 16 squares, 1⅞" x 1⅞". Cut once diagonally into 32 half-square triangles (H).

Cut 1 strip, 1" x 42". Cut this strip into 1¼"-wide segments, to make 32 rectangles, 1" x 1¼" (I).

Cut 1 strip, 3¼" x 42". Cut this strip into 1½"-wide segments, to make 16 rectangles, 1½" x 3¼" (J).

From the tan or gold print:

Cut 9 strips, 2½" x 42", for sashing and inner border. Cut 2 of the strips into 6½"-wide segments, to make 12 rectangles, 2½" x 6½", for sashing pieces. Leave the remaining 7 strips uncut.

From the dark blue print:

Cut 4 strips, 3½" x 42", for outer border.

DIRECTIONS

1. Piece 16 Tin Man blocks as shown.

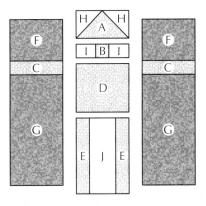

Make 16.

2. Set the blocks together in 4 rows of 4, placing a 2½" x 6½" tan or gold sashing piece between each block as shown.

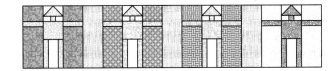

3. Measure the length of the rows and cut 3 of the 2½"-wide tan or gold strips to that measurement for sashing strips. Set the rows together with a sashing strip between each of the rows as shown in the quilt photo; join the rows.

4. Add the tan or gold inner border, seaming strips as necessary. See "Borders with Straight-Cut Corners" on page 243.

5. Add the dark blue outer border as for the inner border.

6. Layer with batting and backing; quilt or tie. See page 271 for a quilting suggestion.

7. Bind with straight-grain or bias strips of fabric.

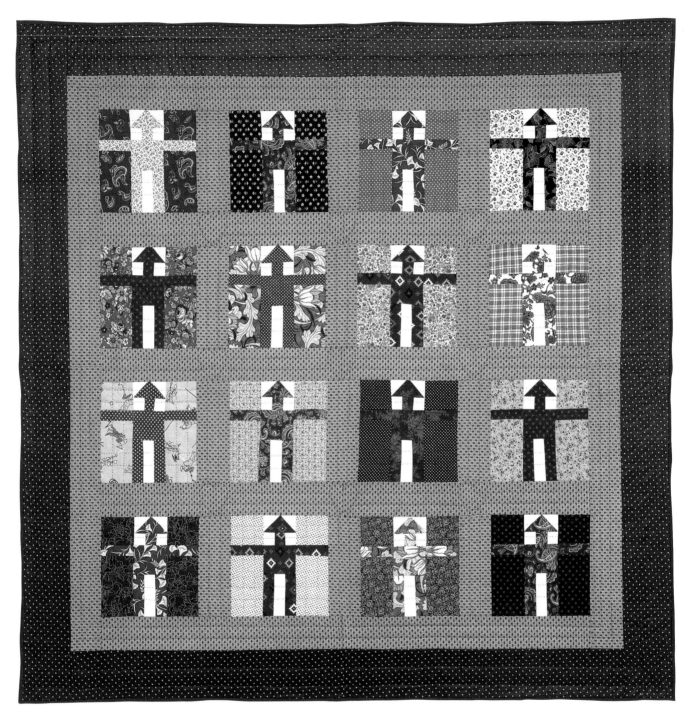

Tin Man *by Bridget Hughes Walsh, 1987, Anchorage, Alaska, 60" x 60". Bridget fearlessly combined prints of all descriptions in this charming representational quilt. Her sturdy, red tin men are softened by a smorgasbord of blue background prints.*
NOTE: The pattern uses a smaller block to produce a 40" x 40" wall quilt.

Union

Union
12" block

Alternate block
12" block

Alternate half block
6" x 12" block

Dimensions: 72" x 72"

25 blocks (13 Union blocks and 12 alternate blocks), 12", set as a bar quilt with alternate half blocks; finished without a border.

Materials: 44"-wide fabric

6 fat quarters of light and dark navy blue patriotic prints

1½ yds. tan background fabric for bias squares

6 fat quarters of tan-background patriotic prints

1½ yds. navy blue star fabric for alternate blocks and half blocks

8 fat quarters of light and dark red fabric for large triangles

½ yd. tan patriotic print for block corners

4⅝ yds. fabric for backing (lengthwise or cross-wise seam)

⅝ yd. fabric for binding

Batting and thread to finish

Cutting: All measurements include ¼" seams.

From each fat quarter of navy blue prints:

Cut 1 piece, 13½" x 18" (6 total) for bias squares.

Cut 2 squares, 4½" x 4½" (12 total), for Piece A.

From the tan-background fabric for bias squares:

Cut 6 pieces, 13½" x 18". Pair each with a navy blue patriotic print. Cut and piece 2½"-wide bias strips, following the directions for making bias squares on page 14. Cut a total of 208 bias squares, 2½" x 2½".

From each of 3 fat quarters of tan-background patriotic prints:

Cut 2 squares, 9" x 9" (6 total), for alternate blocks.

Cut 1 square, 13¼" x 13¼" (3 total). Cut twice diagonally into 4 quarter-square triangles (12 total) for alternate half blocks.

Cut 1 rectangle, 6½" x 12½" (3 total), for side setting pieces.

From each of the 3 remaining fat quarters of tan patriotic prints:

Cut 2 squares, 9" x 9" (6 total), for alternate blocks.

Cut 2 rectangles, 6½" x 12½" (6 total), for side setting pieces.

From the remaining tan background fabric left from bias squares:

Cut 4 squares, 6½" x 6½", for corner setting pieces.

From the navy blue star fabric:

Cut 1 square, 4½" x 4½", for Piece A.

Cut 36 squares, 6⅞" x 6⅞". Cut once diagonally into 72 half-square triangles for alternate blocks and half blocks.

From the red fat quarters:

Cut a total of 26 squares, 4⅞" x 4⅞". Cut once diagonally into 52 half-square triangles. You will need 4 matching dark red Piece D triangles for each block.

Cut a total of 26 squares, 3¾" x 3¾". Cut once diagonally into 52 half-square triangles. You will need 4 matching light red Piece B triangles for each block.

From the tan patriotic print for block corners:

Cut 52 squares, 2½" x 2½", for Piece C.

DIRECTIONS

1. Piece 13 Union blocks as shown.

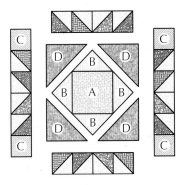

Make 13.

2. Piece 12 alternate blocks and 12 alternate half blocks.

Make 12.   Make 12.

3. Set the Union blocks together in rows with the alternate blocks and half blocks as shown; join the rows.

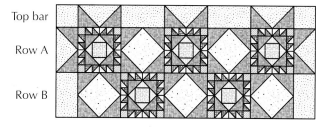

4. Layer with batting and backing; quilt or tie. See page 272 for a quilting suggestion.
5. Bind with straight-grain or bias strips of fabric.

Union *by Nancy J. Martin, 1992, Woodinville, Washington, 72" x 72". This traditional block, executed in a superb collection of patriotic fabrics, was set together with alternate blocks and half blocks to create a spectacular star setting. Quilted by Nancy Sweeney. (Collection of Martingale & Company)*

Walkabout

Walkabout
12" block

Dimensions: 61" x 61"

9 blocks, 12", set 3 across and 3 down with 3"-wide pieced sashing strips and sashing squares; 1¼"-wide inner border, 2"-wide pieced middle border, and 6"-wide outer border.

Materials: 44"-wide fabric

9 fat quarters of assorted blue prints for blocks and pieced border
8 fat quarters of assorted pink prints for blocks
½ yd. white background fabric for nine-patch units
2 yds. pink print for star tips, pieced sashing, and borders
⅜ yd. blue fabric for inner border
4 yds. fabric for backing (lengthwise or crosswise seam)
½ yd. fabric for binding
Batting and thread to finish

Cutting: All measurements include ¼" seams.

From each of the 8 blue print fat quarters: (Reserve 1 for bias squares in border.)

Cut 2 strips, 2" x 22" (16 total), for nine-patch units.

Cut 1 square, 3½" x 3½" (8 total), for star center.

Cut 1 square, 4¼" x 4¼" (8 total). Cut twice diagonally into 4 quarter-square triangles (36 total).

Cut 1 square, 10" x 10" (8 total), for bias squares.

From each of the 8 pink print fat quarters:

Cut 1 square, 10" x 10" (8 total). Pair each 10" pink print square with each 10" blue print square, right sides up. Cut and piece 3½"-wide bias strips, following the directions for making bias squares on page 16. Cut 8 bias squares, 3⅞" x 3⅞", from each pair of squares for a total of 64 bias squares. You will have 4 left over.

From the white background fabric:
Cut 15 strips, 2" x 22".

From the pink print for star tips, sashing, and borders:

Cut 2 strips 2⅜" x 42". Cut the strips into 34 squares, 2⅜" x 2⅜". Cut 2 additional squares from scraps for a total of 36 squares, 2⅜" x 2⅜". Cut once diagonally into 72 half-square triangles for star tips.

Cut 12 rectangles, 3½" x 6½", for sashing.

Cut 1 piece, 18" x 22", for bias squares in border.

Cut 6 strips, 6¼" x 42", for outer border.

From the blue fabric for inner border:
Cut 6 strips, 1¾" x 42".

From the remaining scraps of blue fabric (from fat quarters and inner border):

Cut 13 squares, 5¼" x 5¼". Cut twice diagonally into 52 quarter-square triangles for pieced border.

Cut 22 squares, 3¼" x 3¼". Cut twice diagonally into 80 quarter-square triangles for pieced border.

Cut 4 squares, 3½" x 3½", for sashing squares.

DIRECTIONS

1. Place 2 bias squares of different coloration with right sides together and seam allowances pressed in opposite directions. Make 60 Square Two units, following the directions on page 16.

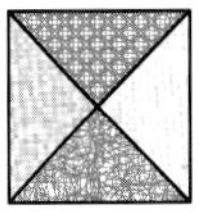

Make 60.

2. Join 2 of the 2" x 22" blue print strips and 1 of the 2" x 22" white background strips; make 7 strip units as shown. The units should measure 5" wide when sewn. Cut the units into 72 segments, each 2" wide.

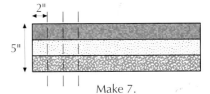

Make 7.

3. Join a 2" x 22" blue print strip and 2 of the 2" x 22" white background strips; make 4 strips as shown. The units should measure 5" wide when sewn. Cut the units into 36 segments, each 2" wide.

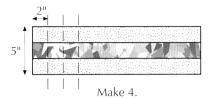

Make 4.

4. Join the segments to make 36 nine-patch units.

Make 36.

5. Join pink print half-square triangles and blue print quarter-square triangles to make the following units.

Make 36.

6. Piece 9 Walkabout blocks as shown.

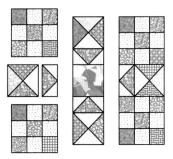

Make 9.

7. Join a Square Two unit to each end of a sashing strip.

Make 12.

8. Join 3 Walkabout blocks and 2 sashing strips to form a row. Make 3 rows.
9. Join 3 sashing strips and 2 sashing squares together to form a row. Make 2 rows.

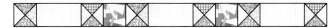

10. Join the rows, alternating rows of blocks and sashing squares.
11. Add the blue inner border, seaming strips as necessary. See "Borders with Straight-Cut Corners" on page 243. The top should now measure 44½" x 44½". To accommodate the pieced border, adjust the width of the strips, if necessary, before proceeding.
12. Using the remaining blue print fat quarter and the pink fat quarter, cut and piece 2"-wide bias strips, following the directions for making bias squares on page 14. Cut 40 bias squares, 1⅞" x 1⅞", for the pieced border.
13. Add the pieced border to the quilt top as shown, using bias squares and large and small border triangles.

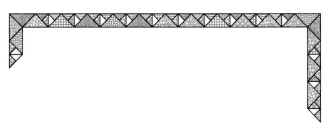

14. Add the pink print outer border as for the inner border.
15. Layer with batting and backing; quilt or tie. See page 272 for a quilting suggestion.
16. Bind with straight-grain or bias strips of fabric.

Walkabout *by Nancy J. Martin, 1992, Woodinville, Washington, 61" x 61". This quilt was named for fabrics collected during a quilt-teaching trip to Australia. It includes various botanical prints, some by Tony Wentzel, featuring vegetation that one might see on a walkabout. Square Two units surround the star centers and form a secondary star pattern in the pieced sashing. An Aboriginal-type print is used for the nine-patch units. A printed handkerchief used for the label on the quilt backing is helpful in identifying the Australian flowers found on the fabric. Quilted by Sue von Jentzen.*
(Collection of Martingale & Company)

Weathervane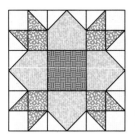

Weathervane
12" block

Dimensions: 74½" x 74½"

25 blocks (13 Weathervane blocks and 12 alternate blocks), 12", set 5 across and 5 down; 2"-wide inner border, 1½"-wide middle border, 3½"-wide outer border.

Materials: 44"-wide fabric

3½ yds. gold print for background, bias squares, and inner border

⅜ yd. red print for 4 blocks

1 fat quarter *each* of 3 assorted red prints for 9 blocks

¾ yd. assorted black prints with dark background for blocks and middle border

1⅞ yds. assorted black prints with light background for blocks and outer border

4½ yds. fabric for backing (lengthwise or crosswise seam)

⅝ yd. fabric for binding

Batting and thread to finish

Cutting: All measurements include ¼" seams.

From the gold print:

Cut 13 squares, 8" x 8", for bias squares.

Cut 12 squares, 12½" x 12½", for alternate blocks.

Cut 52 squares, 2½" x 2½".

Cut 52 squares, 2⅞" x 2⅞". Cut once diagonally into 104 half-square triangles.

Cut 8 strips, 2½" x 42", for inner border.

From the ⅜ yd. red print:

Cut 4 squares, 8" x 8", for bias squares. Pair each 8" red print square with an 8" gold print square, right sides up. Cut and piece 2½"-wide bias strips, following the directions for making bias squares on page 16. Cut 8 bias squares, 2½" x 2½", from each pair of squares for a total of 32 bias squares.

Cut 16 squares, 2½" x 2½".

From each fat quarter of red prints:

Cut 3 squares, 8" x 8", for bias squares (9 total). Pair each 8" red print square with an 8" gold print square, right sides up. Cut and piece 2½"-wide bias strips. Cut 8 bias squares, 2½" x 2½", from each pair of squares for a total of 72 bias squares.

Cut 12 squares, 2½" x 2½" (36 total).

From the black prints with dark background:

Cut 13 squares, 4½" x 4½".

Cut 8 strips, 2" x 42", for middle border.

From the black prints with light background:

Cut 52 squares, 4½" x 4½". Align Bias Square with 3¼" marking at both sides of square and cut away 2 corners.

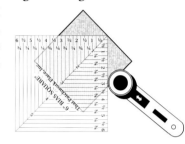

Cut 8 strips, 4" x 42", for outer border.

DIRECTIONS

1. Piece 13 Weathervane blocks as shown.

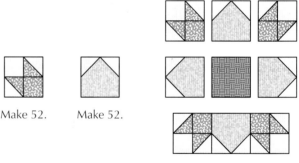

Make 52.   Make 52.

Make 13.

2. Set the blocks together in 5 rows of 5 as shown in the quilt photo, alternating Weathervane blocks and alternate blocks. Join the rows.

3. Add the gold inner border, seaming strips as necessary. See "Borders with Straight-Cut Corners" on page 243.

4. Add the black middle border as for the inner border.

5. Add the black outer border as for the previous borders.

6. Layer with batting and backing; quilt or tie. See page 272 for a quilting suggestion.

7. Bind with straight-grain or bias strips of fabric.

Weathervane *by Nancy J. Martin, 1985, Woodinville, Washington, 74½" x 74½" A warm gold print used in the alternate blocks highlights the delicate feather wreaths. Quilted by Andrea Scadden. (Photo by Carl Murray; collection of Martingale & Company)*

Finishing Your Quilt

This section begins with basic information on squaring up blocks and joining them in either straight or on-point (diagonal) sets, and continues with an in-depth discussion of other finishing techniques: adding borders, marking the quilting lines, preparing backing and batting, layering the quilt, quilting and tying, binding, and adding sleeves and labels. A variety of finishing approaches has been used in the quilts included in this book; the photos are an excellent source of ideas.

SQUARING UP BLOCKS

Some quilters trim or square up their blocks before they assemble them into a quilt. Trimming is risky business and shouldn't be needed if your pieces have been accurately cut and stitched. If you must trim, be sure to leave ¼"-wide seam allowances beyond any points or other important block details that fall at the outside edges of the block.

If your blocks or units become distorted during the stitching process, you can square them up with a freezer-paper guide. Use an accurate cutting square and a pencil or permanent pen to draw a square on the plain side of the freezer paper (finished block size plus seam allowance). Iron the freezer paper to your ironing board cover, plastic side down. Align the block edges with the penciled lines and pin. Gently steam-press. Let each block cool before you unpin it from the freezer-paper guide.

STRAIGHT SETS

In straight sets, blocks are laid out in rows that are parallel to the edges of the quilt. Constructing a straight-set quilt is simple and straightforward. When you set blocks side by side without sashing, simply stitch them together in rows, then join the rows to complete the patterned section of the quilt. If you are using alternate blocks, cut or piece them to the same size as the primary blocks (including seam allowances), then lay out the primary and alternate blocks in checkerboard fashion and stitch them together in rows.

When setting blocks together with plain sashing, cut the vertical sashing pieces to the same length as the blocks (including seam allowances) and to whatever width you have determined is appropriate. Join the sashing pieces and the blocks to form rows, starting and ending each row with a block, then join the rows with long strips of the sashing fabric cut to the same width as the shorter sashing pieces. Make sure the corners of the blocks are aligned when you stitch the rows together. Add the side sashing strips last.

If your sashing includes corner squares of a fabric different from the rest of the sashing (sashing squares), cut the vertical sashing pieces and join them to the blocks to form rows, starting and ending each row with a sashing piece. Cut the horizontal sashing pieces the same size as the vertical sashing pieces. Cut sashing squares to the same dimensions as the width of the sashing pieces and join them to the horizontal sashing pieces to make sashing strips. Start and end each row with a sashing square. Join the rows of blocks with these pieced sashing strips.

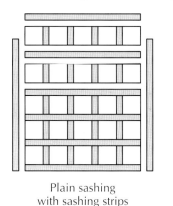 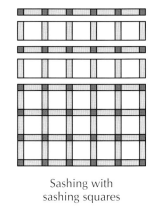

Plain sashing with sashing strips   Sashing with sashing squares

ON-POINT SETS

Quilts that are set on point are constructed in diagonal rows, with half blocks and quarter blocks or setting triangles added to complete the corners and sides of the quilt. If you are designing your own quilt and have no photo or assembly diagram for reference, sketch the quilt on a piece of graph paper so you can see how the rows will go together and how many setting pieces you will need.

Plain setting triangles can be quick-cut from squares. You will always need four corner triangles. To maintain the straight grain on the outside edges of the quilt, use half-square triangles. Two squares cut to the proper dimensions and divided once on the diagonal will yield the four half-square triangles needed for the corners.

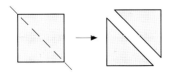

Half-square triangles
for corners

Check your quilt sketch to see how many side triangles are needed. To maintain the straight grain on the outside edges of the quilt, use quarter-square triangles. A square cut to the proper dimensions and divided twice on the diagonal will yield four quarter-square triangles, so divide the total number of triangles needed by 4, round up to the next whole number, and cut and divide that many squares. In some cases, you will have extra triangles to set aside for another project.

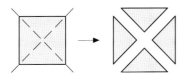

Quarter-square
triangles for sides

How do you determine the "proper dimensions" for cutting these squares? The calculations are based on the finished size of the blocks, and they vary depending on whether the blocks are set side by side or separated by sashing. Though you can use common mathematical formulas (included at right) to calculate the cutting dimensions down to a gnat's eyebrow, Judy prefers the "cut 'em big and trim 'em down" method, which requires mostly simple addition and just one tedious calculation.

The tedious calculation is this: Multiply the finished size of your block by 1.414 to find the finished diagonal measurement of the block. You will need this measurement during the planning stage in order to determine the overall size of the patterned section of an on-point quilt and, later, to calculate the cutting dimensions for setting triangles. If the prospect of translating the result of this calculation from decimals to inches is unnerving, just multiply the finished size of your block by

1.5 to get the approximate finished diagonal measurement of the block. The result will be accurate enough for the "cut 'em big" approach to setting triangles.

For on-point sets where the blocks are set side by side with no sashing, determine the proper dimensions to cut the squares as follows:

Corners: Add 2½" to the finished measurement of the block. Cut two squares to that size; cut the squares once on the diagonal.

Sides: Calculate the approximate finished diagonal measurement of the block (finished block size x 1.5); add 3" to the result. Cut squares to that size; cut the squares twice on the diagonal. Each square yields four triangles.

For on-point sets where the blocks are separated by sashing, determine the proper dimensions to cut the squares as follows:

Corners: Multiply the finished width of the sashing by 2; add the result to the finished size of the block, then add 2½". Cut two squares to that size; cut the squares once on the diagonal.

Sides: Add the finished width of the sashing to the finished size of the block. Calculate the approximate finished diagonal measurement (block + sash x 1.5); add 3". Cut squares to that size; cut the squares twice on the diagonal. Each square yields four triangles.

These somewhat slapdash calculations will work just fine; exact numbers are unnecessary. If you ever need to know how to calculate cutting dimensions for setting triangles with utter precision, here are the gnat's eyebrow formulas mentioned previously. First, some basic geometry:

When you know the length of the side of a square or right triangle, multiply by 1.414 to get the diagonal measurement.   When you know the length of the diagonal of a square or right triangle, divide by 1.414 to get the side measurement.

For on-point sets where the blocks are set side by side with no sashing, determine the proper dimensions to cut the squares as follows:

Corners: Divide the finished block size by 1.414; add .875 (for seams) and round up to the nearest ⅛". (Decimal-to-inch conversions are given on page 240.) Cut two squares to that size; cut the squares once on the diagonal.

Sides: Multiply the finished block size by 1.414; add 1.25 (for seams) and round up to the nearest ⅛". Cut squares to that size; cut the squares twice on the diagonal. Each square yields four triangles.

For on-point sets where the blocks are separated by sashing, determine the proper dimensions to cut the squares as follows:

Corners: Multiply the finished width of the sashing by 2; add the finished block size. Divide the result by 1.414; add .875 (for seams) and round up to the nearest ⅛". (Decimal-to-inch conversions are given below.) Cut two squares to that size; cut the squares once on the diagonal.

Sides: Add the finished width of the sashing to the finished size of the block. Multiply the result by 1.414; add 1.25 (for seams) and round up to the nearest ⅛". Cut squares to that size; cut the squares twice on the diagonal. Each square yields four triangles.

Decimal-to-Inch Conversions

.125 = ⅛"
.25 = ¼"
.375 = ⅜"
.5 = ½"
.625 = ⅝"
.75 = ¾"
.875 = ⅞"

ASSEMBLING ON-POINT QUILTS

As mentioned in the previous section, quilts laid out with the blocks set on point are constructed in diagonal rows. To avoid confusion, lay out all the blocks and setting pieces in the proper configuration before you start sewing. In an on-point set where blocks are set side by side without sashing, simply pick up and sew one row at a time, then join the rows.

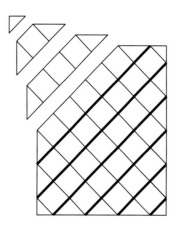

When you use the "cut 'em big" approach for the setting triangles, the side and corner triangles will be larger than the blocks. Align the square corners of the triangle and the block when you join the side triangles to the blocks, leaving the excess at the "point" end of the setting triangle. Stitch and press the seam, then trim the excess even with the edge of the block. Attach the corner triangles last, centering the triangles on the blocks so that any excess or shortfall is distributed equally on each side.

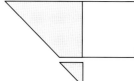
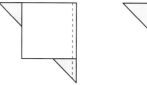

When sewn, your quilt top will look something like this:

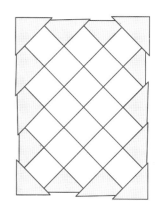

Obviously, you will need to do some trimming and squaring up. At this point, you can make a decision about whether to leave some excess fabric so that blocks will "float" or to trim the setting triangles so that only a ¼"-wide seam allowance remains. Use the outside corners of the blocks to align your cutting guide and trim as desired; make sure the corners are square.

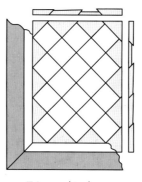
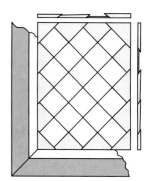

Trimmed to leave
¼" seam allowance
(Border, when added,
will come to the corners
of the blocks.)

Trimmed to allow
blocks to float

The assembly order for on-point sets that include sashing is a little more complex. In the illustration below, notice that the side triangles span a block plus one sashing strip, and the corner triangles span a block plus two sashing strips. Before laying out your blocks, sashing strips, and setting triangles, make a photocopy or tracing of your paper quilt plan and slice it into diagonal rows so you can see which pieces constitute a particular row. Once you have joined the pieces into rows, join the rows from the bottom-right corner and work toward the center. When you reach the center, set that piece aside and go to the top-left corner, again working toward the center. Add the top-right and bottom-left corner triangles last, after the two main sections have been joined.

Add corners last.

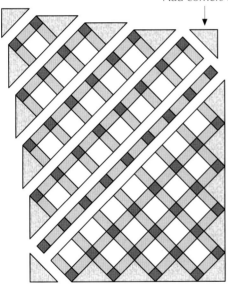

Assembly diagram for on-point set with sashing

Some of us have difficulty getting on-point quilts to lie flat. To minimize potential problems, take a few precautions. Make sure that the individual blocks are absolutely square and are all the same size. Plain or pieced alternate blocks should be square and the same size as the primary blocks. Since the side setting triangles are quick-cut on the bias, sometimes their corners are not square; it's worth double-checking. When you join blocks to setting triangles, feed them into the sewing machine with the block, which has a straight-grain edge, on top and the bias-edge setting triangle on the bottom; any stretching of the bias edge will be eased by the feed dogs.

BAR QUILTS

In a bar quilt, various pieced and plain units are joined into rows, or bars, instead of blocks; the pattern emerges only after the bars are stitched together. Several different bar formats may be combined to form the overall pattern of a particular quilt. Make sure the design, fabrics, and colors will come out as you intended by laying out the pieces for several bars—or for the entire quilt—before you start to sew.

For some quilts, bar construction is the only logical method. For many common quilt designs, changing to a bar-quilt approach simplifies construction, reduces the number of seams, and/or creates large seam-free areas in which to quilt. Study a full-quilt photo or a scale drawing of several rows of a quilt to see if old block boundaries can be eliminated and new units of construction identified, as in the examples below.

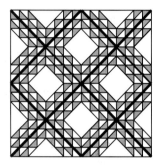

Traditional Ocean Waves blocks in a diagonal set

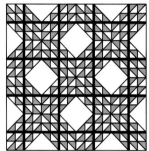

Bar setting simplifies construction.

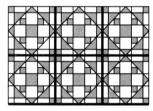

Traditional Old-Favorite blocks

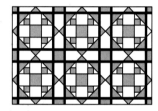

Bar setting reduces number of seams.

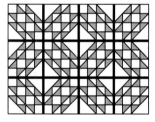

Traditional Hovering Hawks blocks

Bar setting creates large seam-free areas for quilting.

BORDERS

Whether or not to add a border to your quilt is entirely up to you. Some quilts seem to resist borders. If you have tried several different border options and none seems to work, perhaps the piece wants to be finished without at border at all or with a border on only one or two sides. Many quilts will happily accept a "1-2-3" border—an inner border, a middle border, and an outer border in 1:2:3 proportions (1" inner, 2" middle, and 3" outer borders, or 1½" inner, 3" middle, and 4½" outer borders, for example).

Though many of us avoid adding elaborately pieced borders to our quilts because of the additional work involved, some quilts demand them. As an alternative, try a multifabric border. Use a different fabric on each edge of the quilt; use one fabric for the top and right edges and a different fabric for the bottom and left edges; or join random chunks of several different fabrics until you have pieces long enough to form borders. Quiltmakers who buy fabric in small cuts often resort to multifabric borders out of necessity, since they rarely have enough of any one fabric to border an entire quilt.

Because you need extra yardage to cut borders on the lengthwise grain, plain border strips commonly are cut along the crosswise grain and seamed where extra length is needed. Press the seams open for minimum visibility. To ensure a flat, square quilt, cut border strips extra-long and trim the strips to the proper length after you know the actual dimensions of the patterned center section of the quilt.

Most of the quilts in the pattern section of this book have seamed borders with straight-cut corners; a few may have borders with corner squares or with mitered corners.

Straight-cut corners

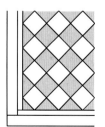
Corner squares

Mitered corners

Borders with Straight-Cut Corners

To make a border with straight-cut corners, measure the length of the patterned section of the quilt at the center, from raw edge to raw edge. Cut two border strips to that measurement and join them to the sides of the quilt with a ¼"-wide seam, matching the ends and centers and easing the edges to fit. Then, measure the width of the quilt at the center from edge to edge, including the border pieces you just added. Cut two border strips to that measurement and join them to the top and bottom of the quilt, matching ends and centers and easing as necessary.

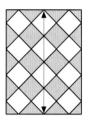 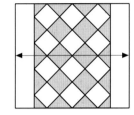

Measure length at center.   Measure width at center after adding side borders.

NOTE: Do not measure the outer edges of the quilt! Often, these edges measure longer than the quilt center due to stretching during construction; the edges might even be two different lengths. To keep the finished quilt as straight and square as possible, you must measure the centers.

Borders with Corner Squares

To make a border with corner squares, measure the length and width of the patterned section of the quilt at the center, from raw edge to raw edge. Cut two border strips to the lengthwise measurement and join to the sides of the quilt with a ¼"-wide seam, matching the ends and centers and easing the edges to fit. Then, cut two border strips to the original crosswise measurement, join corner squares to the ends of the strips, and stitch these units to the top and bottom of the quilt, matching ends, seams, and centers and easing as necessary.

Borders with Mitered Corners

To make mitered corners, first estimate the finished outside dimensions of your quilt, including borders. Cut border strips to this length plus at least ½" for seam allowances; it's safer to add 2" to 3" to give yourself some leeway. If your quilt is to have multiple borders, sew the individual strips together and treat the resulting unit as a single piece for mitering.

Mark the centers of the quilt edges and the centers of the border strips. Stitch the borders to the quilt with a ¼"-wide seam, matching the centers; the border strip should extend the same distance at each end of the quilt. Start and stop the stitching ¼" from the corners of the quilt; press the seams toward the borders.

Lay the first corner to be mitered on the ironing board, pinning as necessary to keep the quilt from pulling and the corner from slipping. Fold one of the border units under at a 45° angle. Work with the fold until seams or stripes meet properly; pin at the fold, then check to see that the outside corner is square and that there is no extra fullness at the edges. When everything is straight and square, press the fold.

Starting at the outside edge of the quilt, center a piece of 1"-wide masking tape over the mitered fold; remove pins as you apply the tape.

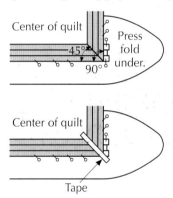

Unpin the quilt from the ironing board and turn it over. Draw a light pencil line on the crease created when you pressed the fold. Fold the center section of the quilt diagonally from the corner, right sides together, and align the long edges of the border strips. Stitch on the pencil line, then remove the tape; trim the excess fabric and press the seam open. Repeat these steps for the remaining three corners.

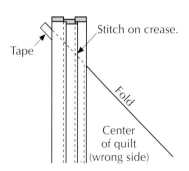

MARKING THE QUILTING LINES

Marking may not be necessary if you are planning to quilt in-the-ditch or to outline-quilt a uniform distance from seam lines. Some quiltmakers do outline quilting "by eye," though many others use ¼"-wide masking tape to mark these lines as they stitch. You can use masking or drafting tape to mark any straight-line quilting design; cut simple shapes from Con-Tact paper. Apply the tape or adhesive-paper shape when you are ready to quilt and remove promptly after you have quilted along its edge; adhesives left on the quilt too long may leave a residue that is difficult to remove.

Mark more complex quilting designs on the quilt top before layering the quilt with batting and backing. A gridded transparent ruler is useful for measuring and marking straight lines and filler grids. You can place quilting patterns from books or magazines or hand-drawn designs underneath the quilt and trace onto the fabric if the quilt fabrics are fairly light. Use a light box or put your work against a window if you have difficulty seeing the design.

If you cannot see through the quilt fabric, you will have to draw the design directly onto the quilt top. Use a precut plastic stencil, or make your own by drawing or tracing the quilting design on clear plastic; cut out the lines with a double-bladed craft knife, leaving "bridges" every inch or two so the stencil will hold its shape. You can also trace the design onto plain paper (or make a photocopy); cover the paper with one or two layers of clear Con-Tact paper and cut out the lines. Try putting small pieces of double-stick tape on the back of the stencil to keep it in place as you mark the quilting lines.

When marking quilting lines, work on a hard, smooth surface. Use a hard lead pencil (number 3 or 4) on light fabrics; for dark fabrics, try a fine-line chalk marker or a silver, nonphoto blue, or white pencil. Ideally, lines will remain visible for the duration of the quilting process and will be easy to remove when the quilting is done. Light lines are always easier to remove than heavy ones; test to make sure that the lines will wash out after the quilting is completed.

If you are using an allover quilting pattern that does not relate directly to the seams or to a design element of the quilt, you may find it easier to mark the quilting lines on the backing fabric and quilt from the back rather than the front of the quilt.

BACKINGS

The quilt backing should be a least 6" wider and 6" longer than the quilt top. A length of 44"-wide fabric (42 usable inches after preshrinking) is adequate to back a quilt that is no wider than 36". For a larger quilt, buy extra-wide cotton, or sew two or more pieces of fabric together. Use a single fabric, seamed as necessary, to make a backing of adequate size, or piece a simple multifabric back that complements the front of the quilt. Early quiltmakers often made pieced backings as a matter of necessity; modern quiltmakers see quilt backings as another place to experiment with color and design.

If you opt for a seamed or pieced backing, trim off the selvages before you stitch and press the seams open.

Calculate the yardage required for single-fabric backings as follows:

For quilts up to 36" wide, any length: length + 6"
For quilts 37" to 78" wide and no longer than 78": width + 6" x 2 (1 crosswise seam)
For quilts 37" to 78" wide and more than 78" long: length + 6" x 2 (1 lengthwise seam)
For quilts more than 78" wide and 79" to 120" long: width + 6" x 3 (2 crosswise seams)

BATTING

Batting comes packaged in standard bed sizes; you can also buy it by the yard. Several weights or thicknesses are available. Thick battings are fine for tied quilts and comforters; choose a thinner batting if you intend to quilt by hand or machine.

Thin batting is available in 100% cotton, 100% polyester, and an 80%/20% cotton/polyester blend. The cotton/polyester blend supposedly combines the best features of the two fibers. All-cotton batting is soft and drapable but requires close quilting and produces quilts that are rather flat. Though many quilters like the antique look, some find cotton batting difficult to "needle." Glazed or bonded polyester batting is sturdy, easy to handle, and washes well. It requires less quilting than cotton and has more loft. However, polyester fibers sometimes migrate through the fabric, creating tiny white "beards" on the surface of a quilt. The dark gray and black polyester battings now available ease this problem for quiltmakers who like to work with dark fabrics; bearding is less noticeable.

Unroll your batting and let it "relax" overnight before you layer your quilt. Some battings may need to be prewashed, while others should definitely not be prewashed; be sure to check the manufacturer's instructions.

LAYERING THE QUILT

Once you have marked your quilt top, pieced and pressed your backing, and let your batting relax, you are ready to layer the quilt. Spread the backing, wrong side up, on a flat, clean surface; anchor it with pins or masking tape. Spread the batting over the backing, smoothing out any wrinkles, then center the quilt top on the backing, right side up. Be careful not to stretch or distort any of the layers as you work. Starting in the middle, pin-baste the three layers together, gently smoothing any fullness to the sides and corners.

Baste the three layers together with a long needle and light-colored thread; start in the center and work diagonally to each corner, making a large X. Continue basting, laying in a grid of horizontal and vertical lines 6" to 8" apart. Finish by basting around the outside edges.

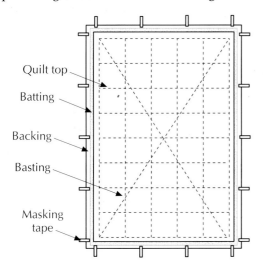

Quilt top
Batting
Backing
Basting
Masking tape

QUILTING

The purpose of quilting or tying is to keep the three layers together and to prevent the batting from lumping or shifting. While several early methods for tying and quilting are being revived, some quiltmakers are stretching tradition by "tying" with eyelets or decorative studs or quilting with unusual materials, including narrow ribbon, wire, and even cassette tape.

Machine Quilting

Machine quilting is suitable for all types of quilts, from simple baby and bed quilts that will be washed frequently to sophisticated pieces for the wall. With machine quilting, you can quickly complete quilts that might otherwise languish on the shelf. The technique provides some creative challenges as well.

Unless you plan to stitch in-the-ditch, mark the quilting lines before you layer the quilt. Consider using a simple allover grid or a continuous-line quilting design. Basting for machine quilting is usually done with safety pins; if you have a large work surface to support the quilt and an even-feed foot for your sewing machine, you should have no problem with shifting layers or untidy pleats, tucks, and bubbles on the back side. Remove the safety pins as you sew. Pull thread ends to the back and work them into the quilt for a more professional look.

Try machine quilting with threads of unusual types and weights, or experiment with the decorative stitch or twin-needle capabilities of your sewing machine. Double-needle quilting produces an interesting, corded effect.

Traditional Hand Quilting

To quilt by hand, you will need short, sturdy needles (called "Betweens"), quilting thread, and a thimble to fit the middle finger of your sewing hand. Most quilters also use a frame or hoop to support their work. Quilting needles run from sizes 3 to 12; the higher the number, the smaller the needle. Use the smallest needle you can comfortably handle: the smaller the needle, the smaller your stitches.

Thread your needle with a single strand of quilting thread about 18" long; make a small knot and insert the needle in the top layer about 1" from the place where you want to start stitching. Pull the needle out at the point where quilting will begin and gently pull the thread until the knot pops through the fabric and into the batting.

Begin your quilting line with a backstitch and continue with a small, even running stitch. Place your left hand underneath the quilt so you can feel the needle point with the tip of your finger when you take a stitch.

Push the needle through all the layers with the thimble on the middle finger of your top hand, using the dimples in the side or end of the thimble (whichever is more comfortable) to support the eye end of the needle. When you feel the tip of the needle with the middle or index finger of the underneath hand, simultaneously rock the needle eye down toward the quilt surface, depress the fabric in front of the needle with the thumb of the top hand, and push the needle tip up with the underneath finger.

When the needle tip comes through to the top of the quilt, relax the top-hand thumb and the underneath finger, rock the needle eye up so it is almost perpendicular to the quilt, and push the needle through the layers to start the next stitch. Repeat the process until you have three or four stitches on the needle, then pull the needle all the way through, taking up any slack in the thread, and start again.

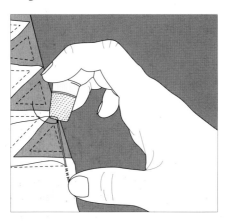

To end a line of quilting, make a small knot close to the last stitch, then backstitch, running the thread a needle's length through the batting. Gently pull the thread until the knot pops into the batting; clip the thread at the quilt's surface. Remove basting stitches as you quilt, leaving only those that go around the outside edges of the quilt.

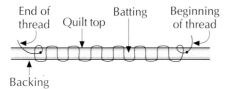

End of thread   Quilt top   Batting   Beginning of thread

Backing

Utility Quilting

Utility quilting is faster than traditional hand quilting but "homier" than machine quilting; you use big needles and heavy threads, such as perle cotton, crochet thread, or several strands of embroidery floss, and take big stitches, anywhere from ⅛" to ¼" in length. This method is well worth considering for casual, scrappy quilts and for pieces you might otherwise plan to machine quilt. Quilts finished with this technique are unquestionably sturdy, and the added surface texture is very pleasing.

You can work freehand, without marking the quilt top, or you can mark quilting lines as usual. Use the shortest, finest, sharp-pointed needle you can get the thread through; try several different kinds to find the needle that works best for you. Judy likes working with #8 perle cotton and a #6 Between needle. Keep your stitches as straight and even as possible.

CROW FOOTING AND OTHER TACKING TECHNIQUES

Judy has an old comforter in her collection that is tied with a technique called "crow footing." Crow footing is done with a long needle and thick thread, such as a single or double strand of perle cotton or crochet thread. Isolated fly stitches are worked in a grid across the surface of the quilt, leaving a small diagonal stitch on the back of the quilt; there are no visible knots or dangling threads. Stitches can be spaced as far apart as the length of your needle will allow.

Put your work in a hoop or frame. Use a long, sharp-pointed needle—try Cotton Darners, millinery needles, or soft-sculpture needles. Make a small knot in the thread and insert the needle in the top layer of the quilt about 1" from A. Pull the needle out at A and gently pull the thread until the knot pops through the fabric and into the batting. Hold the thread down with your thumb and insert the needle at B as shown; go through *all three layers* and bring the needle out at C. Insert the needle at D and travel *through the top layer only* to start the next stitch at A.

Work in rows from the top to the bottom or from the right to the left of the quilt, spacing the stitches 2" to 3" apart. To end stitching, bring the needle out at C and make a small knot about ⅛" from the surface of the quilt. Make a backstitch at D, running the thread through the batting an inch or so; pop the knot into the batting and clip the thread at the surface of the quilt.

Crow Footing

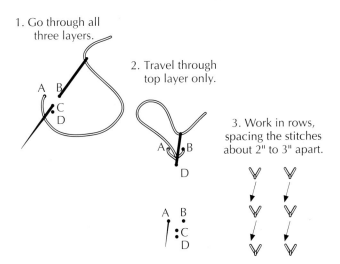

1. Go through all three layers.

2. Travel through top layer only.

3. Work in rows, spacing the stitches about 2" to 3" apart.

Backstitch tacking is another option. Two favorite stitches are the Mennonite tack and the Methodist knot. Both stitches are best worked from the right to the left rather than from the top to the bottom of the quilt; they leave a small horizontal stitch on the back of the quilt.

To do the Mennonite Tack, bring the needle out at A and take a backstitch ¼" to ⅜" long *through all three layers*, coming back up just a few threads from the starting point (B–C). Reinsert the needle at D and travel *through the top layer only* to start the next stitch. The tiny second stitch, which should be almost invisible, crosses over the backstitch and locks the tacking.

Mennonite Tack

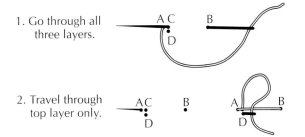

1. Go through all three layers.

2. Travel through top layer only.

3. Work in rows from right to left.

The Methodist knot is done with two backstitches, one long and one short, or both the same length. Bring the needle out at A and take a backstitch *through all three layers*, coming back up beyond the starting point (B–C). Reinsert the needle at A and travel *through the top layer only* to start the next stitch.

Methodist Knot

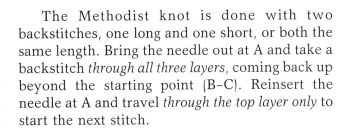

1. Go through all three layers.

2. Travel through top layer only to start the next stitch.

You can lay in any of these tacking stitches at random, rather than on a uniform grid. Early quiltmakers who used these techniques often worked with the quilt stretched full size on a large floor frame, working from both ends and rolling in the edges of the quilt as the rows of tacking were completed, thus eliminating the need for basting. You can tie or tack small quilts without basting if you spread the layers smoothly over a table or other large, flat work surface.

BINDING

When the tying or quilting is complete, remove any remaining basting threads, except for the stitches around the outside edges of the quilt. Trim the batting and backing even with the edges of the quilt top. Use a rotary cutter and cutting guide to get accurate, straight edges; make sure the corners are square.

Make enough binding to go around the perimeter of the quilt plus about 18". The general instructions below are based on ⅜"-wide (finished), double-fold binding, which is made from strips cut 2½" wide and stitched to the outside edges of the quilt with a ⅜"-wide seam. Cutting dimensions and seam widths for bindings in other sizes are given in the chart on page 250.

Straight-grain binding is fine for most applications. Simply cut strips from the lengthwise or crosswise grain of the fabric; one crosswise strip will yield about 40" of binding. For ⅜"-wide (finished) binding, cut the strips 2½" wide. Trim the ends of the strips at a 45° angle and seam the ends to make a long, continuous strip; press the seam allowances open.

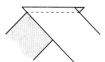

Cut strip ends at a 45° angle and seam.

Press seam allowances open.

Fold the strip in half lengthwise, wrong sides together, and press.

Use bias binding if your quilt edges have curves or if you expect the quilt to get heavy use; binding cut on the bias wears longer. Some quilters cut bias strips from a flat piece of fabric, joining the strips after cutting; others prefer the tubular method for making a continuous bias strip.

To make a flat-cut binding, lay out a length of fabric. Make a bias cut, starting at one corner of the fabric; use the 45° marking on a long cutting ruler as a guide. Then, cut bias strips in the desired width, measuring from the edges of the initial bias

cut. Seam the ends to make a long, continuous strip; press the seams open. Fold the strip in half lengthwise, wrong sides together, and press.

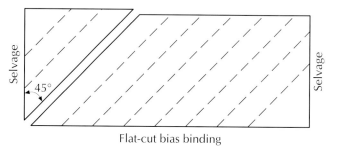

Flat-cut bias binding

Continuous bias binding can be made from a square of fabric. To determine what size square will yield the amount of bias binding you need, multiply the length of bias needed (in inches) by the width you plan to cut it, then use a pocket calculator to find the square root of the result.

Let's say you are planning to finish a 72" x 84" quilt with ⅜"-wide finished binding, which requires 2½"-wide strips. You will need 330" of binding (quilt perimeter plus 18"); 330 x 2½ = 825. The square root of 825 is 28.72. Thus, a 29" to 30" square will yield the 330" of binding you need.

Remove the selvage and mark the top and bottom of the square with pins. Cut the square in half on the diagonal to make two half-square triangles.

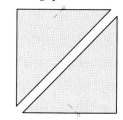

Mark top and bottom of square and divide it on the diagonal.

With right sides together, join the marked sides of the triangles with a ¼"-wide seam; press the seam open.

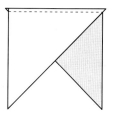

Join the marked sides.

Measure and draw lines the width of the binding strips on the wrong side of the fabric, starting at one of the long bias edges as shown below. If the distance between the last line and the bottom edge is less than the strip width you need, trim to the line above. Slice along the top and bottom lines (at the ends closest to the seam) for a distance of about 6" as shown.

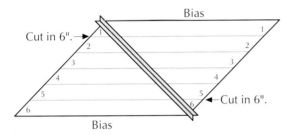

Draw lines on wrong side of fabric.
Slice in 6" along top and bottom lines.

With right sides together *and the edges offset by the width of one line*, stitch the ends together to form a cylinder; press the seam open. Starting at the top, cut along the marked lines to form a continuous bias strip. Fold the strip in half lengthwise, wrong sides together, and press.

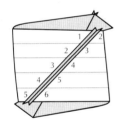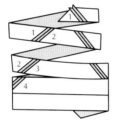

Stitch ends together to form a cylinder, offsetting edges by width of one line.

Cut along lines to form a continuous strip.

The following sections describe two different methods of applying the binding to the quilt. One produces a binding with mitered corners, with the binding applied in a continuous strip around the edges of the quilt. In the second method, measured lengths of binding are applied separately to each edge of the quilt. In both cases, the instructions are based on ⅜"-wide finished binding; you will need to use a different seam width if your finished binding is narrower or wider than ⅜". Refer to the chart on page 250.

Bindings with Mitered Corners

For a binding with mitered corners, start near the center of one side of the quilt. Place the binding on the front of the quilt, lining up the raw edges of the binding with the raw edges of the quilt. Using an even-feed foot, sew the binding to the quilt with a ⅜"-wide seam; leave the first 8" to 10" of binding loose so that you can join or overlap the beginning and ending of the binding strip later. Be careful not to stretch the quilt or the binding as you sew. When you reach the corner, stop the stitching ⅜" from the edge of the quilt and backstitch; clip the threads.

Turn the quilt to prepare for sewing along the next edge. Fold the binding up and away, then fold it again to bring it along the edge of the quilt. There will be an angled fold at the corner; the straight fold should be even with the top edge of the quilt.

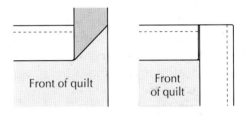

Stitch from the straight fold in the binding to the next corner, pinning as necessary to keep the binding lined up with the raw edge of the quilt. When you reach the next corner, stop the stitching ⅜" from the edge of the quilt and backstitch; clip the threads. Fold the binding as you did at the last corner and continue around the edge of the quilt. Stop and backstitch about 12" from the starting point. Overlap the end of the remaining unattached binding and the tail you left when you started, and adjust them to fit the quilt exactly. Join with a diagonal seam; trim the excess. Stitch this newly joined section to the quilt.

Fold the binding to the back, over the raw edges of the quilt; the folded edge of the binding should just cover the machine-stitching line. Blindstitch the binding in place, making sure your stitches do not go through to the front of the quilt. At the corners, fold the binding to form miters on the front and back of the quilt; stitch down the folds in the miters.

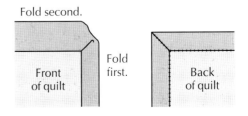

Bindings with Measured Strips

Use this binding method if the outside edges of your quilt need to be eased to the binding so that their finished measurements conform to the quilt's center measurements. Straight-grain binding strips work best for this type of binding.

Bind the long edges of the quilt first. Measure the length of the quilt at the center, from raw edge to raw edge.

NOTE: Do not measure the outer edges of the quilt. Often the edges measure longer than the quilt center due to stretching during construction; the edges might even be two different lengths.

From your long strip of binding, cut two pieces of binding to the lengthwise center measurement. Working from the right side of the quilt, pin the binding strips to the long edges of the quilt, matching the ends and centers and easing the edges to fit as necessary. Use an even-feed foot and sew the binding to the quilt with a ⅜"-wide seam. Fold the binding to the back, over the raw edges of the quilt; the folded edge of the binding should just cover the machine-stitching line. Blindstitch the binding in place, making sure your stitches do not go through to the front of the quilt.

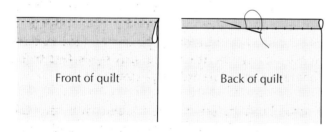

Now measure the width of the quilt at the center, from outside edge to outside edge. From the remainder of your long binding strip, cut two pieces to that measurement plus 1". Pin these measured binding strips to the short edges of the quilt, matching the centers and leaving ½" of the binding extending at each end; ease the edges to fit as necessary. Sew the binding to the quilt with a ⅜"-wide seam.

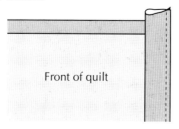

To finish, fold the extended portion of the binding strips down over the bound edges, then bring the binding to the back and blindstitch in place as before.

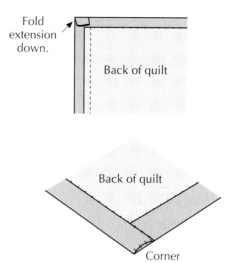

Strip and seam widths for double-fold bindings in various finished sizes are as follows:

Binding	Strip Width	Seam
¼"	1¾"	¼"
⅜"	2½"	⅜"
½"	3¼"	½"
⅝"	4"	⅝"
¾"	4¾"	¾"

QUILT SLEEVES

Quilts that will be displayed on walls should have a sleeve tacked to the back near the top edge, to hold a hanging rod. We put sleeves on all our quilts, even those intended for beds, so they can be safely hung if they are suddenly requested for an exhibit or if their owners decide to use them for decoration rather than as bedding.

Sleeves should be a generous width. Use a piece of fabric 6" to 8" wide and 1" to 2" shorter than the finished width of the quilt at the top edge. Hem the ends. Then, fold the fabric strip in half lengthwise, *wrong sides together*; seam the long, raw edges together with a ¼"-wide seam. Fold the tube so that the seam is centered on one side and press the seam allowances open.

Hem ends, then seam raw edges, right side out.

Center seam and press open.

Place the tube on the back side of the quilt, just under the top binding, with the seamed side against the quilt. Hand sew the top edge of the sleeve to the quilt, taking care not to catch the front of the quilt as you stitch.

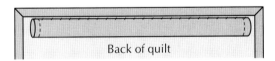

Back of quilt

Tack down top edge of sleeve.

Push the front side of the tube up so the top edge covers about half of the binding (providing a little "give" so the hanging rod does not put strain on the quilt itself) and sew the bottom edge of the sleeve in place as shown.

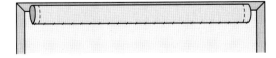

Push tube up and tack down bottom edge.

Slide a curtain rod, a wooden dowel, or a piece of lath through the sleeve. The seamed side of the sleeve will keep the rod from coming into direct contact with the quilt. Suspend the rod on brackets. Or, attach screw eyes or drill holes at each end of the rod and slip the holes or eyes over small nails.

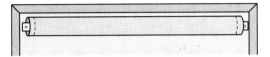

Insert hanging rod in sleeve.

QUILT LABELS

Be sure to sign and date your work! At the very least, embroider your name and the year you completed the quilt on the front or back of the quilt. However, quilt historians and the future owners of your quilts will want to know more than just the "who" and "when." Consider tacking a handwritten or typed label to the quilt back, including the name of the quilt, your name, your city and state, the date, whom you made the quilt for and why, and any other interesting or important information about the quilt.

Press a piece of plastic-coated freezer paper to the wrong side of the label fabric to stabilize it while you write or type. For a handwritten label, use a permanent marking pen; use a multistrike ribbon for typewritten labels. Always test to be absolutely sure the ink is permanent.

NOTE: Hand- or typewritten labels that pass the washing-machine test sometimes run and bleed when they are dry-cleaned.

Quilting Suggestions

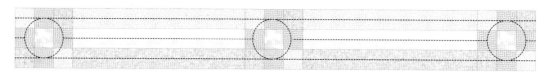

A Brighter Day
1 row

Amish Nine Patch
Corner of quilt

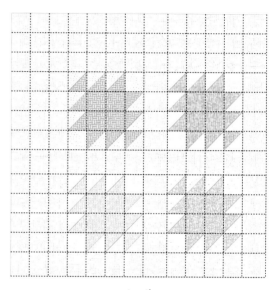

Anvil
Corner of quilt

Anvil Star
4 blocks

Army Star

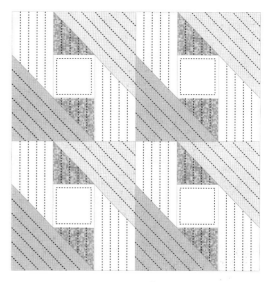

Attic Window
4 blocks

Amsterdam Star
Corner of quilt

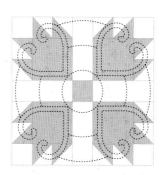

Bear's Paw
1 block

Ann Orr's Rose Garden
Corner of quilt

Birds in the Air
Corner of quilt

Blackford's Beauty
1 block

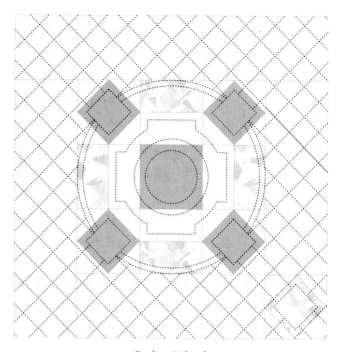

Broken Wheel
Corner of quilt

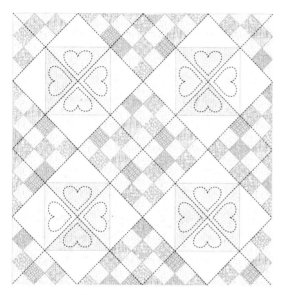

Bridal Path
Corner of quilt

Buckeye Beauty
4 blocks

Broken Dishes
Corner of quilt

Christmas Star
4 blocks

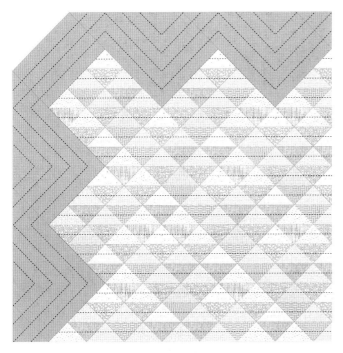

Charm Quilt
Corner of quilt

Cleo's Castles in the Air
Corner of quilt (without border)

City Lights
Corner of quilt (without borders)

Comet
Corner of quilt

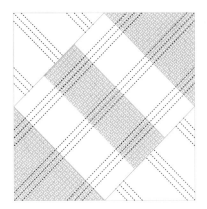

Cracker Box
1 block

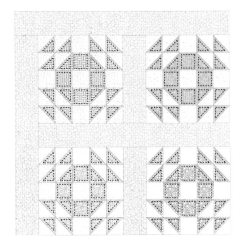

Crown of Thorns
Corner of quilt

Double Pinwheel
4 blocks

Delectable Mountains
Corner of quilt

Double Irish Chain
Corner of quilt

Double Squares
4 blocks

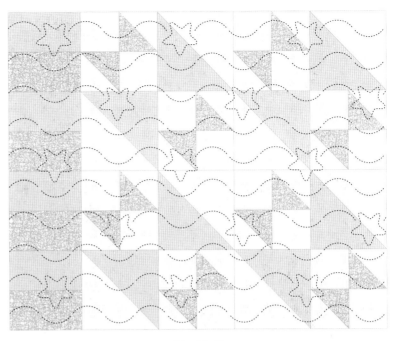

Double X
Corner of quilt

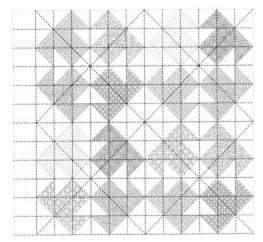

Double T
Corner of quilt

Double Wrench
Corner of quilt

English Ivy
Corner of quilt (without borders)

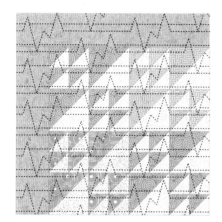

Envelope
4 blocks

Four Corners
Corner of quilt

Flock of Geese
Corner of quilt

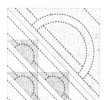

Flying Birds
1 block

Friendship Star
Corner of quilt

Four-Four Time
1 block

Fruit Basket
Corner of quilt

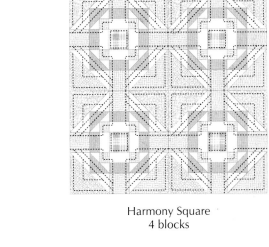

Harmony Square
4 blocks

Gaggle of Geese
4 blocks

Hearts and Hourglass
Corner of quilt

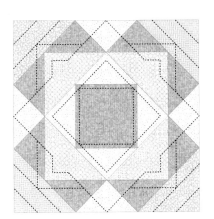

Gentleman's Fancy
1 block

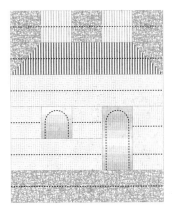

Holly's Houses
1 block

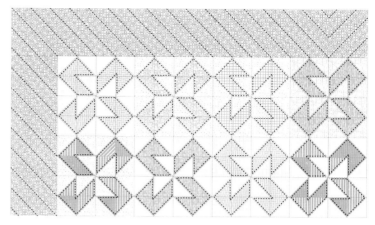

Jack-in-the-Box
Corner of quilt

Homeward Bound to Union Square
4 blocks

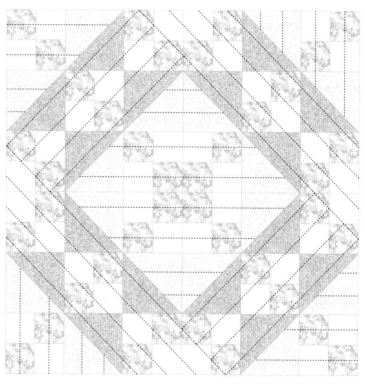

Indian Trails
Corner of quilt

Jacob's Ladder
4 blocks

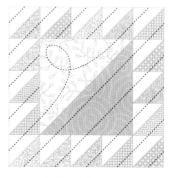

Lady of the Lake
1 block

London Roads
9 blocks

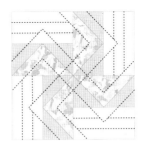

Louisiana
1 block

Magic Carpet
1 block

London Square
Corner of quilt

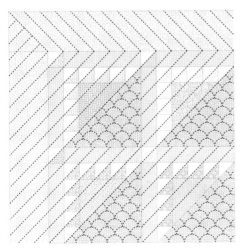

Lost Ships Signature
Corner of quilt

Market Square
4 blocks

Memory Wreath
Corner of quilt (without border)

Pinwheel Mosaic
Corner of quilt

Milky Way
Corner of quilt

Mrs. Keller's Nine Patch
4 blocks

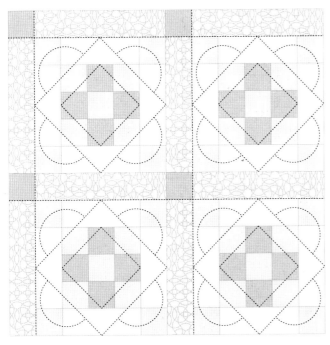

Nine Patch Plaid
4 blocks

Ocean Chain
Corner of quilt

Nine Patch Strippy
Corner of quilt

Ohio Fence
Corner of quilt

Ohio Stars
Corner of quilt

Paths and Stiles
4 blocks (with sashing)

Old Favorite
Corner of quilt (without borders)

Pinwheel Star
Corner of quilt (without border)

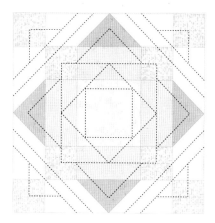

Oregon Trail
1 block

Puss in the Corner I
Corner of quilt

Pot of Flowers
Corner of quilt

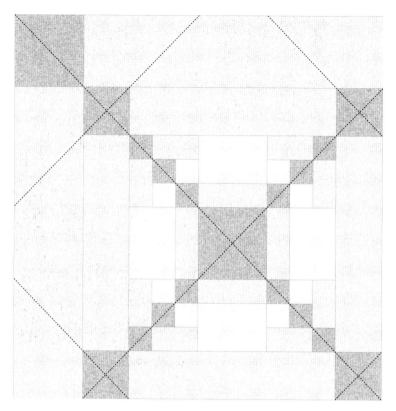

Puss in the Corner II
Corner of quilt

The Railroad
4 blocks

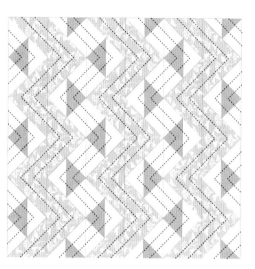

Ribbon Quilt
Corner of quilt

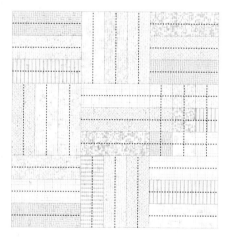

Rail Fence
9 blocks

Rolling Pinwheel
1 block

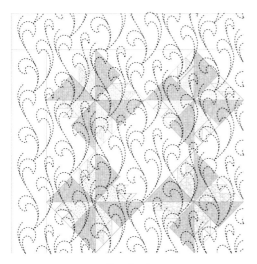

Rosebud
Corner of quilt

Shaded Nine Patch
9 blocks

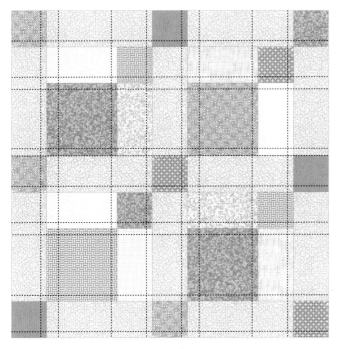

Scot's Plaid
Corner of quilt

Shaded Pinwheel
4 blocks

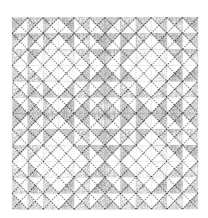

Scrap Angles
Corner of quilt

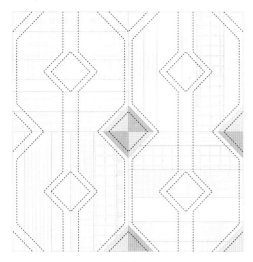

Snowball Strip
4 blocks

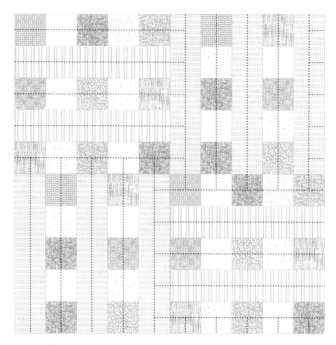

Split Rail Fence
4 blocks

Snowbows
Corner of quilt (without borders)

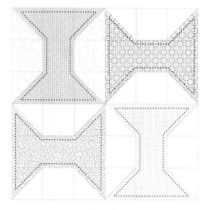

Spools
Corner of quilt

Split Nine Patch
1 block

Square in a Square
Corner of quilt

Square on Square
4 blocks (with sashing)

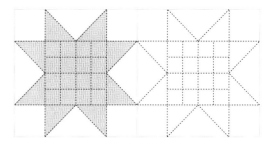

Squares and Points
1 pieced and 1 alternate block

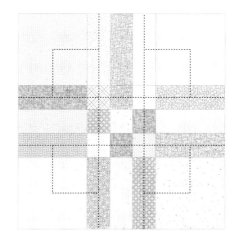

Squares and Strips
1 block

Squares and Ladders
Corner of quilt

Stardancer
Corner of quilt

Stars in Strips
Corner of quilt

Stars in the Sashing
Corner of quilt

State Fair
4 blocks

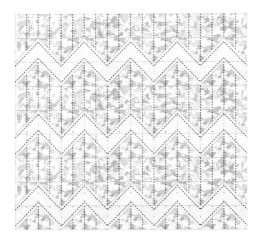

Streak of Lightning
Corner of quilt

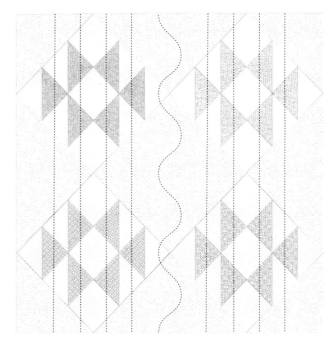

Three and Six
Corner of quilt

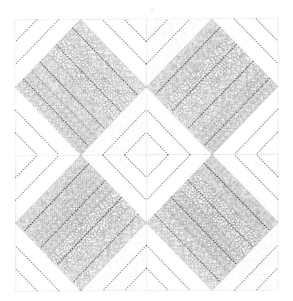

String Square
4 blocks

Tin Man
1 block

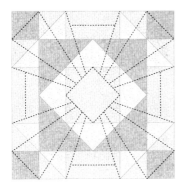

Summer Winds
1 block

Union
Corner of quilt

Weathervane
Corner of quilt

Walkabout
Corner of quilt